MW01071673

THE NEW
AMERICAN
COMMENTARY

An Exegetical and Theological
Exposition of Holy Scripture

General Editor
E. RAY CLENDENEN

Associate General Editor, OT
KENNETH A. MATHEWS

Associate General Editor, NT
DAVID S. DOCKERY

Consulting Editors

Old Testament
L. RUSS BUSH
DUANE A. GARRETT
LARRY L. WALKER

New Testament
RICHARD R. MELICK, JR.
PAIGE PATTERSON
CURTIS VAUGHAN

Production Editor
LINDA L. SCOTT

THE NEW
AMERICAN
COMMENTARY

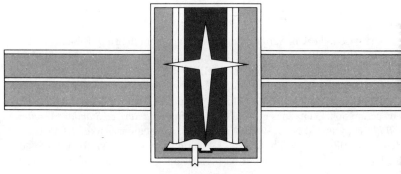

Volume
36

JAMES

Kurt A. Richardson

BROADMAN
&HOLMAN
PUBLISHERS

© Copyright 1997 • Broadman & Holman Publishers
All rights reserved
4201–36
ISBN 13: 978-08054-0136-3
ISBN 10: 0-8054-0136-9
Dewey Decimal Classification: 227
Subject Heading: BIBLE. N.T. JAMES
Printed in the United States of America
10 09 08 07 06 05   10 09 8 7 6

Unless otherwise indicated, Scripture quotations are from the Holy Bible, *New International Version* (NIV), copyright © 1973, 1978, 1984 by International Bible Society. Used by permission of Zondervan Bible Publishers. Scripture quotations marked NEB are from *The New English Bible*. Copyright © The Delegates of the Oxford University Press and the Syndics of the Cambridge University Press, 1961, 1970. Used by permission. Quotations marked RSV are from the *Revised Standard Version of the Bible,* copyrighted 1946, 1952, © 1971, 1973. Quotations marked JB are from The Jerusalem Bible, copyright © 1966 by Darton, Longman and Todd, Ltd. and Doubleday and Company, Inc. Used by permission. Scripture quotations marked RSV are from the *Revised Standard Version of the Bible,* copyrighted 1946, 1952, © 1971, 1973.

In
Memoriam

Bo Ivar Reicke
Christian Gentleman, Professor, Interpreter of James

Editors' Preface

God's Word does not change. God's world, however, changes in every generation. These changes, in addition to new findings by scholars and a new variety of challenges to the gospel message, call for the church in each generation to interpret and apply God's Word for God's people. Thus, THE NEW AMERICAN COMMENTARY is introduced to bridge the twentieth and twenty-first centuries. This new series has been designed primarily to enable pastors, teachers, and students to read the Bible with clarity and proclaim it with power.

In one sense THE NEW AMERICAN COMMENTARY is not new, for it represents the continuation of a heritage rich in biblical and theological exposition. The title of this forty-volume set points to the continuity of this series with an important commentary project published at the end of the nineteenth century called AN AMERICAN COMMENTARY, edited by Alvah Hovey. The older series included, among other significant contributions, the outstanding volume on Matthew by John A. Broadus, from whom the publisher of the new series, Broadman Press, partly derives its name. The former series was authored and edited by scholars committed to the infallibility of Scripture, making it a solid foundation for the present project. In line with this heritage, all NAC authors affirm the divine inspiration, inerrancy, complete truthfulness, and full authority of the Bible. The perspective of the NAC is unapologetically confessional and rooted in the evangelical tradition.

Since a commentary is a fundamental tool for the expositor or teacher who seeks to interpret and apply Scripture in the church or classroom, the NAC focuses on communicating the theological structure and content of each biblical book. The writers seek to illuminate both the historical meaning and contemporary significance of Holy Scripture.

In its attempt to make a unique contribution to the Christian community, the NAC focuses on two concerns. First, the commentary emphasizes how each section of a book fits together so that the reader becomes aware of the theological unity of each book and of Scripture as a whole. The writers, however, remain aware of the Bible's inherently rich variety. Second, the NAC is produced with the conviction that the Bible primarily belongs to the church. We believe that scholarship and the academy provide an indispensable foundation for biblical understanding and the service of Christ, but the editors and authors of this series have attempted to communicate the findings of their research in a manner that will build up the whole body of Christ. Thus, the commentary concentrates on theological exegesis while providing practical, applicable exposition.

THE NEW AMERICAN COMMENTARY's theological focus enables the reader to see the parts as well as the whole of Scripture. The biblical books vary in content, context, literary type, and style. In addition to this rich variety, the editors and authors recognize that the doctrinal emphasis and use of the biblical books differs in various places, contexts, and cultures among God's people. These factors, as well as other concerns, have led the editors to give freedom to the writers to wrestle with the issues raised by the scholarly community surrounding each book and to determine the appropriate shape and length of the introductory materials. Moreover, each writer has developed the structure of the commentary in a way best suited for expounding the basic structure and the meaning of the biblical books for our day. Generally, discussions relating to contemporary scholarship and technical points of grammar and syntax appear in the footnotes and not in the text of the commentary. This format allows pastors and interested laypersons, scholars and teachers, and serious college and seminary students to profit from the commentary at various levels. This approach has been employed because we believe that all Christians have the privilege and responsibility to read and seek to understand the Bible for themselves.

Consistent with the desire to produce a readable, up-to-date commentary, the editors selected the *New International Version* as the standard translation for the commentary series. The selection was made primarily because of the NIV's faithfulness to the original languages and its beautiful and readable style. The authors, however, have been given the liberty to differ at places from the NIV as they develop their own translations from the Greek and Hebrew texts.

The NAC reflects the vision and leadership of those who provide oversight for Broadman Press, who in 1987 called for a new commentary series that would evidence a commitment to the inerrancy of Scripture and a faithfulness to the classic Christian tradition. While the commentary adopts an "American" name, it should be noted some writers represent countries outside the United States, giving the commentary an international perspective. The diverse group of writers includes scholars, teachers, and administrators from almost twenty different colleges and seminaries, as well as pastors, missionaries, and a layperson.

The editors and writers hope that THE NEW AMERICAN COMMEN-

TARY will be helpful and instructive for pastors and teachers, scholars and students, for men and women in the churches who study and teach God's Word in various settings. We trust that for editors, authors, and readers alike, the commentary will be used to build up the church, encourage obedience, and bring renewal to God's people. Above all, we pray that the NAC will bring glory and honor to our Lord who has graciously redeemed us and faithfully revealed himself to us in his Holy Word.

SOLI DEO GLORIA
The Editors

Author's Preface

The Epistle of James is one of the outstanding pieces of the New Testament Scriptures. In a wonderful way, it embodies much of Jesus' teaching in the Synoptic Gospels. Within the canon of the New Testament, the Epistle of James, together with those of Peter and the epistle to the Hebrews, forms a strand of teaching essential to the richness of Christian faith and life. James is famous for its sermonic quality. The letter contains some of the most potent imagery and exhortation in the entire Bible. James is the prominent voice of the New Testament, calling for consistency of faith in Jesus Christ. Complementing Paul's emphasis on justifying faith, James requires the demonstration of faith. Those who claim to be believers must show their faith by what they do. Faith must be useful, rooted in the kind of discipleship motive we find in Jesus' teaching: "Freely you have received, freely give" (Matt 10:8).

As a theologian writing a biblical commentary, I found the rigors of working closely with the biblical text to be a joy. Commenting on James has afforded me a wonderful laboratory where the inseparable unity of doctrine and ethics, theology and church could find fresh expression. Reading the text over and over in Greek and in multiple translations, wrestling with old and new controversies of interpretation, pierced by the convicting work of the Spirit of God, longing for James's wisdom of faith, and applying the message to the contexts of ministry in both seminary and church were all essential dimensions of the production of this commentary.

The last two decades have seen a burgeoning of research into the nature and content of James, and I am indebted to a host of outstanding Jacobean scholars for their ground-breaking contributions. These include J. B. Adamson, P. H. Davids, R. P. Martin, S. Laws, H. Frankemölle, F. Mussner, and above all L. T. Johnson. Their works and abiding scholarly merits expound in detail far beyond the purview of this commentary the state of the art in James research and interpretive debate. The serious student of James is advised to refer to them in due course.

The text of this commentary is typified by theological exposition. With recognition of the carefully argued exegetical debates that have been conducted in helpful ways by the commentators above, I have sought to produce a volume that would help the student of James perceive and grasp the meaning of the message itself. This approach is a modest version of the one applied by the great New Testament scholar C. F. D. Moule in his commentary on Colossians and Philemon:

When the primary task was to establish the text and to discuss the authenticity of the documents, linguistic and historical considerations were foremost. But gradually, as these foundation-tasks were done, it became possible to devote increasing attention to the elucidation of the theological and religious contents of the New Testament, and to see it in the setting of the life and worship of Christian communities. (*The Epistles to the Colossians and to Philemon*, CGTC [Cambridge University Press, 1957], v)

Many persons and churches have played a significant role in my life and work while writing this commentary. This work was conducted largely during the course of my eight years as a teacher of theology at Southeastern Baptist Theological Seminary and as a preacher of the gospel in Southern Baptist churches of North and South Carolina. These years marked the beginning of my ministry career and spanned the course of many notable events. In the midst of these years, David S. Dockery, one of the early editors of the series, invited me to join his team of commentators. His constant encouragement, along with E. Ray Clendenen's, has been of tremendous scholarly and personal value to me. Southeastern Seminary, under three presidents, Lolley, Drummond and Patterson, and its very fine library and ideal location as an academic institution in the South, graciously afforded me the context in which I could work. More recently, Gordon-Conwell Theological Seminary and President Cooley have provided a similarly conducive and congenial environment in which to bring the commentary to completion. Several church congregations in which I ministered as interim pastor, particularly Friendly Avenue Baptist Church of Greensboro, along with Homestead Heights Baptist Church and Guess Road Baptist Church of Durham, faithfully attended and supported scores of Bible studies and sermons on the Epistle of James. Without the participation of these precious "priestly" believers and fellow Bible interpreters, the commentary would have been a much poorer product. Friends and respected colleagues in theological education are many, and those I must mention in appreciation include Timothy George, Glenn T. Miller, Jean-Paul Deschler, Jey Kim, Mark Siefrid, Robert Culpepper, John Morrison, Ed Buchanan, Philip Roberts, Kenneth Hemphill, Thomas Jackson, John Newport, Albert Mohler, James Johnson, Clayton Stalnaker, David Wells, Jack Davis, Rick Lints, Garth Rosell, Peter Kuzmic; along with my esteemed professors: Ronald Russell, Harold O. J. Brown, Jan M. Lochman, Heinrich Ott, and the late Bo Reicke—to whose memory this commentary is dedicated; and helpful students: Michael Deboer, Frank Cone, Kenneth Keathley, Peter Heltzel, Patrick Gray. My secretary at Southeastern, Mary Lou Stevens, performed the invaluable service of typing the first draft of the manuscript. Each of these contributed to whatever might be helpful and beneficial in this commentary; its shortcomings are to be accounted entirely to me.

Above all I must thank my wife, Dolores, for her constancy in love and support through the years during which this work was written. She is my truest companion who has only encouraged me and affirmed the calling we share together in God's Kingdom work. Our children, Erik, Kristin, Matthew, and Kelsey, have each in their own way helped me to keep my focus on the best goal of any Scripture interpretation: contributing to the consistent faith and understanding of the next generation of believers. Our parents, Mort and Melda Richardson, Alwin and Gertrud Kirschbaum, also are vital participants in our task of faithful witness. Together by faith in the Lord Jesus, we form a small part of the immense family of "our father Abraham" (James 2:21) who seek to be useful for the Kingdom of God.

Lamentations 3:27
—Kurt Anders Richardson
Gordon-Conwell Theological Seminary

Abbreviations

Bible Books

Gen	Isa	Luke
Exod	Jer	John
Lev	Lam	Acts
Num	Ezek	Rom
Deut	Dan	1, 2 Cor
Josh	Hos	Gal
Judg	Joel	Eph
Ruth	Amos	Phil
1, 2 Sam	Obad	Col
1, 2 Kgs	Jonah	1, 2 Thess
1, 2 Chr	Mic	1, 2 Tim
Ezra	Nah	Titus
Neh	Hab	Phlm
Esth	Zeph	Heb
Job	Hag	Jas
Ps (pl. Pss)	Zech	1, 2 Pet
Prov	Mal	1, 2, 3 John
Eccl	Matt	Jude
Song	Mark	Rev

Apocrypha

Add Esth	The Additions to the Book of Esther
Bar	Baruch
Bel	Bel and the Dragon
1,2 Esdr	1, 2 Esdras
4 Ezra	4 Ezra
Jdt	Judith
Ep Jer	Epistle of Jeremiah
1,2,3,4 Mac	1, 2, 3, 4 Maccabees
Pr Azar	Prayer of Azariah and the Song of the Three Jews
Pr Man	Prayer of Manasseh
Sir	Sirach, Ecclesiasticus
Sus	Susanna
Tob	Tobit
Wis	The Wisdom of Solomon

Commonly Used Sources for New Testament Volumes

AB	Anchor Bible
ABR	*Australian Biblical Review*
ACNT	Augsburg Commentary on the New Testament
AGJU	Arbeiten zur Geschichte des antiken Judentums und des Urchristentums
AJT	*American Journal of Theology*
AJTh	*Asia Journal of Theology*
ANF	Ante-Nicene Fathers
ANRW	*Aufstief und Niedergang der römischen Welt*
ATANT	Abhandlungen zur Theologie des Alten and Neuen Testaments
ATR	*Anglican Theological Review*
ATRSup	*Anglican Theological Review Supplemental Series*
AusBR	*Australian Biblical Review*
AUSS	*Andrews University Seminary Studies*
BAGD	W. Bauer, W. F. Arndt, F. W. Gingrich, and F. Danker, *Greek-English Lexicon of the New Testament*
BARev	*Biblical Archaeology Review*
BBR	*Bulletin for Biblical Research*
BDF	F. Blass, A. Debrunner, R. W. Funk, *A Greek Grammar of the New Testament*
BETL	Bibliotheca ephemeridum theologicarum lovaniensium
Bib	*Biblica*
BJRL	*Bulletin of the John Rylands Library*
BK	*Bibel und Kirche*
BR	*Biblical Research*
BSac	*Bibliotheca Sacra*
BT	*The Bible Translator*
BTB	*Biblical Theology Bulletin*
BZ	*Biblische Zeitschrift*
BZNS	*Biblische Zeitschrift* New Series
BZNW	Beihefte zur *ZAW*
CBC	Cambridge Bible Commentary
CBQ	*Catholic Biblical Quarterly*
CCWJCW	Cambridge Commentaries on Writings of the Jewish and Christian World
CNT	Commentaire du Nouveau Testament
CNTC	Calvin's New Testament Commentaries
CO	W. Baur, E. Cuntiz, and E. Reuss, *Ioannis Calvini opera quae supereunt omnia,* ed.
ConBNT	Coniectanea biblica, New Testament

Conybeare	W. J. Conybeare and J. S. Howson, *The Life and Epistles of St. Paul*
CJT	*Canadian Journal of Theology*
CSR	*Christian Scholars' Review*
CTM	*Concordia Theologial Monthly*
CTQ	*Concordia Theological Quarterly*
CTR	*Criswell Theological Review*
Did.	*Didache*
DNTT	*Dictionary of New Testament Theology*
DownRev	*Downside Review*
DSB	Daily Study Bible
EBC	Expositor's Bible Commentary
EDNT	*Exegetical Dictionary of the New Testament*
EGT	*The Expositor's Greek Testament*
EGNT	*Exegetical Greek New Testament*
EKKNT	Evangelisch-katholischer Kommentar zum Neuen Testament
ETC	English Translation and Commentary
ETL	*Ephemerides theologicae lovanienses*
EvT	*Evangelische Theologie*
EvQ	*Evangelical Quarterly*
ETR	*Etudes théologiques et religieuses*
ETS	Evangelical Theological Society
Exp	*Expositor*
ExpTim	*Expository Times*
FNT	*Filologia Neotestamentaria*
FRLANT	Forschungen zur Religion und Literatur des Alten und Neuen Testaments
GAGNT	M. Zerwick and M. Grosvenor, *A Grammatical Analysis of the Greek New Testament*
GNB	Good News Bible
GNBC	Good News Bible Commentary
GTJ	*Grace Theological Journal*
HBD	*Holman Bible Dictionary*
HBT	Horizons in Biblical Theology
HDB	J. Hastings, *Dictionary of the Bible*
Her	Hermeneia
HNT	Handbuch zum Neuen Testament
HNTC	Harper's New Testament Commentaries
HeyJ	*Heythrop Journal*
HTKNT	Herders theologischer Kommentar zum Neuen Testament
HTR	*Harvard Theological Review*
HUCA	*Hebrew Union College Annual*
IB	*The Interpreter's Bible*

IBS	*Irish Biblical Studies*
ICC	International Critical Commentary
IDB	*Interpreter's Dictionary of the Bible*
IDBSup	Supplementary Volume to *IDB*
IJSL	*International Journal for the Sociology of Language*
Int	*Interpretation*
INT	Interpretation: A Bible Commentary for Preaching and Teaching
ISBE	*International Standard Bible Encyclopedia*
JAAR	*Journal of the American Academy of Religion*
JANES	*Journal of Ancient Near Eastern Studies*
JAOS	*Journal of the American Oriental Society*
JBL	*Journal of Biblical Literature*
JES	*Journal of Ecumenical Studies*
JETS	*Journal of the Evangelical Theological Society*
JJS	*Journal of Jewish Studies*
JR	*Journal of Religion*
JRE	*Journal of Religious Ethics*
JRH	*Journal of Religious History*
JRS	*Journal of Roman Studies*
JRT	*Journal of Religious Thought*
JSNT	*Journal for the Study of the New Testament*
JSOT	*Journal for the Study of the Old Testament*
JSS	*Journal of Semitic Studies*
JTSA	*Journal of Theology for Southern Africa*
JTS	*Journal of Theological Studies*
LB	*Linguistica Biblica*
LEC	Library of Early Christianity
LouvSt	*Louvain Studies*
LS	Liddel and Scott, *Greek-English Lexicon*
LTJ	*Lutheran Theological Journal*
LTQ	*Lexington Theological Quarterly*
LW	Luther's Works
LXX	Septuagint
MCNT	Meyer's Commentary on the New Testament
MDB	*Mercer Dictionary of the Bible*
MM	J. H. Moulton and G. Milligan, *The Vocabulary of the Greek Testament*
MNTC	Moffatt NT Commentary
MQR	*Mennonite Quarterly Review*
MT	Masoretic Text
NAB	New American Bible
NAC	New American Commentary
NASB	New American Standard Bible

NBD	*New Bible Dictionary*
NCB	New Century Bible
NEB	New English Bible
Neot	*Neotestamentica*
NICNT	New International Commentary on the New Testament
NIGTC	New International Greek Testament Commentary
NIV	New International Version
NovT	*Novum Testamentum*
NovTSup	Novum Testamentum, Supplements
NPNF	Nicene and Post-Nicene Fathers
NRSV	New Revised Standard Version
NRT	*La nouvelle revue théologique*
NTD	Das Neue Testament Deutsch
NTI	D. Guthrie, *New Testament Introduction*
NTM	*The New Testament Message*
NTS	*New Testament Studies*
PC	Proclamation Commentaries
PEQ	*Palestine Exploration Quarterly*
PRS	*Perspectives in Religious Studies*
PSB	*Princeton Seminary Bulletin*
RB	*Revue biblique*
RelSRev	*Religious Studies Review*
RevExp	*Review and Expositor*
RevQ	*Revue de Qumran*
RevThom	*Revue thomiste*
RHPR	*Revue d'histoire et de philosophie religieuses*
RSPT	*Revue des sciences philosophiques et théologiques*
RSR	*Recherches de science religieuse*
RSV	Revised Standard Version
RTP	*Revue de théologie et de philosophie*
RTR	*Reformed Theological Review*
SAB	*Sitzungsbericht der Preussischen Akademie der Wissenschaft zu Berlin*
SBLDS	SBL Dissertation Series
SBLMS	SBL Monograph Series
SBLSP	SBL Seminar Papers
SCR	*Studies in Comparative Religion*
SEAJT	*Southeast Asia Journal of Theology*
SJT	*Scottish Journal of Theology*
SNTSMS	Society for New Testament Studies Monograph Series
SNTU	*Studien zum Neuen Testament und seiner Umwelt*
SPCK	Society for the Promotion of Christian Knowledge
ST	*Studia theologica*
SWJT	*Southwestern Journal of Theology*

TB	*Tyndale Bulletin*
TBC	Torch Bible Commentaries
TBT	*The Bible Today*
TDNT	G. Kittel and G. Friedrich, eds., *Theological Dictionary of the New Testament*
TGl	*Theologie und Glaube*
Theol	*Theology*
ThT	*Theology Today*
TLZ	*Theologische Literaturzeitung*
TNTC	Tyndale New Testament Commentaries
TrinJ	*Trinity Journal*
TRu	*Theologische Rundschau*
TS	*Theological Studies*
TSK	*Theologische Studien und Kritiken*
TU	Texte und Untersuchungen
TynBul	*Tyndale Bulletin*
TZ	*Theologische Zeitschrift*
UBS	United Bible Societies
UBSGNT	*United Bible Societies' Greek New Testament*
USQR	*Union Seminary Quarterly Review*
VD	*Verbum Domini*
VE	*Vox Evangelica*
WBC	Word Biblical Commentary
WEC	Wycliffe Exegetical Commentary
WMANT	Wissenschaftliche Monographien zum Alten und Neuen Testament
WP	Word Pictures in the New Testament, A. T. Robertson
WTJ	*Westminster Theological Journal*
WUNT	Wissenschaftliche Untersuchungen zum Neuen Testament
ZDPV	*Zeitschrift des deutschen Palästina-Vereins*
ZNW	*Zeitschrift für die neutestamentliche Wissenschaft*
ZRGG	*Zeitschrift für Religions- und Geistesgeschichte*
ZST	*Zeitschrift für systematische Theologie*
ZTK	*Zeitschrift für Theologie und Kirche*

Contents

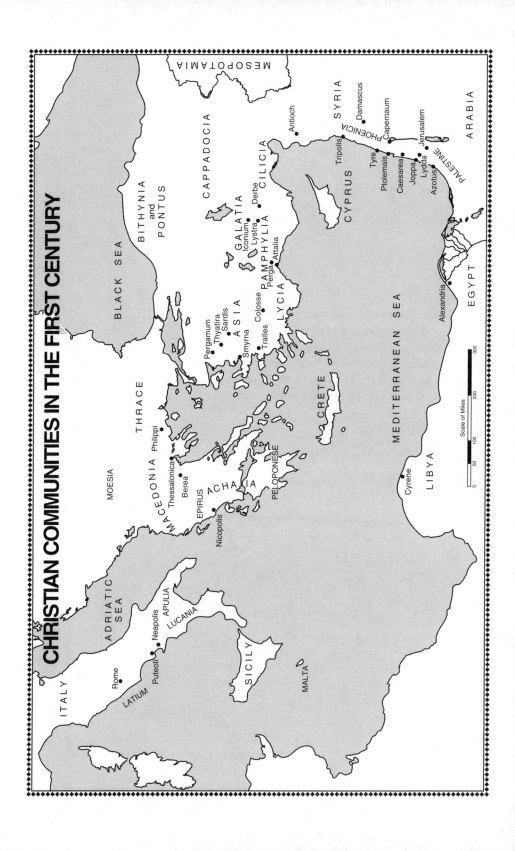

CHRISTIAN COMMUNITIES IN THE FIRST CENTURY

James

1. The Letter of James
   (1) James's Greek and Literary Style
   (2) Structure
   (3) Literary Form
   (4) Literary Context
       The Old Testament
           The Law
           The Prophets
           Old Testament Wisdom
       Intertestamental Jewish Literature
       The New Testament
           The Four Gospels
           The Writings of Paul
2. The Occasion of James
3. The Theology of James
   (1) Eschatology
   (2) Faith and Deeds
   (3) Ethical Teaching: Speech, Trials, Wealth, Mercy
   (4) Law
   (5) Wisdom
   (6) Human Nature
   (7) Church
   (8) God

———————————— INTRODUCTION ————————————

1. The Letter of James

The Epistle of James would serve well as a companion piece to Jesus' teachings recorded in the canonical Gospels. Its strong ethical nature is entirely consistent with the moral teaching of Jesus to his disciples as well as the sometimes harsh denunciations he uttered against religious hypocrisy. Like Jesus' teachings, this letter is a source of both exhortation and comfort, of reproof and encouragement. James is known for being eminently practical; but at the same time, some of the most profound truths of the New Testament emerge from the text.

This commentary is first of all a theological exposition[1] of the Epistle of James. It presses beyond the strictures of exegetical minutiae toward the larger and more fundamental meaning of the epistle. This introduction aims to help the reader of James appreciate contemporary scholarship on the epistle. This survey is by no means exhaustive; indeed, the scholar will immediately recognize the necessity of consulting the sources cited for the mass of detail. This introduction supplies an overview of the major issues confronting the contemporary study and application of James's epistle.

(1) James's Greek and Literary Style

The high quality of James's use of *koine* Greek has long been compared to that of Hebrews.[2] It may be judged of a more literary

---

[1] See the valuable encapsulation of themes in A. Chester, "The Theology of James," in *The Theology of the Letters of James, Peter, and Jude,* ed. A. Chester and R. P. Martin (Cambridge: University Press, 1994), 1–62. Cf. also J. B. Adamson, *James: The Man and His Message* (Grand Rapids: Eerdmans, 1989); P. H. Davids, *The Epistle of James* (Grand Rapids: Eerdmans, 1982); U. Luck, "Die Theologie des Jakobusbriefes," *ZTK* (1981): 1–30.

[2] J. B. Mayor, *The Epistle of St James: The Greek Text with Introduction, Notes, Comments and Further Studies in the Epistle of St. James,* 3rd. ed. (London: Macmillan, 1913), cclv–cclix. Also see the chart in D. B. Wallace, *Greek Grammar Beyond the Basics* (Grand Rapids: Zondervan, 1996), 30.

quality than that of the Gospel of John and does not indulge in the personalized expressiveness found in Paul's letters. When James quoted or alluded to the Old Testament, he used the Septuagint (LXX), a pre-Christian Greek translation (cf. 2:8–11,23; 4:6; 1:11; 2:25; 5:4,17,20). James's vocabulary and frequent use of syntax affected by the Hebrew underlying the LXX[3] are evident throughout his letter. At significant points in chaps. 2–3, knowledge of the LXX would have been necessary for a precise understanding of James's original meaning.

James's close relation to the LXX is significant since much of the negative critical study of the epistle in the modern period (nineteenth and twentieth centuries) has regarded the literary quality of Greek in the letter as the prime argument against Jacobean authorship. The judgment also has been made that the question of the letter's point of origin can be answered by the fluency of its Greek; that is, James was a product of diaspora Judaism.[4] Many Jews in Palestine, however, attained high proficiencies in speaking and writing Greek. Indeed, virtually all Jews of the first century A.D. were Hellenized.[5] Most Palestinian Jews, of course, like Jews of

---

[3] Known as "semitisms"; cf. C. F. D. Moule, *An Idiom Book of New Testament Greek,* 2nd. ed. (Cambridge: University Press, 1959), 171–91; K. Beyer, *Semitische Syntax im Neuen Testament,* 2nd ed., SUNT 1 (Göttingen: Vandenhoeck & Ruprecht, 1968); N. Turner, *Style,* in *A Grammar of New Testament Greek,* vol. 4, ed. J. H. Moulton, (Edinburgh: T & T Clark, 1976), 116–20.

[4] Cf. E. Baasland, "Literarische Form, Thematik und geschichtliche Einordnung des Jakobusbriefes," *ANRW* II.25/5, 3676.

[5] Cf. J. N. Sevenster, *Do You Know Greek? How Much Greek Could the First Jewish Christian Have Known?* NovTSup 19 (Leiden: Brill, 1968); M. Hengel, *The 'Hellenization' of Judaea in the First Century after Christ,* trans. J. Bowden (London: SCM, 1989); E. M. Meyers and J. F. Strange, *Archaeology, the Rabbis and Early Christianity* (Nashville: Abingdon, 1981); R. Riesner, *Jesus als Lehrer: Eine Untersuchung zum Ursprung der Evangelien-Überlieferung,* 3rd. ed., WUNT, 2.7 (Tübingen: Mohr, 1988); and S. E. Porter, "Jesus and the Use of Greek in Galilee," in *Studying the Historical Jesus: Evaluations of the State of Current Research,* ed. B. Chilton and C. A. Evans (Leiden: Brill, 1994, 123–54). Note also the important observation that early Christians often came from middle-class backgrounds and would have had access to Greek forms of education; cf. G. Theissen, "'We Have Left Everything . . .' (Mark 10.28): Discipleship and Social Uprooting in the Jewish-Palestinian Society of the First Century," in *Social Reality and the Early Christians,* trans. M. Kohl (Minneapolis: Fortress, 1992), 60–93.

the diaspora, would have been bilingual with Greek as their second language. The matter of authorship, date, or place of origin simply cannot be decided by appeal to the quality of James's Greek. The Greek of James is polished, but the epistle betrays an intimate knowledge of the LXX and of the teachings of Jesus.

James's style is multifaceted,[6] with several stylistic features working together to produce the overall effect of his message. His prophetic voice is prominent throughout the letter, detectable especially in the short sentences, the use of 59 imperatives in 108 verses, and in rhythmic speech (cf. 4:7–10). James is also didactic; for example, an imperative is usually accompanied by an explanation; and a command, by a rationale. Poetic elements in James include asyndeton,[7] pleonasm,[8] rhyme, alliteration, wordplay, or punning and catchwords.[9] Striking rhetorical features also are present, particularly those of the diatribe:[10] the use of an unidentified interlocutor who gives a sense of the dialogical; the use of stinging epithets, stereotype, question/answer, rhetorical questions to signal necessary agreement, comparisons, even expletives, as well as brevity of expression.

James's use of analogy is particularly striking: wind-tossed waves (1:6), withering plants (1:10–11), self-inspection using a mirror (1:23), a dead body (2:26), bridling of a horse (3:3), turning a ship (3:4), forest fire (3:5–6), taming wild beasts (3:7), impossible fountain of fresh and bitter water (3:11), impossible vine of grape and figs (3:12), ephemeral mist (4:14), clothes consumed by moths (5:2), rust behaving like fire (5:3), farmers waiting for rain (5:7), rain watering the earth (5:18). James also uses the technique of exaggeration to the point of paradox: trials should occasion "pure joy" (1:2); the humble brother "ought to take pride in his high position" (1:9); the rich man should "take pride in his low position" (1:10); "God cannot be tempted by evil, nor does he

---

[6] Cf. E. Baasland, "Literarische Form, Thematik und geschichtliche Einordnung des Jakobusbriefes," 3659–62.

[7] A leaving out of conjunctions between coordinate sentence elements.

[8] Use of redundancy for emphasis.

[9] Repeated words that thus "stitch" separate passages together.

[10] A formal denunciation.

tempt anyone" (1:13); "full-grown" sin "gives birth to death" (1:15); God the Father gives "birth" to believers (1:18); demons "believe . . . and shudder" (2:19); the tongue is "a fire," "a world of evil," "set on fire by hell" (3:6); "your desires . . . battle within you" (4:1). These stylistic components underscore how very powerful is the language of James.

(2) Structure

One of the major debates over how to interpret James concerns the letter's structure. Some have asserted that James is a rather disconnected collection of sayings,[11] while others have contended that it is a well-organized and coherent letter centering on a theme or set of themes.[12] A number of proposals based on overly complex structural or syntactical analyses[13] are not persuasive because they presume a kind of textual control foreign to the characteristics of writing in the ancient world. Structure according to topical arrangement is certainly apparent in some segments: 1:2–12 presents the testing of faith; 2:1–11 presents the contradiction of faith and favoritism; 2:14–26 presents the relation between faith and deeds; 3:1–12 presents the power of speech; 3:13–18 presents the two

---

[11] Cf. esp. M. Dibelius, *James,* Her., rev., H. Greeven, trans. M. A. Williams (Philadelphia: Fortress, 1975), 11.

[12] E.g., J. H. Ropes, *The Epistle of St. James,* ICC (Edinburgh: T & T Clark, 1916), 4–5; F. Stagg, "An Analysis of the Book of James," *RE* 66 (1969): 365–68; F. Francis, "The Form and Function of the Opening and Closing Paragraphs of James and 1 John," *ZNW* 70 (1970): 110–26; P. H. Davids, *The Epistle of James: A Commentary on the Greek Text,* NIGNTC (Grand Rapids: Eerdmans, 1982), 22–29; F. Vouga, *L'Epitre de Saint Jacque,* CNT, vol. 13a (Geneva: Labor et Fides, 1984), 20; R. P. Martin, *James,* WBC (Waco: Word, 1988), ciii–civ.

[13] Cf. the otherwise valuable contributions of P. B. R. Forbes, "The Structure of the Epistle of James," *EvQ* 47 (1975): 147–53; J. Duplacy, "Les divisions du texte de l'épître de Jacques dans B (03) du Nouveau Testament," in *Studies in New Testament Language and Text,* ed. J. K. Elliott (Leiden: Brill, 1976), 122–36; W. H. Wuellner, "Der Jakobusbrief im Licht der Rhetorik und Textpragmatik," *LB* 43 (1978): 5–66; C. B. Amphoux, "Systèmes anciens de division de l'épître de Jacques et composition littèraire," *Bib* 62 (1981): 390–400; H. Frankemölle, "Das semantische Netz des Jakobusbriefes. Zur Einheit eines umstrittenen Briefes," *BZ* 34 (1990): 161–97; and idem, *Der Brief des Jakobus. Ökumenischer Taschenbuch-Kommentar Zum Neuen Testament,* Vol. 17/1–2 (Gütersloh: Gütersloher, 1994), I, 152–80.

kinds of wisdom; 4:1–10 presents the opposition of friendship with the world and friendship with God; 5:7–11 presents the virtue of patience; 5:13–18 presents the power of effective prayer. Other verses and clusters of verses in the letter are not so easy to classify. Nearly all form a bridge of thought between the units just listed, but it is not always clear whether their content is linked more closely to a previous or a following section or whether they have a semi-independent role to play in the transitions of the text. Each of the five chapters of James contains units of teaching that contribute to its overall structure.[14]

Although the structure of the letter is approximated by the outline offered in this commentary, one might still inquire about the organizing idea of the letter. This commentary does not suggest an introductory status for the entirety of chap. 1. There is too much weighty teaching there to set it off from the other four chapters as a mere table of contents. There is certainly an eschatological framing of the letter that stands in the opening (1:2–12) and closing verses (4:6–5:12).[15] These verses contain essential features of an end-time ethic derived from the Old Testament prophets. But this feature belongs to the overarching concern of the letter. Structure and content are inseparable. Partly because James's style was determined by his commitment to brevity and partly because he intended to discuss a number of key themes, the structure of the letter is not readily apparent. No single term repeated through the letter secures for the reader this easy sense of structure.

On the other hand, the question of the structure of James should not be regarded as highly problematic. The fact that structure is something of a sensation for modern exegetes is part of a set of frustrations surrounding the search for the origins of the letter, stemming from the paucity of evidence. Consequently, the contents

---

[14] Contra L. T. Johnson, *The Letter of James,* AB (New York: Anchor, 1995), 13–15. While not asserting a structure based on a complicated analysis, Johnson sees chap. 1 as containing a succession of aphorisms that anticipate and link with the various sections of chaps. 2–5.

[15] Cf. the landmark study in T. C. Penner, *The Epistle of James and Eschatology: Re-reading an Ancient Christian Letter,* v. 121, *JSNT* (Sheffield: Academic Press, 1996), 158–213.

of the letter are the scholar's only resource for identifying the author, date, location of author and addressees, literary dependencies, and relation to other New Testament writings. Unfortunately, none of these questions can be answered definitively because of the absence of internal references other than the name "James" and "the twelve tribes scattered among the nations" (1:1). The Epistle of James comes to us in a given canonical form with its own textual integrity. These limits must be respected, and great care must be taken to avoid constructs that inhibit straightforward readings of the text.

(3) Literary Form

The question of literary form, often referred to as genre, is an important part of determining the meaning of James. James is distinctive in many ways, and much debate has surrounded the attempt to identify the text's literary type.[16] The traditional characterization of James as an "epistle" has much to commend it, although the question of what kind of epistle arises. In the case of the Pauline Epistles, some are addressed to persons, others to churches of an entire city, still others to clusters of churches within a region. There have never been completely consistent rules for identifying the literary type of a composition, nor have the rules of literacy within a given civilization ever been followed with exactness. Nevertheless, key interpretive questions, such as authorial intent and how

---

[16] C. L. Church (*A Forschungsgeschichte on the Literary Character of the Epistle of James* [Ph.D. diss., Southern Baptist Theological Seminary, 1990]) demonstrates the difficulty of positively identifying the genre. He rejects most scholarly proposals, although noting the homiletic character of the composition as rhetorically effective persuasion. He makes an important observation that the question of form and of the coherence of the composition should be linked only indirectly (p. 261). See also E. Baasland, "Literarische Form, Thematik und geschichtlich Einordnung des Jakobusbriefes," 3646–84; T. Kent, *Interpretation and Genre* (Lewisburg: Bucknell University, 1986); K. Berger, "Hellenistische Gattungen im Neuen Testament," *ANRW II*. 25.2 (1984): 1041–44; A. Fowler, *Kinds of Literature: An Introduction to the Theory of Genres and Modes* (Cambridge: Harvard, 1982); A. J. Malherbe, "Ancient Epistolary Theorists," *Ohio Journal of Religious Studies* 5 (1977): 3–77; H. Songer, "The Literary Character of the Book of James," *RevExp* 66 (1969): 379–89.

addressees hear the composition, are dependent upon identifying literary form.

The discernment of literary form, however, cannot be allowed to straightjacket contemporary readings of James for at least two reasons: (1) highly original and lively compositions exhibit extraordinary features that exceed the boundaries of literary typology, and (2) the reading of the text for faith never regards literary conventions as anything more than part of the instruments of effective communication. Faithful reading will be attentive to the affect of the text upon the whole self.

Upon close inspection James evokes the qualities of several literary types. The *epistolary* form[17] is commended by James's directness of speech and dialogical features, and especially by the opening: "James, a servant of God and of the Lord Jesus Christ. To the twelve tribes scattered among the nations. Greetings" (1:1). As Johnson suggests, the lack of more personal characteristics we often find in Paul's letters could be explained by it being a circular letter, its intended audience being "scattered among the nations."[18] The *diatribe*, a pedagogical device to exhort moral reform, is another likely type. A third is *paraenesis,*[19] traditional moral instruction in the form of loose sets of aphorisms or proverbs.[20] Identifying genre can tell much indirectly about the social setting of the addressees.[21] Numerous signs within the text of James give a general sense of the social and economic condition of James's hearers. The warnings against self-deception and inconsistent faith reflect the constant struggle of the people of God to maintain the

---

[17] Cf. S. K. Stowers, *Letter Writing in Greco-Roman Antiquity,* Library of Early Christianity (Philadelphia: Westminster, 1986).

[18] See Johnson, *The Letter of James,* 22–24.

[19] Cf. J. G. Gammie, "Paraenetic Literature: Toward the Morphology of a Secondary Genre," *Semeia* 50 (1990): 41–77; L. G. Perdue, "Paraenesis and the Letter of James," *ZNW* 72 (1981): 241–56.

[20] Cf. A. J. Malherbe, "Hellenistic Moralists and the New Testament," *ANRW II.II* 26.1 (1992): 278–93.

[21] Cf. L. T. Johnson, "The Social World of James: Literary Analysis and Historical Reconstruction," in *The Social World of the First Christians: Essays in Honor of Wayne A. Meeks,* ed. L. M. White and O. L. Yarbrough (Minneapolis: Fortress, 1995), 180–97.

truth of their religious identity. In this sense, some sections of James resonate with such intertestamental Jewish wisdom literature as *Sirach* and the *Wisdom of Solomon*. These and similar pieces written after the close of the Old Testament canon and prior to the birth of Christ helped to maintain the tradition of biblical wisdom found in the Old Testament and to define the communities of diaspora Judaism. That James could exhort his hearers in what appears to be reminders rather than new teaching reflects his hearers' familiarity with this sort of traditional wisdom.[22]

James's canonical "shape" is that of an epistle of the New Testament; and it has been received and interpreted, both inside and outside the church, as a general or catholic epistle. James is a literary whole, has a standing alongside the variety of other New Testament letters, and has close thematic links to the Synoptic Gospels, particularly with Matthew. The wisdom of James is a New Testament embodiment of his exhortation to the early church in epistolary form.

(4) Literary Context

James only indirectly reflects nonbiblical Hellenistic influences. Although James's Greek is very good, this fluency is not necessarily a warrant for any self-conscious relationship to the Greco-Roman forms of moral discourse.[23] From first to last, the Epistle of James is a profoundly Christian document rooted in the depth of Jesus' own teaching and in key Old Testament texts and personages. The obvious parallels and presuppositions of James come from both Old and New Testament texts and teachings and perhaps some intertestamental Jewish literature.

THE OLD TESTAMENT. James has a close relation to the Old

---

[22] Cf. esp. L. T. Johnson, "The Mirror of Remembrance (James 1:22–25)," *CBQ* 50 (1988): 632–45.

[23] No two scholars of James have been more qualified to detect connections with Greco-Roman sources than J. B. Mayor (see note 2) nearly a century ago and most recently L. T. Johnson. I disagree with Johnson's conclusion that James consciously used "common Hellenistic themes and *topoi*," whatever parallels might be suggested. Johnson does admit: "No single Hellenistic composition . . . provides an adequate literary comparison" (*The Letter of James*, 28–29).

Testament while being a fully Christian letter. In 1:1 James, writing to the "twelve tribes scattered among the nations," appropriated an Old Testament image of the people of God to refer to Christians outside Palestine. His usages of "law" (*nomos,* or *Torah*) are conspicuously Christian. "Wisdom" appears in his letter with both Old Testament and intertestamental nuances. Old Testament prophetic themes in a Christian cast characterize parts of the letter as well.

The Law. James called repeatedly for obedience to the law of God by believers; only by doing the word would they fulfill what God requires. He did not concentrate on the ritual law as Paul did in his polemic on circumcision (cf. Rom 3:20,28; Gal 2:16; 3:2,5,10). That James's focus was the moral law is suggested by his appeals to the Decalogue ("Do not commit adultery," and "Do not commit murder" in 2:11). For James the law is more than a prescribed list of commands; it is the revealed will of the one Lawgiver and Judge (4:12; cf. 2:11, "he who said"). The law is synonymous with the word of God. This Word is to be believed; its models of great faith are to be emulated; its wisdom is to be heeded; its commands to perform acts of mercy consistent with the character of the God of the exodus are to be obeyed.

The law as synonymous with God's word is visible in such phrases as "the perfect law that gives freedom"—"into" which the man who does this law looks (1:25). This same liberating law is the standard by which believers will be judged as well (2:12). James connected the law of freedom with mercy: both the divine mercy and a corresponding mercy in the actions of the believer (2:13).

There is, however, another usage of "law" in James: the "royal law" (2:8). This sense is reinforced by the reference to "kingdom" (2:5) within the same context. This law that governs the kingdom of God summarizes the Old Testament law in one of the greatest of all laws, that is, the command to love God and to love one's neighbor (Lev 19:18). Several passages in the Gospels show Jesus' approval of this principle (Matt 22:39; Mark 12:31; Luke 10:27). The summary command is also used in the writings of Paul (Rom 13:9; Gal 5:14) in a way similar to that of James. Fulfilling the royal law of Leviticus 19 is a vital theme in Jas 2:1,8,14–16; 3:13–

4:10–11; 5:4,12. The work of Christ in the New Testament is never an abrogation of God's call to his people to obey his commands. Jesus' own teaching is abundantly clear on this point (e.g., Matt 5:17–20). Faith must be active, and the revealed law of God defines that action.

The Prophets.   James's unmistakably prophetic voice is heard in several texts, especially in 4:4, where he castigates believers who seek "friendship with the world" because it amounts to enmity with God and spiritual adultery. This theme of spiritual adultery is deeply rooted in the exhortations of the Old Testament prophets (e.g., Isa 57:3; Jer 3:9; 13:27; Ezek 16:38; 23:45; Hos 3:1). The rigorous spiritual exercises to which James called his hearers in 4:7–10 (cf. 1:8) reflect the prophetic call to repentance (cf. Ps 73:28; Isa 1:16; Jer 4:14; Zech 1:3; Mal 3:7). Because God "opposes the proud" (Jas 4:6; cf. Prov 3:34), the rich man is like the "wild flower" that is scorched by the sun and quickly destroyed (Jas 1:10; cf. Isa 40:6–7). Indeed, the fierce statements James made against the unmerciful rich emerge out of the prophetic tradition of calling for social justice (Jas 5:1–6).[24]

Significantly, James called his audience to emulate the prophets: "Brothers, as an example of patience in the face of suffering, take the prophets who spoke in the name of the Lord" (5:10). Job, because of his endurance, is said to be one of these prophets (5:11). The prophets served the Word of God rather than the world political order and endured suffering for their service. Jesus' teaching as well as the rest of the New Testament reflected that Christians should follow the Old Testament prophetic model (cf. Matt 5:11–12; Luke 6:23; 11:50; 13:34; 1 Thess 2:15; Heb 11:32–34). Believers should take Elijah as their exemplar in exercising complete trust in God through effective prayer (Jas 5:17–18).

Old Testament Wisdom.   In spite of the extent of exhortation and prophetic witness in James, its simple characterization as "the wisdom book of the New Testament" is inadequate. Although James has

---

[24] Cf. Isa 3:14–15; 5:8–9; 13:6; 50:9; Jer 12:3; 22:13; 25:34; Ezek 16:49; 30:2; Joel 2:23; Amos 2:6–7; 3:10; 4:1; 8:4–6; Mal 3:5.

a prominent sapiential (wisdom) component, the letter is by no means dominated by wisdom themes.[25] Perhaps this sapiential characterization is understandable from the early exhortation to seek wisdom from God in the face of the end-time trials of the believer (1:5; cf. Prov 2:3–6; Ps 51:6). In a way that is reflective of New Testament understandings, James contrasts wisdom from God with wisdom from the world (Jas 3:13–18). Sapiential elements are present throughout the letter. The problem of double-mindedness is pondered by the Old Testament teachers of wisdom (1:8; cf. Ps 119:113). The transience of wealth and well-being is a sapiential theme (1:10; cf. Job 14:2; Pss 102:4,11; 103:15–16). Temptation comes from within the self (Jas 1:14; cf. Prov 19:3); self-mastery is a common wisdom theme. The perfect gifts of creation come from God the Father (Jas 1:17; cf. Pss 85:12; 102:27; 136:7). A slow response avoids anger (1:19; cf. Prov 10:19). The law is perfect and a vehicle of blessing (1:25; cf. Ps 19:7). The tongue should be kept under restraint (1:26; 3:2; cf. Pss 34:13; 39:1; 141:3; Prov 10:19). Orphans and widows should be visited in their distress (1:27; cf. Job 31:16,17,21; Ps 146:9). Favoritism is to be rejected (2:1; cf. Prov 24:23). The poor are subjects of special divine favor (2:5; cf. Job 34:19). Boasting is a great sin of human speech (3:5; cf. Pss 12:3,4; 73:8–9). The tongue can be compared to a fire (3:6; cf. Prov 16:27) and a deadly poison (3:8; cf. Ps 140:3). Wisdom from God bears righteous fruit (3:18; Prov 11:18). God will not answer prayers wrongly motivated (4:3; cf. Ps 66:18). "God opposes the proud but gives grace to the humble" (4:6; cf. Prov 3:34). God desires deep repentance (4:8; cf. Pss 24:4; 73:28; 119:113). Human life is like a dissipating mist (4:14; cf. Job 7:7). Job endured in view of God's compassion and mercy (5:11; cf. Job 42:10,12–17; Ps 103:8). Oil imparts well-being (5:14; cf. Ps 23:5).

These examples show the importance of wisdom themes in James. Close inspection of these verses and their contexts, however, reveals

---

[25] Cf. T. C. Penner's critique (*The Epistle of James and Eschatology: Re-reading an Ancient Christian Letter,* JSNT, n. 121 [Sheffield: Sheffield Academic Press, 1996], 220) of B. Witherington, *Jesus the Sage: The Pilgrimage of Wisdom* (Minneapolis: Fortress, 1994), esp. 236–47. I am persuaded by Penner's arguments concerning the overall eschatological character of James, characterized by the imminent expectation of the Lord's return, rather than an "operational eschatology," which lacks this expectation.

that sapiential themes are embedded within others (e.g., nomistic and prophetic themes) that serve James's larger purpose of exhorting his hearers to consistent behavior as believers in the Lord Jesus Christ.

INTERTESTAMENTAL JEWISH LITERATURE.   The literary materials of Judaism from about 200 B.C. to the New Testament era are vast. Commentators recognize many resonances of this literature in James as well as in the rest of the New Testament. The present commentary points out these allusions in the footnotes. Some commentators seek this kinship from materials that were written up until about A.D. 200. This should not be regarded as wholly illegitimate since the time line of literary development in the ancient world worked on a much slower basis than today. Thus, a text like the *Pirke Aboth,* compiled around this later date and included within the *Mishna,* would nevertheless contain rabbinical sayings that easily were two centuries older than the composition.

How one views James's literary form or genre as well as its dominant themes affects how one sees James's closest literary kin from this period. This problem becomes evident with respect to the apocalyptic/eschatological elements in James. If one is more inclined to regard James as basically a wisdom text and to discount the eschatological, then illuminating parallels from Jewish apocalyptic literature may be overlooked. Occasional citations from this body of intertestamental Jewish wisdom literature, especially from *Sirach, Philo, 1–4 Maccabees, The Testaments of the Twelve Patriarchs, Wisdom of Solomon,* do not imply that James was in any way directly dependent upon them. They can be helpful, however, in highlighting themes in James that resonate with these noncanonical texts.[26]

---

[26] Cf. R. W. Wall, "James as Apocalyptic Paraenesis," *ResQ* 32 (1990): 11–22; H. von Lips, *Weisheitliche Traditionen im Neuen Testament, WMANT* 64 (München: Neukirchener, 1990); H. Frankemölle, "Gesetz im Jakobusbrief: Zur Tradition, contextuellen Verwendung und Rezeption eines belasteten Begriffes," in *Das Gesetz im Neuen Testament,* ed. K. Kertelge, *QD* 108 (Freiberg: Herder, 1986), 175–221; E. J. Schnabel, *Law and Wisdom from Ben Sira to Paul,* WUNT 2.16 (Tübingen: Mohr, 1985); Baasland, "Literarische Form, Thematik und geschichtliche Einordnung des Jakobusbriefes"; C. H. Hope, *Wisdom, Law and Social Concern in the Epistle of James* (Ph.D. diss., Union Theological Seminary, 1982); R. Hoppe, *Der Theologische Hintergrund des Jakobusbriefes. FzB* 28 (Wurzburg: Echter, 1977); J. A. Kirk, "The Meaning of Wisdom in James: Examination of a Hypothesis," *NTS* 16 (1969–70): 24–38; B. R. Halston, "The Epistle of James: 'Christian Wisdom'?" *SE* 4 (1968): 308–14; O. J. F. Seitz, "James and the Law," *SE* 2 (1964): 472–86.

THE NEW TESTAMENT. James manifests a close relationship to the other New Testament writings, especially the Synoptic Gospels. But this intimate relationship must be defined. It is not clear that other New Testament texts reflect knowledge of James's epistle. This is not a unique circumstance, for most New Testament works lack clear references to other New Testament documents. A work like Acts with clear dependence on another New Testament document (Luke's Gospel) is the exception rather than the rule. The themes that James did not include are somewhat surprising: for example, the person and work of Jesus Christ, the work of the Holy Spirit, the practice of baptism and the Lord's Supper, and the gifts of the church and its nature as a spiritual body. The following paragraphs, however, trace some of the parallels with other New Testament texts, wherein it becomes clear that James really could only be a Christian composition.

The Four Gospels. Especially from Matthew[27] the following texts contain vocabulary and concepts similar to that of James: Matt 4:17, the nearness of the kingdom of heaven (cf. Jas 5:8); Matt 5:3, the blessedness of the poor (cf. Jas 2:5); Matt 5:7, the blessedness of the merciful (cf. Jas 2:13); Matt 5:8, purity of heart (cf. Jas 4:8); Matt 5:9, peacemaking (cf. Jas 3:18); Matt 5:11–12, persecution and trials (cf. Jas 1:1; 5:10–11); Matt 5:16, the light of good works glorifying the Father (cf. Jas 1:17); Matt 5:17, the law fulfilled in Jesus (cf. Jas 1:25 and the perfect law); Matt 5:34–37, the command against oaths (cf. Jas 5:12); Matt 5:48, the command to be perfect (cf. Jas 1:4; 3:2); Matt 6:11, the petition for daily bread (cf. Jas 2:15–16); Matt 6:19, the counsel against hoarding wealth, which will decay (cf. Jas 5:2–3); Matt 6:22, "good" and "bad" eyes, which reveal the heart (cf. Jas 4:4,8); Matt 6:29, the perishability of earthly goods (cf. Jas 1:11); Matt 6:34, the uncertainty of tomorrow (cf. Jas 4:13–14); Matt 7:1, the prohibition against judging (cf. Jas 4:11–12); Matt 7:7–8, the command to ask

---

[27] Cf. P. J. Hartin, *James and the Sayings of Jesus, JSNT 47* (Sheffield: JSOT, 1991); P. H. Davids, "James and Jesus," in *Gospel Perspectives: The Jesus Tradition Outside the Gospels,* ed. D. Wenham (Sheffield: JSOT, 1985), 63–84; M. H. Shepherd, "The Epistle of James and the Gospel of Matthew," *JBL* 75 (1976): 40–51; R. Cooper, "Prayer: A Study in Matthew and James," *Encounter* 29 (1968): 268–77.

God (cf. Jas 1:5; 4:3); Matt 7:16, fruit that reveals true character (cf. Jas 1:21; 3:10–13,18); Matt 7:21–23, the warning against mere profession (cf. Jas 1:26–27; 2:14–26; 3:13–14); Matt 7:24, the security of a life built upon Christ's commands (cf. Jas 1:22–25); Matt 8:29, the demons' fear of the Lord (cf. 2:19); Matt 10:22, the promise of salvation to those who endure (cf. Jas 1:12); Matt 12:32, the forgiveness of sins (cf. Jas 5:15); Matt 12:36, account-ability for every spoken word (cf. 3:1–2); Matt 18:4, the necessity of humility (cf. Jas 1:9–10; 4:10); Matt 24:33, the image of the Lord at the door (Jas 5:8–9).

The Gospels of Mark and Luke also contain material similar to that found in James: for example, Mark 12:28–31, the greatest commandment (cf. Jas 2:8–10,19); Luke 6:24, the warning against the rich and their wealth (cf. Jas 2:6; 4:9; 5:1–5); Luke 8:1–15, the seed of God's Word (cf. Jas 1:18–21); Luke 12:16–21, the pre-sumptuous rich (cf. Jas 4:13–15); Luke 16:19–31, the contrast of a rich man and a poor man (cf. Jas 2:2–7).

The Gospel of John and the Johannine Epistles also contain comparable material: John 1:4; 3:19–21; 8:12, that life is in and from the Lord (cf. Jas 1:17–18); John 3:3,8,13, to be born of God (cf. Jas 1:17–18); John 6:63, the life-giving word of the Lord (cf. Jas 1:21); John 13:17, the blessedness of obeying the Lord's com-mands (cf. Jas 1:25; 4:17); 1 John 1:5, the light of God (cf. Jas 1:17); 1 John 1:10, the denial of God's culpability for our sin (cf. Jas 1:16); 1 John 2:5, maturity in obedience (cf. Jas 3:1); 1 John 2:8, the falsehood in claiming faith while hating one's brother (cf. Jas 2:1–4,15–16; 3:13–18); 1 John 2:15, the protest against love of the world (cf. Jas 4:4–6); 1 John 2:24–25, endurance and the prom-ise of eternal life (cf. Jas 1:12); 1 John 3:17, lack of mercy as a lack of love for God (cf. Jas 2:5; 15–16); 1 John 2:21–22, confidence in obedience (cf. Jas 1:6–7).

The Writings of Paul.   The history of Christian biblical inter-pretation is fraught with many controversies over how to square one saying or assertion with another, but none has been so broad ranging or theologically embattled as that dealing with the relation between James and the Pauline Epistles. The perception of a radical tension between the teachings of Paul on justification by faith apart from works and those of James that require faith and works comes largely from the Reformation conflicts between Luther and his Roman Catholic opponents. Counter-reformation polemics at times yielded to proof-texting James against Paul, which infuriated a younger Luther. In the first edition preface to his German translation of the New Testament, Luther published the now infamous remark that James was "a right strawy epistle,"[28] which he would just as well remove from the canon of Scripture. The disparaging statements were removed from all later editions of the "Luther Bible." Nevertheless, the teaching of James dogged Luther,[29] and throughout his life he let it be known, somewhat jokingly, that he would give his doctor's cap to whoever could show how Paul and James's teachings could be reconciled.[30] In recent decades biblical scholarship has been effectively showing how Paul and James meant different things by their vocabulary based upon their different purposes. Once we begin thinking theologically about "saving faith," statements that seem to imply faith apart from works and faith inseparable from works do seem at odds with each other. Fortunately, this apparent conflict is not where precise interpretation of James must rest.

As will be seen later in the commentary, particularly at 2:14–25, James was not making a pronouncement about who is "saved" and who is not. Instead, he was speaking about the necessity of demonstrating faith. Paul in his writings was most concerned with describing how God has saved his people in Christ. Paul was intent upon disclosing the divine plan of salvation through history in his Epistle to the Romans and the freedom of God in reconciliation in Galatians. James touched upon none of this. From the overall perspective of the New Testament, he surely was presupposing these matters. Their point of closest relation is on what it means for God to "save" the believer. Otherwise, how James and Paul employed

---

[28] Cf. the helpful article by T. George, "'A Right Strawy Epistle': Reformation Perspectives on James," *RevExp* 83 (1986): 369–82.

[29] Luther chafed over the epistle because it does not contain "even once the great doctrine of the suffering, the resurrection, the Spirit of Christ; he names Christ a couple of times, but teaches nothing about him, but speaks only of a general belief in God" [author's translation] (WA.DB 7,384,19–22).

[30] Cf. F. Schmidt-Clausing, "Die unterschiedliche Stellung Luthers und Zwinglis zum Jakobusbrief," *Reformation* 18 (1969): 568–85.

the vocabulary they have in common is very different, for example, in the case of words such as "faith," "law," and "works." Paul's vocabulary, however, is so rich in meaning that we can distinguish between usages that do and do not correlate with that of James.

The case of the term "works" is most instructive. Paul's use of the phrase "works of the law" in contrast to the righteousness that is by faith was unique to him. But in the majority of cases in Paul, "works" in the sense of behavior that is good or right takes on a positive meaning in the life of faith (e.g., Rom 13:3; 15:18; 1 Cor 3:13ff.; 9:1; 15:58; 16:10; 2 Cor 9:8; 11:15; 1 Thess 1:3; 5:13; 2 Thess 2:17). Paul taught that the works of believers will come under judgment and that they must correspond to that which is commanded by the law of Christ (cf. Ps 61:13; Rom 2:5; Jas 5:3). Both Paul and James, in fact, were in agreement that the law is summed up in the command to love (Lev 19:18). Paul could write, "It is those who obey the law who will be declared righteous" (Rom 2:13) and sound very similar to James. According to Rom 2:25–27 circumcision is of no value (cf. Jas 2:9–11) if the law is not kept, and there are those who obey it without being circumcised who will be declared righteous. Both Paul and James recognized the internal battle of desires within the believer, which characterize the "double-minded" whom James warned (cf. Jas 1:8; 4:1; Rom 4:20; 7:23; 14:23). The only antidote is the fruit of the wisdom from above (Jas 3:17–18) that Paul called the fruit of the Spirit (Gal 5:22–23).

These important comparisons should be emphasized when reading Paul next to James. The apparent contradiction regarding works is just that, only apparent. James was not struggling against Judaizing Christianity, which sought to require the ritual aspects of Old Testament law in addition to faith in Christ. He was not trying to "correct" Paul at key points (e.g., Rom 3:20; Gal 2:16). He was concerned with the consistency of genuine faith as evidenced by its results,[31] that faith should be active, not a mere profession covering a life of sin.

---

[31] Cf. the careful argument in D. J. Verseput, "Reworking the Puzzle of Faith and Deeds in James 2.14–26," *NTS* 43 (1997): 97–115. See also J. C. Lodge, "James and Paul at Cross-Purposes? James 2:22," *Bib* 62 (1981): 195–213; T. Lorenzen, "'Faith without Works Does Not Count before God!' James 2:14–26," *ExpTim* 89 (1977–78): 231–35; W. Nicol, "Faith and Works in the Letter of James," *Noet* 9 (1975): 7–24; U. Luck, "Der Jakobusbrief und die Theologie des Paulus," *Theologie und Glaube* 61 (1971): 161–79; J. Jeremias, "Paul and James," *ExpTim* 66 (1955): 368–71.

2. The Occasion of James

Not being a church planter in Gentile territory as Paul was, James was not battling the same problems. A fairly clear picture of the context surrounding James and his audience could highlight the particular features of his epistle. Unfortunately James, like most of the writings of the New Testament, offers little for the historical researcher to use to identify its social context. Thus, what the greeting of 1:1 ("To the twelve tribes scattered among the nations") offers in the way of a historical referent is completely undetermined. Almost everything that can be discerned about the addressees of the Letter of James is derived from the text itself.[32] The concept of diaspora when applied to Christians will have an interesting theological meaning, but discerning its sociohistorical import is impossible unless the details of the context can be uncovered.

The text of James yields meager traces of information about its sociohistorical setting. The local congregation was led by teachers (3:1) and by a plurality of elders (5:14). The audience can be located somewhere within the socioeconomic middle. The story of the rich and poor visitors to the local congregation (2:1–4) suggests that at least the majority of James's audience identified with neither. They had suffered personal and legal persecution by the rich, who may have been professing believers (2:6; 4:13–5:6). There are of course other passages, for example, the traveling merchants in chap. 3 and the unpaid fieldhands and oppressive landowners in chap. 5. There is no consensus over whether all James's addressees were in fact in the congregation. The Hebrew prophets sometimes preached to absent foes. What is sure is that James's audience could "appreciate" preaching against the oppressive rich, whether or not the rich were Christian. Little more is offered by the epistle.

---

[32] Cf. W. Popkes, *Adressaten, Situation und Form des Jakobusbriefes. Stutgarter Bibelstudien,* 125/126 (Stuttgart: Katholisches, 1986); C. Burchard, "Gemeinde in der strohernen Epistel: Mutmassungen über Jakobus," in *Kirche: Festschrift für Günther Bornkamm,* ed. D. Lührmann and G. Strecker (Tübingen: Mohr, 1980), 315–28; J. B. Polhill, "The Life-Situation of the Book of James," *RevExp* 66 (1969): 369–78.

To go much beyond these inferences requires speculation and probably is not helpful to the proper interpretation of the text.

If the epistle's author is James the Lord's brother, then it was written before A.D. 62, perhaps in the previous decade. James is the only likely candidate for authorship, as, indeed, Christian tradition has affirmed. Did he write to Christians inside or outside Palestine? The allusion to the diaspora in the first verse is ambiguous. The reference likely indicates an original destination to Christians outside Palestine.

Whether or not James's audience was Jewish Christian rather than Gentile Christian can only be answered by conjecture. In the recent history of interpretation, impressive arguments have been offered for both positions. The letter itself is both Christian and reflective of the Jewish origins of the first Christians. It bears the marks of an author who belonged to the circle of Jesus' disciples. This was true of James, who did not belong to the Twelve but, like Paul, represented the earliest Christian teaching in its standard form.

Throughout much of the history of interpretation Paul's reference to "James, the Lord's brother" in Gal 1:19 was not taken to mean that James was born of the same mother. Older Roman Catholic interpretation was concerned to protect the perpetual virginity of Mary and to identify another James as the author of the epistle.[33] The problem with proposing another James to have written the letter is finding a more likely candidate. James the son of Zebedee (Matt 10:2) was killed by Herod Agrippa (Acts 12:2) and does not figure significantly in the New Testament. Neither does James the son of Alphaeus (Matt 10:3), nor James "the Less," a son of Mary and brother of Joses (Matt 27:56), nor James the father of Judas, although there is some lack of clarity in the New Testament on this unknown figure. What Origen had in mind in identifying the author as James, the Lord's brother, is not known, but he was the first Christian author to do so.[34] The simple identification "James, a servant of God and of the Lord Jesus Christ" (1:1) seems to signify a leader who was so well known within the first generation church

---

[33] Cf. Ropes, *James,* 54–62.
[34] *Com. ep. Rom.* IV.8.

that no further designation was required. The linkage with Jude's Epistle reveals the same dynamic, "Jude, a servant of Jesus Christ and a brother of James" (1:1; cf. Matt 13:55; Mark 6:3).

The figure of James the brother of Jesus looms large. He is mentioned among the brothers of Jesus in the Gospels (Matt 13:55; Mark 6:3). In Acts the brothers of Jesus were among the disciples awaiting the Spirit at Pentecost (1:14). When Peter was delivered from prison, he requested that this James be alerted (12:2–17). James became dominant in the Jerusalem church in Acts. He seems to be chief among the elders in Jerusalem at the first council of the church (Acts 15:12–21). At his initiative the letter to the Gentile Christians was drafted (Acts 15:23–29). By taking Paul's side in the controversy, James thwarted the Judaizing opinions prevalent in the Jerusalem church. Indeed, James is shown as Paul's ally here and was among the elders who affirmed the results of Paul's last missionary journey (Acts 21:18–19). The problem of Paul's apparent "law-breaking," however, was broached by James, not as something James believed but what others believed who were zealous for the law. This conservative movement was threatening the unity of the church. In order to overturn the opinion that Paul was a lawbreaker, James, along with the entire body of elders, suggested that Paul demonstrate his attention to ritual matters by paying for the sacrifices of pilgrims who had completed their Nazirite vows (Acts 21:24). The accounts in Acts show James's prominence in the early church and his fascinating and positive relationship with Paul. No little controversy surrounded Paul's ministry, as Galatians testifies. During Paul's ministry, no other James than the Lord's brother was a figure of comparable recognition.

Paul acknowledged that this James was one of the preeminent witnesses of the resurrected Christ (1 Cor 15:7). But James also was associated in some way with those Judaizing believers who were causing such disruption among the churches of Galatia. Early in Paul's ministry, three years after his Damascus road vision, "James, the Lord's Brother" (Gal 1:19) was one of those he visited. Paul considered him one of the chief leaders of the Jerusalem church (Gal 2:2,6,9), whose approval Paul sought and received. Paul was clear about their unity of purpose and understanding (Gal 2:7–9). His account of the unfortunate occasion of Peter and Barnabas's hypocrisy upon the arrival of "certain men . . . from James" (Gal 2:12) does not lay blame for the incident with James. Paul was giving here an example of how he had confronted this inferior understanding of the gospel in the past. The Galatians, in turn, were to follow his lead and give no room to the Judaizers and their ways. The situation at Galatia was tense, but nothing in the story should be taken to imply a rift between Paul and James or the Jerusalem church. Throughout the New Testament and extrabiblical literature,[35] no other James looms as large within the church of the first century.

The cumulative evidence points clearly to James the brother of Jesus as the author of this epistle. It is unlikely that the letter was written in response to Paul or any other New Testament author. Anything that might be suggestive of an interdependency or even conflict of ideas is strictly speculative. Much commends the letter as a very early piece of New Testament writing: close resemblances to Jesus' teaching, the simplicity of church organization, the simplicity with which the author identifies himself, and most of all, the lack of reference to wider church conflicts. All of these argue for an early dating of James, perhaps sometime in the decade after A.D. 50. Anything more precise would be mere conjecture. The massive literature treating the authorship and dating of the epistle ventures out of reach of solid historical critical scholarship.[36] The precise sociohistorical setting of James remains a mystery for scholars to

---

[35] Cf. Josephus, *Ant.* 20.200; for sources that report on James's death, cf. D. H. Little, *The Death of James, the Brother of the Lord* (Ph.D. diss., Rice University, 1971); A. Böhlig, "Zum Martyrium des Jakobus," *NovT* 5 (1962): 207–13; Eusebius, *Hist.Eccl.* II.1.5; III.23.1–18, referring to him with his title "James the Just," as bishop of Jerusalem (II.1.3); a number of Gnostic writings also contain references to James, e.g., the *Apocryphon of James, First and Second Apocalypses of James, Gospel of the Hebrews;* beyond these are early pseudepigraphical pieces that include the *Pseudo-Clementines, Epistle of Peter to James, Epistle of Clement to James.* These materials are of only minimal use beyond ascertaining the wide respect and honor James the brother of the Lord received in the early church.

[36] Cf. P. H. Davids, "The Epistle of James in Modern Discussion," *ANRW* II. 25.5 (1988), col. 3621–45; B. Pearson, "James, 1–2 Peter, Jude," in *The New Testament and Its Modern Interpreters*, ed. E. J. Epp and G. W. MacRae (Philadelphia: Fortress, 1989), 371–406.

pursue. In the life of the church, however, James's clear exhortations, teachings, and warnings need to be heard continually.

3. The Theology of James

The outline that follows serves as something of a road map to the epistle by highlighting major themes, giving a sense of James's theological direction.

(1) Eschatology

James's message is shaped throughout by an eschatological perspective. The trials and testings of 1:2–4 are presented in terms of the revelation of the end-time rule of God. It is this prospect over which believers are called to rejoice. In 5:7–9 the Lord's coming is said to be imminent, and he alone is adequate to judge. There is thus no room for believers judging one another (2:12–13; 4:11–12). In view of a judgment that God alone can render, the present must be characterized by acts of mercy, a heart of humility, and a life of purity. Judgment is certain, especially upon the rich who have oppressed others with no regard for God's future judgment (5:1–6). Nor have the rich considered the transience of their wealth. None of it will survive the final day, nor even their own deaths; still the rich have put their trust in earthly treasures rather than in God alone, thus making them double-minded (1:9–11; 4:13–15). Blessings, on the other hand, await those who have believed in the Word of God (1:12). Such have sought the wisdom of God for patient endurance in the present time (1:5) and as a result have the inward peace (3:17–18) to persevere to the end.

(2) Faith and Deeds

James juxtaposes faith and works for a particular instructional purpose: deeds (or works) demonstrate the genuineness of faith (cf. 2:14–26). The life of faith is fundamental for James and can be traced throughout the entire letter (1:19–26; 2:1–13; 3:13–18; 4:11–12). The way believers live must correspond to the claims they make for their faith. The harshness of James's language is evident everywhere he attacks the contradiction between faith and life. At the center of his heated warnings is his declaration of an impending "judgment without mercy" for all those who do not live according to mercy (2:12–13).

James extols those who both hear the Word of God and do what it says (1:19–26; 3:12–18). Such doers of the word have received it with humility, and its liberating power enables them to live lives that bear peaceable fruit. Rather than judging others or showing partiality (2:1–7), consistent believers fulfill the law through Christian love (2:8,12) and exercise the religion that "God our Father accepts as pure and faultless" (1:27). They provide care for persons in distress, especially orphans and widows, and avoid the moral pollutants of the world. This life of service to those in need and of commitment to eternal values has become their way of life and proves to be the very nature of faith. Unless professed faith is alive and active in this way, it is really useless and dead. The chilling example of showing special hospitality to a visiting rich man while disgracefully ignoring the visiting poor man presents the case in the most forceful way. A mere profession of faith in God is wholly inadequate, for even the demons express the same (2:19). Instead, a faith like Abraham's and Rahab's (2:21,25), which contained a readiness to do the will of God, is upheld as the faith that makes a difference.

In view of James's requirement of active faith, one assertion about the relation between faith and deeds in James is that works are essential. Deeds are the only way of demonstrating genuine faith. Faith and the law of freedom (1:25) are inseparable; thus, for example, neighbor love is indispensable to faith. Second, faith is integral. It is not a simple but a complex reality; faith requires deeds to be whole or complete. Faith is primary in James, but only true, active, consistent, genuine faith. Faith must be useful and so requires active obedience. It cannot be useful if it is standing alone apart from works of mercy and love. Third, the word "faith" has both positive and negative senses in James. The positive sense involves active trust in God exhibited through works of mercy and love. The negative sense involves an empty profession accompanied by empty assurances of help (2:16), by a harboring of envy and selfishness in the heart (3:14), and by prayers with wrong motives (4:3; cf. 1:6). Such faith will not endure trials with joyful expectation but instead will live in a way that actually invites divine punishment (5:5).

James's perspective on faith, then, is shaped by God's judgment of believers according to their works (cf. Matt 25:31–46; Rev 20:11–13). His task is not to make a determination regarding who will be saved—although he does say that believers are saved by the Word of God (1:21). Instead, his task is to urge the true life of faith upon all believers, one that God "accepts" (1:27). This clarifies what James meant by justification (2:24). The sense here is not what is found in Paul's argument in Romans or Galatians based upon the death and resurrection of Christ. Instead, justification in James has a narrow sense, the coherence of deeds "working together" (2:22) with faith. Men and women are justified in making the claim to faith when they actively trust in God. Active trust, like Abraham's or Rahab's, is a matter of performing deeds—deeds never without faith, of course, but most importantly, never faith without deeds. The faith of believers will be judged by God, and in James's view God will not accept anyone with an empty, useless faith, one where no deeds are present. Certainly there are tensions here with what Paul teaches about justification, but it is a healthy tension, one that is reflected within Paul's epistles themselves. James here echoes the teaching of Jesus in the Gospels.

(3) Ethical Teaching: Speech, Trials, Wealth, Mercy

The Epistle of James evidences a concern for reforming Christian behavior. James effectively develops several ethical topics: speech, trials, wealth, and mercy.

The problem of speech (the "tongue"), its power to bring good or to bring harm, is a well-known emphasis. Speech is the primary instrument of the teacher, and teaching is the context for James's treatment of speech (3:1–12). There is a duty to use the power of speech according to the good purposes of God, that is, for his praise rather than for the cursing of others (3:9). Unless speech is brought under control by wisdom from God, it will reign over the entire body and over all of one's relationships, causing conflict and division (3:15). The best general rule is to avoid all exaggeration in oath-taking. Simplicity of speech is the prime virtue here (5:12).

James's teaching on trials is also prominent. The believer, like the mass of humanity, faces much suffering in the world. Sometimes these trials even involve suffering at the hands of professing Christians who hold positions of power (5:1–6). Though such suffering may seem senseless, it should not be taken only as loss but as divinely purposeful and should thus be patiently received. James pointed to the example of the prophets, who endured all for the sake of obedience to God (5:10); faithful believers should see themselves as in their company. Suffering is not the only kind of trial, however, in James's thinking. Temptation to sin, to serve money and evil desire instead of God, is just as real (1:6–15; 2:1ff.). Believers must be watchful over their own hearts. They must endure the struggle against their own desires, which will surely lead them into sin if they do not maintain the constant meditation upon the Word of God and what it commands them to do (1:22–25). Trials "perfect" the believer, not in the sense that a person becomes sinless but that it drives him or her to mature, complete faith. Trials are used by God to strengthen the believer's resolve to do what God requires, trusting him for the wisdom to accept these trials accordingly. Any suggestion that James might teach a sinless perfectionism must deal with his own admission that all believers stumble in many ways (3:2).

The contrast between rich and poor is very obvious in the text of James. Like the Old Testament prophets, James attacked wealthy members of the people of God who contradicted the truth of their faith by withholding the acts of love and mercy required of them. James unambiguously condemned economic injustice (5:1–6) and harshly condemned the presumptuousness of clever entrepreneurs who fantasized about their own total control of their time and investments. This latter attitude is actually a sign of misplaced faith and therefore of unbelief (4:13–17).

If the majority of James's audience was not rich, however, one might wonder why all the denunciations. The need for such denunciation becomes abundantly clear in the shameful example of a church showing favoritism toward the rich visitor at the expense of the poor visitor (2:17). God has chosen the poor as special objects of his mercy (2:5). But this they completely disregarded. Instead, their behavior revealed their greed and envy of the rich even though the rich were oppressing them too (vv. 6–7). Their longing for special favors from the rich and for their own advantage, if unchecked, would lead them to commit sins against their brothers and sisters as great as any committed by the hard-hearted rich. If they were not circumspect, they would fall short of the religion God accepts, which is to show particular care for the poor, especially orphans and widows (1:27).

Instead of falling prey to greed and envy, believers must cultivate humility, mercy, and love. Everyone stands under the judgment of God, but only "mercy triumphs over judgment" (2:13). If believers are counting on the mercy of God, they are required to show that same mercy toward others (cf. Matt 6:12). This fruit is the sum of wisdom (3:17) and the only means to counteract the divisions and striving that result from evil motives.

(4) Law

Pointing out what James did not include under the rubric "law" (2:8–13) is as important as pointing out what he did include. James's concept of the law draws upon Lev 19:18, which sums up the whole law in the command to love God and neighbor (Jas 2:8; cf. Rom 13:10; Gal 3:10). This law is integral to faith, for it leads to the mercy and love God requires of those who trust in him. The ceremonial and political aspects of Old Testament law are not given the slightest attention by James. This "royal" law, the "law that gives freedom," is that which gives content to faith. It is the spring of action by which faith lives (cf. 2:17).

(5) Wisdom

Wisdom is the gift of God (1:5–8,17; 3:13–18). By wisdom believers translate their present trials into opportunities to trust in and do the will of God. The necessity of wisdom deepens as James comes closer to the description of true faith that contrasts with the foolishness of those who imagine that living faith does not necessarily express itself in obedience (2:20). What Paul meant by the fruit of the Spirit is not identical to what James meant by the fruit of wisdom "from heaven" (3:15,17). James did not make thematic connections with the spirit of wisdom known from the Old Testament (e.g., Prov 8:22–31) or from the writings of John and Paul. The practical outworkings of wisdom and of the spirit, however, are strikingly similar.

(6) Human Nature

James made the point that the conflicts of faith and the temptations to sin find their source within fallen human nature (1:13–15; 3:9; 4:1). Human beings are created in and possess the qualities of the image of God (3:9), but they are also their own sources of evil desire and contentiousness. James's epistle shows a consistency with the rest of the New Testament on this point. The devil and his demons are a reality (2:19), but they are in no way the cause of human contradiction and sin. "Each one" (1:14) is his own tempter whose evil desires, if they are given free reign, are more powerful than the weak will to resist. Only trust in God for the practical wisdom of faith can convert this situation into an occasion for deep repentance (4:7–10) and for deeds done in love.

(7) Church

The Letter of James does not supply direct teaching on the nature of the church but presupposes it. The local church possessed a plurality of elders upon whom the sick were to call for prayer (5:14), but James gave no indication of the nature of their authority. There were teachers, whose number was to remain small, for a harsher judgment awaits those lacking true competence or maturity for this role (3:1). Whether they held an office or simply exercised a spiritual gift is not apparent, nor is it indicated whether they were only male or could include females among their number.[37] The practice of prayer and the centrality of the Word of God are evident throughout James. But since ecclesiology is only a background factor in the message of our epistle, themes such as baptism and the Lord's Supper are not discussed.

---

[37] It is worth bearing in mind, however, how male-centered some of the references in this letter are; cf., e.g., 1:7; 2:20; 5:10; 4:4.

(8) God

God the Creator receives praise throughout the body of the letter. That he has created the universe and sustains it by continuing to give "perfect" gifts is summed up in the title "Father of lights" (3:9; 1:17). God is generous and merciful, but he is also the Judge and Lawgiver who is "able to save and destroy" (4:12). The doctrine of God, like that of the law or of Christ, is presupposed in James rather than extensively developed.

(9) Christ

Although Christology is one of the key doctrines of the faith that is presupposed in the letter, James did make it clear that Jesus Christ is the Lord whom he served (1:1). Significantly, Jesus Christ is said to share this title with "God" (the Father). He is also called "glorious" (2:1), fully sharing in the glory that belongs to God alone. With these twin titles, Christ is identified with God. Why is it that interpreters willingly accept the letters of Paul, which contain only minimal references to the story of Jesus' life, yet are unwilling to accept the same from James, claiming that it is not a truly Christian letter?

Given the uniqueness of James's letter, it is imperative that it be read on its own terms as a distinctive witness to Christian faith. Interpreters misread James when they read him according to standards that are foreign to him. A right understanding of his teachings is accessible only if readers let him speak and pay careful attention to the actual contents of his text.

──────────── *OUTLINE OF THE BOOK* ────────────

GREETING TO THE "DIASPORA" (1:1)

I. THE TRIAL AND FULFILLMENT OF FAITH (1:2–27)

1. Faith for Wisdom (1:2–8)
    (1) Joy for Maturity (1:2–4)
    (2) Faith without Doubt (1:5–8)
2. Faith Reversing Status (1:9–11)
    (1) The Boast of the Poor (1:9)
    (2) The Reduction of the Rich (1:10–11)
3. The Matter of Life and Death (1:12–18)
    (1) Trial as Life Giving (1:12)
    (2) Temptation as Life Taking (1:13–15)
    (3) The Element of Deception (1:16)
    (4) The Father and the Firstfruits (1:17–18)
4. The All-inclusive Doing of the Word (1:19–27)
    (1) Going Fast and Slow (1:19)
    (2) Discarding Offense and Accepting the Word (1:20–21)
    (3) The Liberating Mirror (1:22–25)
    (4) Worthless Religion and Genuine Religion (1:26–27)

GREETING TO THE "DIASPORA" (1:1)

¹James, a servant of God and of the Lord Jesus Christ,

To the twelve tribes scattered among the nations:

Greetings.

The Letter of James opens with a greeting contained in a single verse (cp. the seven-verse greeting that begins Romans). This apostolic salutation heads the chapter (vv. 1–17) of the letter. Stylistically, the greeting[1] is Greek and has a form that is unusual in the

---

[1] The infinitive of χαίρω, "to rejoice," used here elliptically as a formal beginning of a letter; cf. Acts 15:23; 23:26; also the inscriptions of the Ignatian letters; *Eph.; Mag.; Trall.; Rom.; Smyr.; Poly.; Barn.* 1.1.

New Testament (e.g., in Acts 23:26 in official Roman correspondence). But this assertion is unfounded, for the greeting can be found in intertestamental and early Christian literatures.[2] More important is that precisely the same greeting is used in the letter to the Gentile Christians in Acts 15:23, a letter almost certainly authored by James, the brother of Jesus (cf. 23:26; 2 John 10–11). Other letters of the New Testament bear distinctively Christian greetings "through the Lord Jesus Christ." This one is quite general, perhaps out of respect for the Hellenistic readership of the letter.

1:1   The greeting connects with the rest of our letter as part of its formal and thematic unity.[3] The repeated use of the word "God" in the text (cf. 1:5,13,20,27; 2:5,19,23; 3:9; 4:4,6–8) actually functions in a connective way.[4] "Lord," which can refer either to God the Father or to Christ the Son, also is woven throughout the letter (cf. 1:7; 2:1 with Christ; 3:9; 4:10,15; 5:4,10–11,15). Probably the most important bond between the greeting and the body of the letter is the wordplay between "greetings" *(charein)* in this verse and "joy" *(charan)* in the next.[5] This delightful linkage also moves the addressees directly into the practical/spiritual perspective of the epistle.

The one who addresses the readers so authoritatively is none other than James,[6] the Lord's brother, although the identification is not made explicit. The lack of further identification reflects, perhaps, James's determination not to allow his extraordinary familial relationship to imply unique authority for his teaching. Yet from the vantage point of the New Testament and the early church, this relationship was of signal importance. Part of the long questioning about the compatibility of Paul's teaching with that of James is rooted in the question of how prominent James was at the forma-

---

[2] Cf. *1 Macc* 10:25; *Euseb. Praep. Ev.* 9.33–34.

[3] H. Frankemölle, "Das semantische Netz des Jakobusbriefes. Zur Einheit eines umstrittenen Briefes," *BZ* (1990): 161–97.

[4] Although the full name "Jesus Christ" only occurs here and in 2:1, it will become fairly clear that the three references to "Lord" in 5:7–8,14 should be ascribed to the Lord Christ, who is coming in judgment.

[5] This connection unfortunately is incapable of being exposed in the English translation.

[6] Ἰακωβός, "James," unmistakably was the brother of the Lord and leader in the Jerusalem church.

tive stages of the church. James's teaching does represent the more Hebraic form of Christianity that would become eclipsed by the Hellenistic one. Fourth-century Christianity recognized its essential agreement with Jesus' teaching and could discern the indispensability of James's epistle. For our purposes it is enough to recognize who the author of the letter is in order to hear it and assimilate its teachings.

The title "servant"[7] James adopted for himself was one used to describe many of the Lord's chosen.[8] Throughout biblical history such persons—usually prophets—led the people of God because they were divinely selected to be his servants. Since an attitude of service is what distinguishes biblical leadership, there is no contradiction between service and leadership. What distinction there would be between reader and apostle is de-emphasized through the use of "servant" and through the repeated use of "brothers" when directly addressing the readers. This was James the Righteous, James the servant.

Although James's service was rendered to "God and to the Lord Jesus Christ," the text could bear the sense of affirming the deity of Christ. This sense appears again in 2:1, where Jesus can be said to be the glory of God. It is grammatically possible that James was saying he served "Jesus Christ who is God and Lord," which would be one of the great affirmations of the deity of Jesus Christ in the New Testament.[9] Titus 1:1, the only other New Testament greeting

---

[7] δουλός ("slave," a better translation than "servant") indicates full subjection to the authority of another. Note the use of this title rather than that of "apostle." Jude, the brother of Jesus, also employed the title "slave" at the beginning of his letter. This simple title indicates the familiarity of all with the author. No reference then is being made to Jesus in his earthly life (cf. 2:1). Instead, James was putting himself in the same relation of faith in Jesus as other believers (cf. 3:1–2).

[8] This title has a wide application: Moses in Deut 34:5; 1 Kgs 8:53; Dan 9:11; Mal 4:4; Josephus, *Ant.* 5:39; David in 2 Sam 7:5; 1 Kgs 8:16; Jer 33:21; Ezek 37:25; the prophets in Jer 7:25; 44:4; Amos 3:7. The apostles also, particularly Paul, employed the title in combination (Rom 1:1; Gal 1:10; Phil 1:1).

[9] Cf. F. Vouga, *L'epitre de s. Jacques,* CNT, Vol. 13a (Geneva: Labor et fides, 1984), 35; and more recently M. Karrer, "Christus der Herr und die Welt als Stätte der Prüfung: zur Theologie des Jakobusbriefs," *KerDo* 35 (1989): 166–88. Second Peter 1:2; Jude 4; Titus 2:13 could be seen as supporting texts.

to use the term "servant of God," does not add the name of Jesus Christ, whereas Rom 1:1, 2 Pet 1:1, and Jude 1 use "servant of [Jesus] Christ." The Book of Acts expresses the close relation between God and Jesus Christ (cf. 11:17; 15:26; 28:31). We should not turn away too quickly from this suggested interpretation.

James, however, may have been intending to exalt both God the Father and Christ. There is no doubt that such an ascription of deity to Jesus Christ would be a sensitive issue—though not as much in a Gentile as in a Jewish context. We must remember what an exalted status "Lord" carries and how it can be applied to both God and Jesus (1:27 and 3:9). Perhaps there is a kind of openness in this text for a reading that both distinguishes and identifies God and Christ. Against this ambiguity, however, is the use of the word "God," which in James always refers to the Father (1:27; 3:9). In serving Christ as Lord, James served God the Father.

The recipients of the letter, who possessed a messianic faith and therefore were the church, are named (lit.) "the twelve tribes in the dispersion *[diaspora]*." The Greek word *diaspora* is related to the verb *diaspeirō*, "sow, scatter"; hence the NIV rendering "scattered among the nations." Dispersion points first of all to Israel since the time of the Assyrian captivity of the ten tribes (cf. John 7:35). The connection is surely made here with believers in terms of the Old Testament anticipation of the restoration of Israel.[10] The use of the term here, however, has been extended to apply to all the people of God in Christ. The three uses of the verb *diaspeirō* in the New Testament all refer to the scattering of the church (Acts 8:1,4; 11:19). The noun *diaspora* also occurs three times. In John 7:35 it refers to Jews living among the Gentiles. But here and in 1 Pet 1:1 the reference is to the inclusive people of God who are scattered throughout the earth.[11] James wanted to affirm the closest connection between Jewish and Gentile Christians. They were all related by faith through Christ and through "our father" Abraham (cf. 2:21 and Gal 3:9). The idea of the church as the restored Israel appears in the New Testament in several key passages (Matt 19:28; Luke 22:30;

---

[10] διασπορά: "dispersion"; cf. Deut 30:1–4; Neh 1:8–9; Jer 30:3,11; 31:8–14; 32:37; Ezek 37:19–24; and also intertestamental literature; e.g., *Sol* 17:28.

[11] Cf. F. S. Rothenberg, "διασπορά," *DNTT* 1:686.

Rom 4; 1 Cor 10:1; Gal 4:21–31; 3:16; Phil 3; Rev 21:12). The sense here is that the church is the continuation of God's people Israel in a representative sense (Rom 9:24–26; Gal 6:16; 1 Pet 2:9).[12]

Significant passages in the Old Testament and the intertestamental literature identify certain Gentile nations who hosted the "diaspora" people of God: Babylon (Jer 29:4–23), Assyria (*2 Apoc. Bar.* 78–287), and Egypt (*2 Macc* 1:1–10a; 10b–2:18). The apostolic letter was sent abroad to the Gentile believers with the true diaspora people of God by James at the Jerusalem Council of Acts 15:23–29. In 1 Peter the Gentile addressees are treated as partners in a new Judaism. This letter describes them according to the Jewish stereotypes: election, stigma, suffering, future vindication. Election is seen to cause estrangement with the world and to require a sojourning mode of life. It is likely then that James's "diaspora" audience contained both Jewish and Gentile believers.

James identifies believers as the "twelve tribes." No matter how one views Israel in its ongoing relation to God, the term here is unequivocally being applied to the church of Jesus Christ (cf. 5:14). In comparison with Paul's view of the church from Ephesians 2 and Romans 11, we see that, far from displacing Israel as God's beloved, the church participates in a new covenant that will ultimately be the fulfillment of the original Abrahamic/Mosaic covenant. Through Christ believers are adopted into the family of the Heavenly Father and father Abraham (cf. Rom 4:11). Through Christ, with respect to his humanity, believers are spiritually adopted into the family of Abraham. This becomes most explicit in Gal 3:7, where all believers are directly called "children of Abraham."

It may also be suggested that "twelve tribes" is meant to correspond with the diversity of Gentile origins or identities that are present in the church.[13] This diversity is reflected in the seven churches of Revelation and in the many prophetic allusions to the

---

[12] S. Laws, *A Commentary on the Epistle of James* (New York: Harper & Row, 1980), 48.

[13] This notion appears within Christian circles as early as A.D. 140 in *Herm. Sim.* ix. 17.

multitude of people, languages, and nations that will participate in the kingdom of God. This diversity is also reflected in Peter's Pentecost sermon in Acts 2, where the diaspora are indirectly tied to the moment of the descent of the Spirit upon "all people" (Acts 2:17). Everyone heard the same word of praise to God but in each of the languages represented. They would all be baptized into one people in Christ on a single day. The jump from the many languages of diaspora Jews to the "all people" upon which the Spirit was poured out was a major event for the Jerusalem church of James's day. The church was growing among the many "tribes" of the Gentiles in all its ethnic diversity into one people of God.

However, there also is a negative aspect to "diaspora," the exile that is a wandering away from God. The theme of self-deception on the part of the people of God who actually contradict the truth of God is preponderant in the epistle.[14] The Lord remained faithful to his people even in the strange lands into which they had been dispersed, but their estrangement from him caused by their unrepentant sin got them there. Through faith in Christ, believers are no longer friends of the world (cf. 4:4) but experience a kind of exile existence whether Jew or Gentile.

Thus the theme of diaspora governs the entire letter. Indeed, its closing verse emphasizes the return to God from wandering in sin. But all of God's people share together the experience of exile, where trials and temptations are characteristic of the life of faith. Only through the profound wisdom and leading of God can they and will they endure. Indeed, in this way the letter presumes an interpretive standpoint for all of Scripture for believers of whatever origin, for they are part of the twelve tribes of the true Israel in Jesus Christ.

——— I. THE TRIAL AND FULFILLMENT OF FAITH (1:2–27) ———

This first section of James presents trials in their positive and negative aspects. Trials are to be seen overall as a ground for rejoic-

---

[14] Cf. T. B. Cargal, *Restoring the Diaspora: Discursive Structure and Purpose in the Epistle of James* (Atlanta: Scholars Press, 1993), 50.

ing since vital faith is required by God, and trials serve as its stimulus. Trials encourage a continuing dependence upon God and maturation toward the greater worship of God in the activities appropriate to faith in him. Wisdom is required for maintaining a vital faith relation to God and his Word. A kind of "perfection" (1:4,17,25 in KJV) is assured to believers who progress in wisdom. Great reward is promised to the believer who has great discernment for practicing "pure and faultless religion."

1. Faith for Wisdom (1:2–8)

This subsection teaches a rudimentary aspect of faith: allowing God to use trials in believers' lives to accomplish his purpose. Believers are encouraged to turn to God in the prayer of faith for divine wisdom. Wisdom from God (i.e., the Holy Spirit) in the New Testament is the special gift from above that strengthens faith. Wisdom, however, unlike the Spirit, is what "the word planted in you" (1:21) is all about. One source of great testing for faith is wealth, but "faith is the great equalizer,"[15] and trials will test rich and poor believers alike.

In these verses contrasts are set up between faith and doubt. This distinction is key. There is no belief/unbelief dichotomy in James. As we will see in the next chapter, the great problem is not unbelief but inactive faith (cf. 2:18). Doubt characterizes human nature, especially before God. Doubt is not contrasted here with certainty but rather with joy. For James joy is not the product of circumstances but rather the most fundamental expression of faith. Faith is not so much a means of accomplishment but rather a means by which to become open to the instructive wisdom of God. Wisdom is not so much a question of evaluating a person's performance as a means toward acquiring the maturity in faith that characterizes a true child of God.

---

[15] P. H. Davids, *The Epistle of James: A Commentary on the Greek Text* (Grand Rapids: Eerdmans, 1982), 65.

(1) Joy for Maturity (1:2–4)

²Consider it pure joy, my brothers, whenever you face trials of many kinds, ³because you know that the testing of your faith develops perseverance. ⁴Perseverance must finish its work so that you may be mature and complete, not lacking anything.

1:2 James began with pure encouragement, commending to believers the "pure [lit. "all"; NRSV "nothing but"] joy" that was theirs in the face of "trials of many kinds." Being brothers in Christ means sharing in the testing of their faith. James encouraged them to embrace their trials not for what they were but for what God could accomplish through them. As in the admonitions of Rom 5:2–5 and 1 Pet 1:6–7, James here teaches that trials serve as a test for genuine faith. Earthly hardships and losses put believers on display. Trials form an essential part of God's plan for his people. The God who will save us from the fate of the world will sustain us with joy in the midst of it. An eschatological joy is in view here (cf. v. 12). Believers know all the more by their suffering (Matt 5:11–12) that they belong to God.[16] The knowledge of this truth is the cause of their "pure joy," which rests upon the future revelation of God and the reversal of their circumstances (Mal 3:17–18).

The wordplay between "greetings" *(chairein)* and "joy" *(charan)* establishes the connection between James's greeting and his introduction, which suggests something of a title for his letter: Joy in serving God. James's reference to trials has in view specific sufferings of his readers (cf. 2:6; 5:1–6). The real artistry of the wordplay and other features of James's text indicate a crafting for the sake of moral persuasiveness.[17] The use of numerous verbal imperatives also accomplishes this. The first imperative of the letter, "consider it pure joy," initiates a series that continues through to the final chapter with "take the prophets," whose faith proved genuine

---

[16] Cf. Heb 12, where unambiguously trials are called the discipline of the Lord. In James trials are not merely a demonstration of genuine faith but also proof of divine love for the believer.

[17] A. Schlatter, *Der Brief des Jakobus* (Stuttgart: Calwer, 1956), 84–85. The doubling of words based on λείπω, "lacking nothing"/"lack wisdom" (cf. 4:5), is like the doubling "greetings-joy" of vv. 1–2, of ὑπομονή in vv. 3–4, and τέλειος in v. 4.

after "testing" (cf. 5:11).[18] Above all, Abraham (cf. Gen 22; Jas 2) is that one who endured the trial and was proven in the test. Many fail the tests of God, as in the example of Israel (cf. Num 14), but all of these tests are part of the larger scriptural context of our letter. In every trial the people of God should see their preparation for greater things God has planned for them.[19]

What exactly did James mean by "trials"?[20] Although the word *periasmos* can be understood in other contexts to mean a leading into evil, that is, "temptation" in the passive sense (cf. *peirazo*, "tempt," in 1:13), this is not the case here. These are testings in the active sense of experiences that prove a person's intentions. James's hearers were undergoing trials in the permissive will of God to prove the genuineness of their faith. Such trials come close to the crossbearing Jesus required of his disciples (Matt 10:38; 16:24). There would be trouble for them as they lived for him and his gospel. These trials involved persecution "because of righteousness" (Matt 5:10; cf. 1 Pet 3:14).

Like the great exemplars of faith, disciples should joyfully accept as tests the opposition they encounter to serving God. This is also in line with Paul's "many hardships" (Acts 14:22) by which we enter the kingdom of God (Acts 16). In such testing, the basic truth of discipleship in Jesus' own thinking must be kept in view: "If the world hates you, keep in mind that it hated me first" (John 15:18; cf. Matt 10:22; 24:9). Disciples are not greater than their Master, and essential to serving him is the testing that strengthens faith. Thus, because Jesus was tested (cf. Heb 2:10), his followers

---

[18] Important pieces of intertestamental literature help us see on what basis James employed OT references and values for his understanding of trials. James was the elder brother of his addressees. But his addressees had many other more elder brothers who had exhibited the same joyful service. On the basis of the OT exemplars, Sirach could declare that wisdom is promised to those who endure trials (2:1–6; 4:17–18); *4 Macc* focuses on endurance in the face of persecution (*4 Macc* 1:11; 9:30; 17:12; cf. Job 19:8; *T. Jos.* 2:7). In all of these references, faith and service are inseparable.

[19] Cf. *Jdt* 8:25; Luke 2:10; Matt 5:10–15; 1 Pet 4:12–14; 1 Thess 3:3; Acts 5:41.

[20] We often think of trials as merely troubles, but this is not the full sense of the word. In this verse God is the one testing the faith of believers; cf. 1 Pet 1:6; 4:12; 1 Cor 4:9; 2 Cor 9:23; *Sir* 6:7; 27:5,7; *Herm.* 9:7. Wealth and poverty also can be sources of trial as we see in v. 10 and in 1 Tim 4:9.

should expect and accept the troubles that test them.

James also referred to "trials of many kinds." A multitude of afflictions are in view: conflicts from opponents, doubts, fears, and tribulations. These trials are mostly external in comparison with those discussed later in the chapter. Enduring trials is something the servant of Christ must do in view of the inheritance of glory. The end of the ages has come in Christ, and service to him brings opposition. This is the very cause of trials in the Christian life. The biblical text presents no strong demarcation between the tribulations near the end and the tribulation in the end.[21]

In the face of these many kinds of trials, James pointed to God, who was ready to bestow blessing.[22] Joy is a reality for those who serve. We see a reciprocal dynamic here. The servant of Christ swims against the stream of unbelief in his or her service. No time is free of conflict. The servants of God point to the only way of serving God, and this is a scandal, a stumbling block to the followers of other religions. The world, which is primarily religious but pagan, opposes the servants of Christ. But this is to be expected.

1:3 God proves the genuineness of faith in his servants: this is a fundamental biblical theme. The believer endures such testing of faith and service because of what is promised: divine favor in the judgment (i.e., the reward of life in 1:12). As discussed in the introduction, judgment is the end of the trajectory of faith. But the servant of Christ faces that judgment and the trials of the present with joy because of the promise of God's mercy (cf. 2:13). The teaching on trials in the Christian life, like that found in Hebrews 12,[23] focuses on trials as proving our parent-child relation with God and as the discipline necessary for walking in the way of faith. The true

---

[21] δοκίμιον: "testing," in v. 3 rather than the "means of testing," which is its meaning in 1 Pet 1:7, with the result that true faith is proven to be authentic; cf. also Prov 27:21; Luke 8:13ff.; 2 Cor 8:2; 13:3; Rom 5:4; *Sir* 2:1.

[22] Cf. the beatitude "blessed is. . ." in v. 12.

[23] Along with testing, trials are viewed as discipline:

My son, do not make light of the Lord's discipline
  and do not resent his rebuke,
because the Lord disciplines those he loves,
  as a father the son he delights in. Prov 3:11–12

pattern of service that must be kept in view by faith is the service of Jesus himself, "who, for the joy set before him endured the cross" (Heb 12:2). He was the true Son and was tested; thus every servant of Christ should bear up under trial as the proving of his or her identity as a true child of God. Indeed, Jesus accepted discipline, thereby growing "in wisdom and stature, and in favor with God and man" (Luke 2:52).

This proving of filial identity supplies us with a key to understanding this section of James (1:2–8). The proof that those who suffer trials are God's children is necessary from God's perspective, for it will provide a threefold witness: to himself, to the believer, and to the world. God's interest in the witness to himself can be seen in the testing of Abraham: "Now I know that you fear God, because you have not withheld from me your son, your only son" (Gen 22:12).

One of the interpretive challenges of this section of James is to show the relation between "trials" and "temptations" (v. 13) and to account for the shift in meaning between them. The temptation narratives of Jesus in the Gospels, however, furnish a possible solution. With temptations there is also the test: "If you are the Son of God . . ." (cf. Matt 4:3,6). In an astonishing way, Jesus succeeds in demonstrating his identity to Satan rather than to the world by enduring his temptations. The devil wanted Jesus to put his power on display for the world and in turn submit to him. Jesus obeyed his Father and gave no demonstration to the world at the devil's behest. If he had done so, he would have failed the test.

James had an underlying confidence that believers would pass their testings. In every confrontation in service, the believer should see a basis for joy in trials in that they are acquiring the perseverance[24] necessary for greater service and also are proving that they belong to God.

But James's readers knew the good reason God allows such tri-

---

[24] ὑπομονή: "fortitude," or "patient endurance," which is what Job exhibited in 5:11 (cf. Job 4:5). This word also bears the sense of a fortitude that comes from communion with Christ. Cf. 2 Thess 3:5, where Paul referred to "Christ's perseverance"; 2 Cor 1:6; 6:4; Rom 5:3; 2 Thess 1:4; Heb 11:27.

als (v. 3).[25] God intends for them to result in a mature and complete faith; perseverance is faith's first product. But perseverance is not a minimal virtue. Rather, it is elemental to that fortitude of the soldier who braves all in his life-and-death struggle on the field of combat. Praised by Paul (1 Thess 1:3) and by the author of Revelation (cf. 14:12), perseverance characterizes the godly both before and after Christ. The gradual and painful acquisition of this virtue is also unmistakable. Perseverance, though essential to faith, is not infused immediately in a moment of conversion. Only through great ardor and the stumbling pursuit of the goal laid before it and only through sustained service in spite of opposition does perseverance come.

1:4 The perseverance of faith is a virtue in and of itself. Indeed, perseverance characterizes genuine faith. Faith, one of the "good and perfect" gifts of God (v. 17), grows up to produce perseverance in the believer; indeed it makes the believer a perfect (*teleios;* "mature," NIV) work. Believers have been birthed by God (v. 18), and they grow up to full maturity in him.[26]

What James said about persecution must be balanced with what he said in 3:2 about all of us stumbling in many ways. Immediately following, James spoke of someone who is "perfect" in speech. Completeness of faith is meant here whereby profession and behavior are inseparable—this is the maturity of faith James wanted for them.

"Perfect" *(teleios)* was an extremely important word for James, occurring in 1:4 twice (cf. KJV, "Let patience have her perfect work, that ye may be perfect") and in 1:17,25; 3:2. It has three aspects: the character of individuals in all their acts, a divine model

---

[25] γινώσκω: "know," by faith. James's reference to what they knew is an important hint at a great deal that is presupposed in James's letter; cf. Rom 6:6; Heb 10:34; 2 Pet 1:20; 3:3.

[26] Note the parallelism observed by Cargal (*Restoring the Diaspora*, 61) at work here:

1:2–4 trials and tests	1:13–16 temptation
1:5–8 the gift of God is wisdom	1:17–19a the "perfect gift" of God is the "word of truth"
1:9–12 culminates with a "crown of life"	1:19b–21 culminates with the salvation of the soul

or purpose that is under construction or in process, and the ultimate realization of that purpose in the eschaton or the last things.[27] The use of *holoklēros* ("complete")[28] along with *teleios* ("perfect") implies a gradual process of adding virtue upon virtue[29] until one is "not lacking anything." Thus faith becomes complete in the fullest sense, ready to stand before God in the judgment, which is faith's goal.

(2) Faith without Doubt (1:5–8)

[5]If any of you lacks wisdom, he should ask God, who gives generously to all without finding fault, and it will be given to him. [6]But when he asks, he must believe and not doubt, because he who doubts is like a wave of the sea, blown and tossed by the wind. [7]That man should not think he will receive anything from the Lord; [8]he is a double-minded man, unstable in all he does.

1:5 Naturally, every believer still "lacks" that which would make him or her perfect and whole in faith. Wisdom[30] is required

---

[27] Cf. Matt 5:48; Eph 3:19; 4:13; Phil 3:1; Col 1:28; 4:12; 1 Cor 14:20; Heb 5:12–14; note especially how it is said that Christ was made perfect through suffering in Heb 2:10. The meaning of "perfect" is seen reflected in the life of Noah, who was said to be "righteous and blameless . . . walking with God" (Gen 6:9). Noah followed the pattern of righteousness marked out for him by God and did not waver from his way. This resulted in a "full-blown character of stable righteousness" (Davids, *Epistle of James*, 70) that forms the identity of the righteous person. Although for Paul perfection is reached only in the resurrection (cf. 1 Cor 2:6; Eph 4:13; Col 4:12; Phil 3:15), it also applies to the imitation of God/Christ theme in discipleship (cf. Matt 9:21).

[28] ὁλόκληρος: "whole," "complete," as in the man who was healed in Acts 3:1 but also in the metaphorical sense of *Wis* 15:3; 1 Thess 5:23. Here it stands in relation to the necessity of keeping the whole law in 2:9–10.

[29] The lack of wisdom in the believer's life requires a constant striving for the maturity that will allow for greater faith as in 1 Cor 1:7; Phil 3:9. Cf. 2 Pet 1:5–8, where this linking of the parts of faith that will lead to a whole person are delineated (cf. Col 4:12; Matt 21; cf. F. Mussner, "'Direkte' und 'indirekte' Christologie im Jakobusbrief," *Catholica* 24 [1970]: 117).

[30] σοφία: "wisdom" of a practical nature; cf. Prov 2:6 and also *Sir* 4:17; *Wis* 9:6; 5:6–14; 7:7; 8:21. Wisdom often is connected with perfection (cf. 1 Cor 2:6; Col 1:28). James defined true wisdom in 3:13. Other important NT references for wisdom are Luke 2:40; 7:35; 11:49; 1 Cor 1:17; Col 1:9; esp. Eph 1:10–17.

because the faithful do not always know how to persevere nor do they easily find the will to rejoice in future blessings while enduring present trials. A divine vision or perspective is needed in the present to aid the believer in the journey and to fortify the self against temptation. The believer is enjoined to turn to God for the internal and practical means to endure the diverse trials of faith.[31] Wisdom must come from God and is akin to the implanted Word of this chapter (v. 18; cf. 1 Kgs 10:24; Ps 51:6). It is not automatic, however, but must be sought (cf. Prov 1:2; 2:1–12; 4:5–7; 16:16).

Wisdom is given out of God's generosity and gentleness. He is not like the ruler of Prov 23:1–3 whose desirable delicacies are "deceptive." God gives "without finding fault." To request wisdom in the midst of trial is precisely what God intends for his people. Wisdom is always God's gift to his own. Wisdom also is necessary to endure the testing of faith. By such wisdom Jesus himself endured his sufferings (cf. 1 Cor 1:24). Jesus promised his disciples that they would be granted wisdom in the face of the opposition of the world to their message (cf. Matt 12:42; Luke 11:31; 21:15). The New Testament is emphatic about the need for this wisdom and gives special attention to those in possession of it.[32] Later on in the letter the qualities of this wisdom will be defined in contrast to a destructive worldly "wisdom" (3:13,15,17).

God's generosity is emphasized and is central to Jesus' own teaching (Matt 7:7 and parallels; 18:19; 21:22 and parallels; cf. Jer 29:12–13). Using a term for "generously" that means "simple, open, sincere action,"[33] James begins to tear away at false ideas his audience has about God (cf. 1:7,13,17,20,27). The generosity of

---

[31] Cf. D. E. Gowan, "Wisdom and Endurance in James," in *HBT* 15 (1993): 145–53, 149.

[32] Stephen's Spirit-endowed wisdom, e.g., not only confounded his opponents but also enabled him to endure their fatal attack (Acts 6:10–7:60).

[33] ἁπλῶς: "generously"; cf. 2 Cor 8:2 and 9:11. The truth is God gives to *all* generously rather than the opposite and wrongly held view that God gives only to the deserving. God's "liberality" in his provisions for the life of faith is to be imitated in the life of believers, as in 2 Cor 8:2; 9:11,13; Rom 12:8. A possible translation of μγ ὀνειδίγοντος, "without reproach," is "not grumbling." Thus, God does not display "a special kind of reproach . . . the manifestation of displeasure or regret that too often accompanies the giving of a gift" (BAGD, 570).

God is nondiscriminatory. God does not criticize the humble suppliant. That is, his wisdom is given not just to a particular class of persons within the whole people of God but rather to everyone who belongs to him.[34] However poor, ignorant, mistaken, or confused believers may be, they are commanded to pray for wisdom.[35] This command is matched by the certainty of receiving wisdom from God. Every believer then is called to turn to God directly to consider the word that has been planted in the heart. In this way the believer wakens to a new understanding of the world and history. God, who is the source of all good (v. 17), is correspondingly generous to all who exercise humility and ask of him.

1:6 But of course this promise of wisdom from God belongs only to those who have faith. In v. 3 faith was that which identifies one as a believer (cf. Luke 18:8). This faith, which comes from God alone, is like a door that had once been shut but has now been opened (cf. Acts 14:27). What was once secret—kept between God and his very own Israel—now is a mystery disclosed (1 Tim 3:9). The fruit of the gift of wisdom is the understanding that faith is all-encompassing.[36] This faith is essential to the true piety or genuine religion James enjoined at the conclusion of this chapter (v. 27). Here is active trust or confidence in God.[37] Abraham (5:15) was one who modeled such faith. Jesus taught about the potency of faith to move the immovable (Matt 17:20) and about the overcom-

---

[34] μὴ ὀνειδίζοντος, "without reproach/finding fault," is a great comfort to all believers struggling with temptation, for God does not regard them with contempt for their feelings or difficulties with sin. Instead, he is always welcoming them to pursue a purer life of faith through greater wisdom from him; cf. Isa 42:3; Matt 12:20; *Sir* 41:22; *Herm. Man.* 9.3; *Herm. Sim.* 9.23, 24; *Const. Ap.* 7.7.

[35] δίδωμι: "give"; cf. 1 Kgs 3:9–12; Prov 2:3; *Wis* 7:7f.; 9:4f.; *Sir* 1:1f.; 51.13f.; *Barn* 21.5; these references reflect the wisdom that is "from above" expressed later by James in 3:17.

[36] For important background discussions of biblical wisdom cf. D. Garrett, *Proverbs, Ecclesiastes, Song of Songs,* NAC (Nashville: Broadman & Holman, 1995); G. von Rad, *Wisdom in Israel* (Nashville: Abingdon, 1972), 195–203; E. Baasland, "Der Jakobusbrief als Neutestamentliche Weisheitsschrift," *ST* 36 (1982): 119–39.

[37] Thus, never merely the act of praying but only the prayer of faith is that by which believers certainly receive what they ask for. Faith toward God prays according to what is appropriate to friendship with God (4:4f.); cf. Mark 11:22; Acts 19:20; Heb 11:1; 1 Pet 21; 1 Thess 1:8; *Wis* 8:21.

ing of doubt (Matt 21:21). God is always the source of the power of faith. The will of God always distinguishes true faith from false faith. Faith to do amounts to nothing if it is not in accord with the revealed will of God. And so this faith is an exercising of trust in the generosity and power of God.

A close connection exists, therefore, between faith, prayer, and wisdom. The one who asks for wisdom asks in faith; asking in faith requires divine wisdom; to ask for wisdom is itself wise and is part and parcel of persevering in faith and growing in wisdom. Growth in wisdom is to understand that everything of faith is from God. Prayer is both accepting and asking. Prayer accepts the gift of faith. Prayer likewise asks for the means to work out that faith through the gift of wisdom. In the asking mode of prayer, the believer seeks that which will secure persevering wisdom. And asking without doubt[38] is at the heart of James's understanding of prayer.

This attack against doubt is not irrational. This doubting is not about the existence of God but about what kind of God the believer serves. Throughout the letter all James's corrections and warnings are finally concerned with his addressees' misapprehensions of God. True faith is what it is because God is who he is. Since faith is always a matter of personal trust in God, to doubt God in any way is to call his character into question. In actuality, of course, doubting also calls the believer's character into question. And this was what James was concerned with: combating the corrupt faith of worldly Christians.

The believer is called to God and to his purposes, which encompass every aspect of life. God's promise is in accord with his nature: he is generous, and he gives what he promises. The divine gift of wisdom, like the faith God alone can give, aids the believer in rendering unwavering attention to his service to God. To waver in the presence of God (cf. Matt 21:21; Rom 4:20) is to hold oneself back from him. To waver is not a problem of doubting the existence of God. Rather, faith must trust in God without hesitat-

---

[38] διακρίνω: "doubt," from the sense of a willful dividing of what should remain joined together; a going in opposing directions, thus often used in reference to interpersonal conflict; cf. Jer 15:10; Ezek 20:35f.; Matt 21:21; Mark 11:23; Luke 11:18; Acts 10:20; 11:2; Rom 14:23; 1 Cor 4:7; Jude 9. See esp. Jas 2:4 and Matt 6:24.

ing. This hearkens back to the temptations of Israel in the wilderness, always looking back to Egypt while looking forward to God (also Lot's wife in Gen 19:26). This doubting then is the believer holding back from acting. Keeping faith with God is the issue. Being loyal to God, who is faithful to keep his promises, is at stake. Doubt then is an act of distrust when action is called for by the loving God (cf. Matt 21:2–11).

The believer who doubts in his relationship with God exposes the instability of his faith. Here James inserts the analogy of the wave.[39] The doubter is like the ocean surface blown this way and that by the wind. Doubt becomes a moral problem here, for doubt becomes willful disobedience to God, and the believer becomes like the wicked (cf. Isa 57:20; Eph 4:14). By nature human beings are, at the least, extremely vulnerable to the evil influences all about them. In unbelief the sinner has no direction nor the strength to withstand these influences. But doubt renders the believer subject to these same forces. Lacking confident trust in God, how can the believer make a request of God? In doubt that which is contrary to faith and trust in God leaves the believer entirely exposed to its random assaults upon the will. Among James's addressees doubt was particularly the temptation to trust in wealth (v. 11). Because of doubt the believer no longer suffers the trial of faith but rather the excruciating instability of a life torn by two loyalties. Elsewhere James pronounced this a conflict between loving God and loving the world (cf. 4:4).

1:7 James comments about the expectations of a believer whose faith is adulterated by doubt. Persistent doubt nullifies faith. Faith receives because it trusts. Doubt, which also is directed toward God, is totally rejected by him. Prayer accompanied by doubt is much like the problem of claiming to have faith but showing no works (cf. 2:17). There may be expectations, but they are unfounded in relation to God and his will. Such doubters will receive nothing from God. The "not . . . anything" may imply that what was expected was other than what was promised, that is, wis-

---

[39] κλύδωνος: "wave," which is tossed about in any direction the stormy wind may blow; cf. a number of texts that reflect this image or its opposite (Isa 57:20; Jude 13; Matt 11:7; Luke 8:24; Eph 4:14; Heb 6:19; *Sir* 33:2).

dom. The doubting believer misunderstands God and fails to appre-
hend the blessing of God. He suffers from self-delusion about the
relationship of faith and prayer. In the next chapter the root problem of self-deception is disclosed as a culpable misleading to
which we fall prey. For indeed we receive gifts from the Lord in
personal relationship with him. Doubting is a refusal or a denial of
this relationship. We call him "Lord" but do not do what he says,
thus putting no confidence in him.[40]

1:8   Here we find the famous reference to the double-minded
man.[41] The way of true faith in God is with the whole heart, mind,
or soul. To pursue both the evil way and the good way is to divide
oneself and to corrupt all the good. The result is a divided loyalty
to God that can proclaim faith only superficially. The doubting
"believer" is always in two minds and therefore always hypocritical. Paul's reference to "carnal" and "spiritual" minds reflects this
same concern (cf. 1 Cor 2:14–15). Such a double-minded man
attempts to live with a contradictory blend of desires from two
worlds: pleasure and virtue. But he cannot serve both God and self,

---

[40] Cargal (*Restoring the Diaspora*, 69) offers an interesting pattern here:

Positive	Negative
1. Having "faith"	1. Having "doubt"
2. Asking for "wisdom	2. Not asking for "wisdom from God" or asking with "doubt"
3. Receiving "wisdom" from God	3. Receiving nothing from God

[41] ἀνήρ δίψυχος: lit. "man of two souls" (cf. 4:8), surprisingly not found in the
LXX and not in Greek literature before the time of James. This is a semitic pleonasm
(redundancy, i.e., a "two-personed person"). Throughout his letter (1:12,23; 2:2; 3:2)
James used "man" rather than "person." This use can be found in Psalms and Proverbs, e.g., "Happy is the man . . ." (Ps 32:2), which along with many other texts presents the simple fact of the male-centeredness of Jewish wisdom. This term appears
nowhere else in the NT but draws upon such references as Ps 12:2 ("with deception"
is lit. "with heart and heart"; KJV "a double heart") and 1 Chr 12:33 ("with undivided
loyalty" is lit. "not with heart and heart"); cf. also "two opinions" in 1 Kgs 18:21.
The need for wholeheartedness in relation to God is at the center of Deut 4:29;
Rom 7; *Wis* 1:1; *Herm. Man.* 9.4.5; *1 Clem* 23:2, along with many other early Christian writings that are clearly influenced by James's introduction of this concept. Cf.
S. Marshall, "*Dipsychos:* A Local Term?" *SE* 6 (1973): 348–51, and S. E. Porter, "Is
dipsychos (James 1,8; 4,8) a 'Christian' Word?" *Bib* 71 (1990): 469–98; O. J. F.
Seitz, "Afterthoughts on the Term 'Dipsychos,'" *NTS* 4 (1957–58): 327–34, and
"Antecedents and Significance of the Term *Dipsychos*," *JBL* 66 (1947): 211–19.

the spirit and the flesh, the law of life and the law of death, the wisdom from above and the wisdom from below (cf. 3:15,17). That the double-minded believer is a "believer" is already clear, for he is challenged to understand trials not as the interruption of pleasure by suffering but as the pathway toward a mature faith. This pathway will require endurance, but this is secured by the wisdom God always provided to those who ask for it in faith.

James was emphatic: double-mindedness mars a "believer's" life. No part of it remains unsullied. Filled with ulterior motives, a "believer's" divided thinking is only indicative of divided loyalties. His entire relationship with God, especially in prayer, is marred by his self-perverted faith. The source of the "believer's" struggle with doubt is divided loyalties to the self and to God.

But a "Christian doubter" is an oxymoron. In this case "doubt" is in a special class by itself. The doubting believer holds back from active trust. Although such people claim to trust in God, they in fact do not. They may pray the prayers of profession, but they do not pray authentically, that is, the prayers of surrender to God's will. James described such a believer as unstable and restless in everything.[42] The fickleness and instability James had in mind here is connected with real danger and destructiveness because loyalty to God is at stake. Granted, one can live without wholehearted devotion to God, but such a one will become warped—because faith is unauthentic.

Why should such a person expect anything from God through prayer? If wisdom is God's best blessing, why isn't he praying above all for wisdom? Like blessing and cursing from the same mouth, this "should not be" (cf. 3:10). If nothing can be expected from God, then there is the real question of whether anything can be expected from doubting "believers." James's intent was to point out that doubting believers constantly manifest an ineffectiveness of faith that suggests the nonauthenticity of belief. This exposure of inadequate faith is the primary burden of the first chapter, and James reiterates it throughout.

---

[42] ἀκατάστατος: "unstable," "irresolute." This same modifier will be used later to describe the tongue as a restless evil (3:8; cf. 3:16; Isa 54:11; Luke 21:9; 2 Cor 6:5; 12:20; *Herm. Man.* 5.2.7).

The Book of James is both deeply spiritual and painfully practical, providing a rich resource for the Christian doctrine of humanity. For who has not sensed the tug of good and evil impulses within the self? Later in the chapter the source of temptation will be taken up, expanding upon the theme of double-mindedness (vv. 14–15). James was determined to show that there is no safe middle ground between faith and unbelief. Embedded in this passage, however, is much that is encouraging. Although the doubter cannot expect to receive anything from the Lord, the wholehearted believer should expect to receive wisdom for the journey of faith—this is the divine promise. With simple and undivided faith in God, wisdom is his treasure lavished upon the humble believer.

2. Faith Reversing Status (1:9–11)

In this passage James introduces a cardinal teaching of the gospel: the eschatological reversal of status experienced now in fellowship with Jesus (cf. Matt 19:30; Luke 1:46–55). "Lift up the poor believers now; require the rich believers to humble themselves" would be a correct understanding of James's intent. By means of an extended metaphor, including a short parable, the text calls for a kind of spirituality consistent with the coming reversal. The asymmetry of James's assessments of different human states of life is well known. James was especially hard in his judgments of the wealthy. Such judgment coming so early in the letter serves as a strong critique of prideful affluence in the modern world.

(1) The Boast of the Poor (1:9)

⁹The brother in humble circumstances ought to take pride in his high position.

1:9 The man in the humblest[43] condition should boast in the high position that will be his in the future with God. For James there was a close relationship between being humble in status and

---

[43] ταπεινός: "humble," a matter of status here (cf. Luke 1:52; Rom 12:16; 2 Cor 7:6) rather than of attitude (cf. Matt 11:29; 2 Cor 10:1; Jas 4:6; 1 Pet 5:5).

being humble in spirit, at least within the context of genuine faith, which he assumed. Low social standing was had on many levels for those who were poor. James exhorted those of low standing as believers to boast or to "take pride" in their coming exaltation.[44] They had brothers in the church who were of high socioeconomic standing, and the opposite exhortation was directed toward them. Although these poor men and women had nothing visible to boast in, their boast was nevertheless greater than those who boasted in themselves.[45] Their poverty, then, had turned into a double benefit, for it encouraged the humility and faith God requires.

A kind of spiritual exercise is outlined here (cf. 4:7–10). In preparation for the coming kingdom of God, the whole church should encourage those poor and destitute, who in everyday life were rejected and kept at the margins, to come forward and to lead the rejoicing of the church in its future hope. They were to have the "most important seats in the synagogue" of the Lord (cf. Luke 20:46). James offered poor believers special encouragement to appropriate their dignity as elect members of God's kingdom.[46]

Paul had boasted in his weakness in view of the Lord's greater strength (Rom 5:3; 2 Cor 10:15). In a similar way the poor and lowly are encouraged to glory in the rich heavenly reward that has been promised to them. Thus, they become a sign of the Lord's salvation. That salvation includes the reversal of status of poor and rich, of wise and foolish, of strong and weak, and of noble and despised. Faith and the mercy of God are always determinative for salvation, and James was determined to show that the poor believer has a special place in

---

[44] ὕψος: "height," "high position." In the eschaton the believing poor will be raised up by God above those who in the present age had known earthly happiness. On the socioeconomic interpretation, which is helpful but pays too little regard to the churchly context of the epistle, cf. P. U. Maynard-Reid, *Poverty and Wealth in James* (Maryknoll, N.Y.: Orbis, 1987), 40–41; for a better understanding of "humility," cf. J. P. Louw and E. A. Nida, eds., *Greek-English Lexicon of the New Testament Based on Semantic Domains,* §88.51 (1:748). Here the poor are indeed humble because they are humbled by the condition of their lives and by their neglect on the part of the wealthy.

[45] καυχάσθω: "boast," another way to "consider it pure joy" of v. 2 rather than to be double-minded; cf. Jer 9:23.

[46] Cf. Luke 1:52; 2 Cor 7:6; Isa 49:13; Rom 12:16.

God's plan by exhibiting this essential relation (cf. 2:5).

(2) The Reduction of the Rich (1:10–11)

¹⁰But the one who is rich should take pride in his low position, because he will pass away like a wild flower. ¹¹For the sun rises with scorching heat and withers the plant; its blossom falls and its beauty is destroyed. In the same way, the rich man will fade away even while he goes about his business.

1:10 The spiritual exercise continues for the rich.[47] Knowing that in the judgment the rich of the world will be stripped of their perishable wealth and influence, rich believers should "take pride" (the Greek depends on the previous verse for the verb) in their "low position";[48] that is, they should humble themselves now. The condemnation of those whose pride is in their wealth is a common biblical theme.[49] Such pride is an overwhelming temptation. This danger is captured in the proverb "The wealth of the rich is their fortified city; they imagine it an unscalable wall" (Prov 18:11). A surprising irony is contained here, since what is imagined to be so powerful is so obviously a delusion. The rich do not need to work to survive. Thus in the midst of a world of misfortune and flux, they boast in the semblance of their security and undisturbed comfort. Yet death comes to rich and poor alike, and faith acts now in view of this common destiny. The shadow of death already hangs over the poor. Their lives are full of trouble and woe. But the rich bask in the artificial light of the borrowed time their wealth has brought them. In truth they should be humbling themselves to guard against the temptation of trusting in wealth.

---

[47] Cf. G. M. Stulac, "Who Are 'The Rich' in James?" *Presbyterion* 16 (1990): 89–102.

[48] ταπείνωσις: "down-grading," "humiliation." As the poor believer learns self-respect, the rich believer must learn self-abasement. I do not agree with some interpretations that suggest God's rejection of all rich persons because they are rich. James's harshness with them in 2:19; 4:4; 5:1–6 must not be read as a blanket condemnation but a reiteration of Jesus' warnings (Matt 6:19–21; 16:26; Mark 10:24; Luke 12:15–21; 16:9–31) and of Paul's (1 Cor 7:29–31; and in a milder form in 1 Tim 6:17–18; also cf. *Herm. Sim.* 2.4ff.).

[49] E.g., 1 Sam 2:7; Ps 103:15–16; Jer 9:23.

The faith of a rich man must be expressed in a radically different way from that of the poor man. Because the life of the rich is so radically different, they must exercise self-abasement. This self-denial of the rich believer is their way to participate in the total trust required by God. There is, otherwise, no room for the faithless influence of the rich in the church (Isa 53:8; Acts 8:33). The specter of death hangs over the poor as the wretched end of a wretched life—what a wonderful reversal when the hearts of the poor are filled with the joy of the Lord! But the spectacle of the ruination of beauty possessed of the wealthy is the motive for the self-humbling exercise that submits in trust to God. The rich must consider very soberly that the distinguished position they have enjoyed above common folk will disappear in the kingdom of God.

The rich are compared to a wild flower, a familiar Old Testament image of fragility.[50] As the exaltation of the poor believer will appear like life from the dead, the lowering of the rich believer to a place among the least rewarded will be its own kind of spectacle. This metaphor of the falling flower is part of an apocalyptic vision of dying creatures under the judgment of God. James as well as other New Testament writers sharply applied to the rich the quick passing away of people in their bodily lives. Like the transitory beauty of gold (1 Pet 1:7) and the other splendors of this life (Rev 18:14; cf. Jer 10:11; Dan 7:17), the rich will pass out of existence in submission to the God who holds life and death.

1:11 The process of "fad[ing] away"[51] is harsh. The Middle Eastern sun "rises,"[52] and its heat scorches[53] the anemone and cyclamen flowers, quickly causing their beauty to fade. They become mere withered grasses to kindle fires. Their appearance is

---

[50] ἄνθος χόρτου, lit. "a flower of grass." James's language, also quoted in 1 Pet 1:24, is drawn from Isa 40:6; Pss 89:6; 103:15, where it applies to temporal life in general. The power of the image is intensified because of the greater losses of the rich.

[51] παρέρχομαι: "pass by," or "pass away"; cf. Mark 13:31.

[52] A gnomic or proverbial aorist; cf. v. 24. See also Isa 40:7.

[53] καύσωνις: "scorching wind." Cf. the LXX, where the hot wind or sirocco, rather than the sun, scorches the plant as in James (Job 27:21; Ps 103:16; Isa 49:10; Jer 18:17; Ezek 17:10; Hos 12:1; Jonah 4:8; and also Jesus' teaching (Matt 20:12; Luke 12:55).

gone forever under the sun. The beauty of the flower is compared to the beauty of a wealthy man's busy life. All of the hurrying about to maintain success and influence is soon lost. And it is fairly clear here that the rich are made busy by their wealth. James portrayed the hustle of the wealthy. He is much like the industrious rich farmer who is told in his own apocalyptic moment that he is utterly poor toward God and his life is at its end (Luke 12:15–21).[54] Similarly, the affairs[55] of the rich in James now amount to nothing. Surely something so favorable and disarming as wealth and beauty (cf. 2:1–4) would have been more enduring. But those who possess them fall quickly under the harsh heat of this perishable life.

The rich man should beware, according to James, because he "will fade away"[56] together with all his undertakings. In the very movement and manner (v. 8) of displaying the beauty of a wealthy life, all will be lost (cf. 4:13–16). This is the order of things (cf. v. 24). Perishability and loss rule over all of life, but obviously the losses of the wealthy are greater. The biblical meaning of this loss is reflected in 1 Cor 3:12–13, which says that a believer can build a life of service upon the perishables of worldly value, and all of it will be consumed in the fire of judgment.

Nothing of earthly possessions contributes in itself to the kingdom of God. Indeed, the allure of wealth is illusory and invites disaster because of the high cost of making and protecting it. Using riches for their own sake exposes the total lack of lasting value in wealth. Thus the life of the rich and their wealth together fade away. The stark contrast with the call to persevere in vv. 2–3 could not have been made more pronounced. James later confronted the rich again with the sins of injustice they had committed in amass-

---

[54] This parable illuminates whether our passage is a sapiential wisdom saying or an eschatological one. Jesus' teaching implies that it is both. Death can come at any time, plucking a person out of the midst of life. At the same moment, this person stands at his own personal end *(eschaton)* before the judgment of God. Although James had the universal judgment in mind in the whole of his letter, personal eschatology may have been part of his teaching here.

[55] "Even while he goes about his business" is lit. "on his journey," although πορεία can also mean "way of life, conduct." See the related verb πορεύομαι in 4:13 describing the self-abased merchants. The noun ὁδός, "way," in 1:8 is a synonym.

[56] Here is the only place the verb μαραίνω ("fade, waste, disappear") occurs in the NT. Cf. 1 Pet 1:4; *Herm. Vis.* 3.11.2; *Herm. Sim.* 9.23.2.

ing their fortunes (5:1–6). An eternal perishing awaits them.

The overall context for this hard truth about the wealthy and their wealth is the instruction of the Christian community; the rich can be a coequal part of the community of believers. But let their holding and use of the wealth and position be carried under an umbrella of humility. The rich cannot boast in their wealth because confidence in wealth belongs to the enmity of the world system against God's values. James offered a proper way of relating and worshiping among believers of different economic statuses through a kind of spiritual exercise. Drawing from Paul's similar thought, let the rich brother exercise the "as if's" of 1 Cor 7:29–31, "for this world in its present form is passing away."

3. The Matter of Life and Death (1:12–18)

In this section an added dimension is given to the meaning and purpose of trials. Temptations are discussed as well as the great danger they pose toward the Christian life when they are allowed to rule or dominate. The great reward promised to those who live life by persevering faith also appears here. This promise completes the series of assurances to the faithful that James wished them to focus upon. The care of the Heavenly Father evident in the lives of believers is presented from the standpoint of his care over the entire universe. The majesty and goodness of his reign is great cause for the rejoicing of this passage. How can the standards and staples of the world possibly compare to those of the Heavenly Father?

(1) Trial as Life Giving (1:12)

12Blessed is the man who perseveres under trial, because when he has stood the test, he will receive the crown of life that God has promised to those who love him.

1:12 This verse returns to the theme of steadfastness or endurance in the midst of trials (cf. 5:7–11). Because of the faithfulness of the believer under trial, James declared that such a person is "blessed."[57] Such "macarisms" (a term based on the Greek word

---

[57] μακάριος ἀνήρ: "blessed man"; cf. v. 8; 5:11; Pss 1:1; 34:8; 40:4; 84:5; Prov 28:14; also Ps 94:12; Jer 17:7, where the generic "man" in the sense of "human being" is found; Job 5:17; Sir 34:8.

makarios for "blessed") or "beatitudes" (cf. Matt 5:3–11) reflect the person's right relation to God. These are often used in the Old Testament (Deut 33:29; Pss 1:1; 2:12; 144:15; Prov 3:13) and by Jesus in the Gospels (Matt 13:16; 24:46; Luke 6:20–22; 12:37–38; 14:14; John 13:17; 20:29). James's macarism (cf. 5:11) indicates an important conclusion and direction for him. The guiding principle of his entire first chapter is the right understanding of wisdom. Right understanding means a life that puts faith and action together. Right understanding means putting the promise of God ahead of the cares of this life and receiving assurance of life to come beyond death. Right understanding about wise action is blessedness. Anything can be endured with this wisdom because the reward of divine life has been secured for the believer.

Wisdom has been requested and given (Jas 1:5; cf. Luke 11:9), and wherever wisdom is truly received, believers endure testing until the test is finished. They are blessed because they posses the living hope of the salvation of the soul (Matt 5:12; Luke 6:23). Much like the testing spoken of in 1:3, patient endurance results in approval ("when he has stood the test" is lit. "having been approved")[58] when the test is over.[59] God wishes to use trials to produce believers (cf. 2 Cor 10:18; 13:7; 2 Tim 2:15) who stand their ground through a devout life shaped by the Word of God. The testing is finished when the present life is over.[60] Approval does not entail a faultless endurance, as if sinlessness were expected (cf. 3:2a). Rather, it acknowledges a faith that perseveres in the love of God, who promises life.[61]

---

[58] δόκιμος: "approved," relates to δοκίμιον, "testing," in v. 3.

[59] The participial clause means when the trial has been endured and is thus over. This implies that believers who out of love for God seek his wisdom are believers who are enabled to banish doubt from their minds and endure the test of this life. They therefore will be blessed by the God who has promised and who makes such faith a reality.

[60] This is a primary theme in the OT (cf. Exod 20:5–6; Deut 7:9; 30:20; Pss 18:1–2; 69:36; 97:10), which also expresses love for the commands of God (cf. Ps 119:47–48,97,113,159).

[61] Cf. Luke 24:49; Acts 2:33; 17:17; Rom 4:13–21; 9:4; 2 Cor 1:20; Gal 3:14–29; Eph 1:13; 1 Tim 4:8; 2 Tim 1:1; Titus 1:2; Heb 4:1; 6:13.

This love for God is an obedient love (cf. 2:5).[62] Obedience through love is the nature of right relationship with God, a relationship of wholehearted participation in the covenantal love of God. Although the love of God for his people is emphasized by Paul and John (Rom 8:37; Eph 2:4; 5:2; 1 Thess 1:4; 2 Thess 2:16; John 14–16; 1 John 4:7–10), human love for God also can be expressed. First John 5:2 states this as plainly as James does: "This is how we know that we love the children of God: by loving God and carrying out his commands."

For the promised reward James used the exceptional term "the crown [stephanos] of life" (cf. Rev 2:10).[63] The present life is characterized by the testing of every child of God. This testing is much like the disciplining to be endured that is described in Heb 12:7–13. According to James the poor endure the troubles of their poverty; the rich endure their temptation to trust in their wealth rather than in God alone and therefore to be double-minded; those between the two extremes are tempted by their desires and rationalizations to imitate the wealthy. These lifelong tests are relieved at the end of life with the reward of divine life. In the meantime each is to pursue genuine love for God that issues in the true religion (v. 27).

(2) Temptation as Life Taking (1:13–15)

[13]When tempted, no one should say, "God is tempting me." For God cannot be tempted by evil, nor does he tempt anyone; [14]but each one is tempted when, by his own evil desire, he is dragged away and enticed. [15]Then, after desire has conceived, it gives birth to sin; and sin, when it is full-grown, gives birth to death.

In this cluster of verses, James shifted to a mode of strong warning. This is called paraenesis, an ancient form of exhortation

---

[62] Promises that belong to those who love God are many (e.g., Exod 20:6; Deut 7:9; 30:16,20; Judg 5:30; Ps 5:11; 1 Cor 2:9; 2 Tim 4:8). Note also that love for God in the Synoptic Gospels is found in the context of acknowledging Israel's devotion to the one and only God (Matt 22:37; Mark 12:30; Luke 10:27).

[63] The expression refers to the life to come with God in his kingdom and includes the sense of reigning together with Christ in his victory and lordship; cf. 2:5; Dan 7:27; Zech 6:14; Luke 12:32; 22:28; Rom 5:17; 2 Tim 2:12; 4:8; 1 Pet 2:9; 5:4; Rev 1:6; 2:10; Wis 3.8; 5.16.

designed to draw one's audience to belief and denial. The root problem—as it is throughout this first chapter—is that of proper understanding. But James here introduced a fact about the cause of misunderstanding: self-deception.

James contributed one of the most penetrating discussions of the nature of temptation in the whole Bible. But with this section of the letter also comes ambiguity. Where do trials come from? Are some from God, but not others? Are they from God at all? If not, how can we say he rules the universe? Are all trials from God and therefore his goodness is compromised? Other biblical references might be brought in to bolster the claim that God can justifiably be questioned for his testing of persons or even accused of provoking them to do evil. Would this be the case with the command to Abraham to sacrifice his son Isaac (Gen 22:1; cf. Jas 2:21–23)? What of God's testing his people in the wilderness (cf. Deut 8:2; 13:4)? These questions show how the implied question of the text, "Is God tempting me?" could be a very real concern to those who have followed James's teaching—and much of the Bible—up to this point.

1:13 The context of the word "tempt" *(peirazō)*[64] connotes a provocation to sin. Along with v. 14, which clearly focuses on the psychological conflict within the person, the problem of some believers with divine testing comes into view. The ambiguity of what is meant here by "tempt" stems from use of the related word *peirasmos* ("trial") in v. 2, where the context does not entail an incitement to sin. The faith of the doubter in the face of trial is viewed here. This person's incomprehension of the wisdom of God leads him to view trials as a provocation to sin; therefore he sees trials as evil. What he has failed to understand is the truth about himself. This is why the phrase "no one should say" is an important signal for interpreting the problem James now addressed. This kind of signal appears again with the problem of faith and works in 2:18. The lack of wisdom and of undivided trust in God results in a terribly distorted view of one's relationship with God. Trials come not for the ill of God's own but for their good. Such a lack of

---

[64] The verb πειράζω, "test, tempt," occurs in James only in vv. 13–14, but the related noun πειρασμός, "trial," occurs in vv. 2,12. Here enduring temptation corresponds to the rejoicing under trial of v. 2. Blessing comes only to the one who endures. Other outcomes to trial are stated in the following verses.

appreciation of the place of trials in the history of God's covenant people is desperately in need of warning and correction.

James strongly denied that God is the origin of temptation, for "God cannot be tempted [lit. he is "without temptation"] by evil, nor does he tempt anyone." This aphorism places together references to God's personal character or disposition and to his activity. No evil can have its way with God.[65] He is immune to any of its provocations.[66] There can be nothing evil about that which concerns God. Therefore there can be nothing evil about his ways with his people. It is a flat error to regard any testing as a temptation to sin. No doubt, in a world of sinners who often succumb to the temptation to aggrandize the self, many believers feel inclined to misinterpret their trials as God-given opportunities for sin.

Temptation to sin is the operation of evil forces and the devil. In this case the believer himself is the source of temptation. There is already something within the self by which any temptation can arise. Just comprehending this is difficult for the believer who is lacking wisdom. The Gospel account of Jesus' provocation by Peter and the terrifying retort "Get behind me Satan!" starkly illumine the source of temptation. Peter, whose assertion that Jesus not allow himself to be attacked, was regarded by Jesus as an evil tempter. But then Jesus added a clarifying and stunning statement: "You are a stumbling block to me; you do not have in mind the things of God, but the things of men" (Matt 16:22–23; Mark 8:32–33).

The interchangeable "Satan" and "men" as opponents of God is arresting. The thoughts and actions of men become satanic or demonic in their rank opposition to the trials of Jesus as the means of the saving purposes of God. This human opposition to God is quite apart from any demonic possession. The appearance of "stumbling block" in Matt 16:23 also is significant. God acts as a cause of stumbling toward no one. But because of the spiritually

---

[65] ἀπείραστος: "not subject, without temptation" to evil. This word appears only here in the NT, but cf. Matt 4:7; Heb 12:8; 1 Pet 1:15; 2 Pet 2:14 for examples.

[66] The sentiment stated in *Const. Ap.* II,8,2, "an untempted man is untried," expresses well the meaning of trials in James. A close connection exists between temptation and its purpose within God's permissive will. The untemptability of God is the rationale for the conclusion that he tempts no one. Believers should be "imitators of God" (Eph 5:1) and so "in regard to evil be infants, but in your thinking be adults" (1 Cor 15:22).

degrading effects of sin, people often regard him, and his Son, as
the cause of stumbling: "Happy is the man who finds no cause for
stumbling over me." The world stumbles over the gifts of God
because it is at enmity with him (cf. Jas 4:4) and reverses the truth
of God's intent because its own ways are a refusal of God's ways.[67]
How easy it is to stumble over the divine intent of trials! Trouble
and temptation are indistinguishable to the double-minded believer
whose loyalty to God is already compromised with evil motives.
There is no room for any accusation that God causes temptation.[68]

1:14 Just as arresting as the objection of v. 13 is the absence of
a reference to Satan in the following verses. Instead of a demonic
influence, one's own "evil desire," or "deformed desire,"[69] is the

---

[67] The reference to evil and its source is extremely important, for the temptation
to sin is strictly a case of "being dragged into sin." This sense of dragging or luring
into sin is central in the next verse. The cause of temptation also is much like Paul's
expression "inventors of evil" (KJV), referring to those who teach their evil to others
(Rom 1:30–32). Cargal's helpful schema contrasts the positive knowledge of the
nature of temptation rather than the negative knowledge of the double-minded
(*Restoring the Diaspora*, 78). The steps that follow from the misapprehension of
being tempted by God have dire consequences for faith.

[68] Is Jesus' petition in his great prayer—"lead us not into temptation, but deliver
us from the evil one" (Matt 6:13)—at odds with our text? Paul possibly was thinking
of this saying of the Lord when he wrote: "No temptation has seized you except what
is common to man. And God is faithful; he will not let you be tempted beyond what
you can bear. But when you are tempted, he will also provide a way out so that you
can stand up under it" (1 Cor 10:13). The temptation aspect of trials is a dimension
of the permissive will of God. Escape from sinning and the determination to endure
are the actual intent of God in all trials-become-temptations.

[69] There is no word for "evil" in the text but rather ἐπιθυμία, "desire," or "strong
desire." The term can have a neutral sense (cf. Luke 22:15; Phil 1:23; 1 Thess 2:17).
But because its meaning is so connected with the appetites of the body, particularly
of sexuality, it readily expresses itself in lust when its object is a forbidden one. This
negative sense of "desire" appears more frequently in the NT than the neutral one (cf.
Mark 4:19; Rom 1:24; 6:12; 13:14; Gal 5:24; Col 3:5; 1 Tim 6:9; 2 Tim 3:6; 4:3;
1 Pet 1:14; 2 Pet 2:10; 1 John 2:16–17; Jude 18). James describes these desires in
4:1. Here "desire" is personified as though believers have another mind within them
at work against the mind of faith. L. T. Johnson (*The Letter of James,* AB [New York:
Doubleday, 1995], 194) makes an important observation that James showed no evidence of drawing upon the psychology of the "two inclinations" (evil and good) of
Qumran, of the *Testaments of the Twelve Patriarchs,* and of later rabbinic traditions
(contra Davids, Martin, Marcus et al.). For a helpful and fascinating interpretation of
the origin of deformed desire in the creation narratives utilizing the insights of
R. Girard, cf. R. G. Hamerton-Kelly, *Sacred Violence: Paul's Hermeneutic of the
Cross* (Minneapolis: Fortress, 1992), 92–99.

cause of temptation. What is forbidden creates a double opportunity: to desire God's pleasure or to corrupt desire (Rom 7:7–12; 2 Pet 1:4; Col 3:5). This active desire is rooted solely in the self. Deformed desire powerfully draws the sinner away to the forbidden object or activity.[70] James's recognition of the power of desire to lead the self into sin is remarkable for its insight into the human soul. Where we might expect the "devil, like a roaring lion" (1 Pet 5:8), to be dragging off the unguarded believer into sin, it is the believer who drags himself off. How opposite could the case be from falsely accusing God of causing temptation? We are our own cause of temptation, not something outside us, devil or human.[71] This is not to say that Satan is not involved in the temptations of the world. But James was concentrating here on the role of the believer's own desires in all temptations as one who has been born of God (cf. 1:18).

Along with the power of desire is the enticement[72] of desire. Desire and the object of desire combine to produce real attraction and appeal. Temptation is never simply a problem with the object of desire. Temptation entices or lures us by our own appetite or imaginative relation to the object of desire. Every temptation to sin is a temptation to reinvigorate the appeal of past sins. New sins can be learned through acquiring a taste for them through the deceptiveness of temptation. But the enticement to sin is actually not in the object involved in sin. James was describing a thoroughly internalized process. The source of all temptation is the self and its desire for the sake of desire.[73] Thus the complex between thinking, feeling, and willing bound up in this process of temptation is made plain. We entice ourselves with the object we desire. The blame for

---

[70] ἐξέλκω: "drag away," a physical, even violent sense of dragging away; cf. 2 Pet 2:14,18. The power of the experience of such temptation might lead the double-minded to imagine that God must be behind it—or the demonic. This is strictly a statement about the powers of the self to lead one into sin.

[71] Thus the devil can never be the power of temptation but only human desire. The reality of demons is presented in James, although they are subject to the power and authority of God.

[72] δελεάζω: "entice" by the use of bait, even "to lure"; cf. the temptation of Eve in Gen 3:1–5, where the tempter first distracts and then the object of desire becomes the fixation of the one who is tempted.

[73] Note Luther's view of sinful desire "curved in on itself" *(incurvatus in se)*— that every gesture toward others is always self-serving.

temptation then can never rest upon God, but entirely upon us. All temptation originates within us. Temptation is an activity of our own evil desire.

The passive sense—"is dragged away and enticed"—is also important for understanding the need for God and his wisdom. Compare Paul's insight that the weak self is subjugated to the more powerful forces of its own evil desire (flesh) "so that you cannot do what you will" (Gal 5:17). In this passage too there is no mention whatsoever of the tempter, the devil, or Satan. For Paul life in the Holy Spirit was the antidote to the power of evil desire. Although wisdom in James should not be seen as another way of speaking about the Spirit, it too is the gift of God for overcoming temptation and for a living obedience to God. Temptation to sin is the problem of the person's own condition as a sinner. Thus the personal struggle with evil desire is not usually one of a confrontation with the devil but rather a confrontation with our own worst enemy, namely, our very selves. The pain of temptation is a self-inflicted attack. This is the sense of being "dragged away." Our own desires are like a marauding beast that would consume us. Also, being "enticed," our own evil impulses are like the tempter himself, luring us into self-destructive enjoyments. This is an alarming truth, but it is an essential aspect of the wisdom of James.

1:15 The self-tempting process is inseparably tied[74] to the doing of sin itself.[75] Desire conceives its offspring, sin. James used the metaphor of conception for describing the development from temptation to sin. What is always so difficult for the believer, for any sinner, is the truth about one's own sin. No matter how extraordinarily destructive sin is discovered to be, the believer can never find a source of sin outside of himself. Desire is like a creature with a reproductive life of its own. Desire has become pregnant, and sin is now alive within the self. Again, unlike the external trials that come from God, this entire movement from temptation to sin is internal to the self. Temptation, self-induced by the power and

---

[74] The connection between desire and sin is also made in such texts as *4 Macc* 1:25–26; Philo, *On Husbandry* 22–25.

[75] συλλαμβάνω: "conceive"; cf. 3:6; 4:7; Ps 7:14; *T. Ben.* 7; *T. Reub.* 3, commenting on Gen 6:2ff.

appeal of desire, is now producing sin on the way to death.[76] Unrestrained evil desire then engenders a process of three closely connected stages: temptation, sin, and death.

Here is the full portrayal of the self moving against itself in the divided mind and heart of believers, represented in the metaphor of two births. Desire gives birth[77] to sin. Sin,[78] the offspring of desire, grows up, matures, and is ready for fertilization and conception. Finally, sin gives birth to death.[79] Desire is the alien opponent within the self. But once the self has acquiesced to desire, sin is its offspring, owned by the self.

The awful image of the parasite is suggested by this text. The parasite, desire, has found its hospitable environment. When sin has been birthed, the new parasite, nurtured by the life of the self, is tightly intertwined with it. Sin engenders death. The full growth of sin issues in the slaying of the host. This juxtaposition of birth and death, with death arising from birth, is one of the most powerful statements about sin in the New Testament. The progression toward death is rather complex.

- Temptation to sin is not a divine activity but an evil one.
- Temptation begins with the potential of the believer's own desire to satisfy self or God.
- Evil desire is a powerful attraction.
- Temptation is effected within the self.
- Sin lives within the self.
- Sin in the self grows to maturity.
- Sin slays the host—the self.

---

[76] ἀποτελέω: "come to maturity," here "complete." The NIV translates "when it is full-grown." In this sense sin itself is completely ready to reproduce.

[77] τίκτω: "give birth to," "bear"; cf. Matt 1:21; John 16:21; Rev 12:4.

[78] In the singular "sin" becomes the personification of the dynamics of sin; cf. 2:9,22; 4:17; John 1:29; 16:8; Rom 5:12–13; 1 Cor 15:56. James used the plural to indicate specific sins (5:15–16,20); see also Rom 7:5; 1 Cor 15:3; Gal 1:4. Interestingly, Philo, in *Leg. All.* and *De Prof.*, argues that desire is passive until reason or the mind takes hold of it. The mind then becomes the vehicle of the power of desire.

[79] ἀποκεύω: "give birth"; in the metaphorical sense it means "engender," "bring into being," "produce." Note how this verb is used to express God's activity in 1:18; cf. Matt 7:13f.; Rom 6:21–23; *Barn* 18.1. Sin and death are often closely related in Scripture; cf. John 8:21; Rom 5:12,21; 1 Cor 15:56; Eph 2:1.

(3) The Element of Deception (1:16)

[16]Don't be deceived, my dear brothers.

1:16   The complexity of temptation and sin in the Christian life requires the warning against self-deception[80] (cf. 5:19). If the great temptation of the sinner is unbelief, then the great temptation of the believer is misbelief. The believer may have a very rudimentary faith in Christ but has adopted falsehoods about the life of faith. Some among James's audience had adopted the idea that God is the cause of temptation. And yet, in no case can a role be assigned to God in relation to evil, temptation, and sin.

James's "beloved brothers" were to hear his strongest appeal so as to develop whole-hearted trust in God. They must be on their guard against self-deception. They should accept trials from God; he has a right to test them. But God does not tempt them, that is, entice them to do evil. To be mistaken in one's judgment is also a common theme in the teaching of Jesus and is one of the bases for his rejection of all human judgment. Self-directed believers are either like sheep without a shepherd or are incapable of recognizing the signs of the times. There is an insidious connection between misjudging the role of God in temptation and perverting the truth about God's nature.

(4) The Father and the Firstfruits (1:17–18)

[17]Every good and perfect gift is from above, coming down from the Father of the heavenly lights, who does not change like shifting shadows. [18]He chose to give us birth through the word of truth, that we might be a kind of firstfruits of all he created.

1:17   James proclaimed God as the true giver of "every good

---

[80] πλανάω: "mislead," "deceive," here "do not be deceived" or "make no mistake." Cf. Deut 4:19; 11:28; Matt 18:12–13; 22:29; Mark 12:24,27; Luke 21:8; 1 Cor 6:9; 15:33; Gal 6:7; Ign. *Phila.* 3; *Eph.* 16.

and perfect gift."[81] This means that everything with God as its source is good. God is not involved in the evil we do when we are tempted; instead, he is only the source of good in our lives. He is the source of the good fight within us that resists temptation, recognizes what the law of Christ shows us about ourselves, and firms our resolve to pursue the works that belong to faith. The gifts of God are good because they never foster evil desire or sin. The gifts of God are perfect because they are the fulfillment of his will for his people.

James's statement also means that everything good, whether intrinsically so or arising from good motives, comes from the goodness of God.[82] The range of God's giving includes both the goodness of the created world in general and that of the perfect (cf. 1:4) gifts bestowed upon all who put their trust in him and seek his wisdom. A similar kind of assertion can be found in 1 John 4:7: "Everyone who loves has been born of God and knows God." Wisdom can do nothing other than refer beyond to God, who is the giver of everything good.

God generates goodness in all his works and is therefore called "Father."[83] He is the originator and ruler of all things as "Father of lights."[84] Good gifts find their origin "from above"[85]—their good-

---

[81] This is perhaps the best way to translate the combination of words: δόσις, "giving," "gift," "favor," and δώρημα, "gift," with the adjectives "good" and "perfect." This terse and beautiful saying could well be a quotation of some familiar text (cf. John 4:35; Acts 17:28; 1 Cor 15:33; Titus 1:12; Heb 12:13; *Tob* 4:14; *Wis* 2:23). The two words for "gift" are found in 2 Chr 32:23; Dan 2:6; 5:17; cf. John 4:10; Acts 2:38; 8:20; 10:45; Rom 5:16; 2 Cor 9:15; Eph 3:7; 4:7; Heb 6:4, the former perhaps signifying the many gifts of wisdom needed throughout a lifetime of faith; the latter, the gift of eternal life promised to those who persevere.

[82] All goodness, as in the fertile soil of Luke 8:8 or that which is beneficial as in Matt 7:11 and that which is useful in edification as in Eph 4:29, is from God.

[83] πατήρ: "father," as in Creator; cf. Job 39:28; Ps 27:1; John 8:44; 1 Cor 1:3; Eph 1:17. In the metaphorical sense God is likened to the sun who originates rays of light; cf. Ps 35:9; Isa 60:1,19–20; Mal 4:2; 1 John 1:5; Rev 21:23; *Wis* 7:26.

[84] φῶς: "light." In the plural it denotes the heavenly bodies of sun, moon, and stars; cf. Gen 1:3,14–18; Job 38:7,28; Pss 119:105; 135:7; 136:7; Isa 14:12; Jer 31:35; Matt 5:14; Luke 16:8; John 5:35; Phil 2:15.

[85] ἄνωθεν: "from above." Cf. the wisdom from above (3:15; Matt 24:29; Mark 13:25; Luke 5:16,29; 9:18; John 3:31).

ness is intrinsic to them. Like the wisdom from above of 3:15,17, all good gifts "come down"[86] in a revelatory and saving event. Good gifts do not come "from below"—where they are misused because of evil desire—from the created order, but only "from above," from the Creator of heaven and earth. Thus nothing withheld from God's children or forbidden in God's Word is good, regardless of the enticement of desire.

The NIV translation, "who does not change[87] like shifting shadows," grapples with a notoriously difficult text.[88] The term "change"[89] picks up the astral realm of the phrase "Father of lights." God, as Creator of the "heavenly lights," is incomparably greater than they are (cf. Ps 135:6; Jer 4:23). The God who orders the stars and their changes to indicate "seasons and days and years" (Gen 1:14) and who controls all the changes in his creation does not himself change. His governance over all things is impeccable and benevolent, bringing them to the end he has willed for them.

1:18 The decision[90] of God to birth believers through his Word is not the same as his general working within creation. God performs a special kind of work in the life of human beings according to his divine plan.[91] Believers have faith because God gave them spiritual birth (cf. John 1:13; Phil 1:29). Of his perfect gifts, the new

---

[86] καταβαίνω: "come down," as the sun's rays descend to the earth, again the metaphoric sense of God's activity toward his creatures. Cf. also the sheet in Acts 10:11–15 or the new Jerusalem (Rev 3:12; 21:2–10) or even the descent of the Holy Spirit (Mark 1:10).

[87] τροπή ("change," "alteration"), together with ἀποσκίασμα ("shadow"), especially in astrological contexts, refers to the shifts of the heavenly bodies, such as solstices and eclipses. James's point was that God is invariably good. A similar thought appears in 1 John 1:5: "God is light; in him there is no darkness at all." Cf. Deut 33:14; Job 38:33; Mal 3:6; Heb 13:8, where the unchangeability of God is likewise the emphasis.

[88] There are six textual variants for this phrase in the UBS, 3rd edition.

[89] παραλλαγή: "change, variation." There is no other appearance of the word in the NT. Here even the sun's changes throughout the day make it inferior to God and his eternal light (cf. Wis 7:29; Sir 17:26; 27:11).

[90] βούλομαι: "wish," "will," in its form here, "by an act of will," "deliberately" (NIV "chose"); God's will does not cause evil desire, but he does cause the new birth in the believer; cf. Deut 32:18; Pss 7:14; 22:9; 80:18; 87:4–6; 99:25; John 1:13; 3:3–8; Rom 12:2; 1 Cor 4:15; Gal 4:19; 1 Pet 1:3; 1 John 4:10.

[91] Cf. Luke 10:22; 22:42; 1 Cor 12:11; Heb 6:17. Cf. Num 11:12; Deut 32:18; Pss 22:9; 90:2; Isa 66:13.

life he engenders is consummate. God does not cause temptation; he engenders life. The contrast could not be more pointed. This spiritual impartation of life is a giving birth (cf. v. 15)—a remarkable metaphor juxtaposed to the name "Father." Obviously, birthing is a feminine activity, but here the image is applied to God the Father. This application is in no way a pagan contribution but one that frequently appears in Scripture.[92] Indeed, the frequent New Testament reference to the "new birth" implies God giving birth to believers. In contrast to death birthed by sin, life is produced by God.

God gives birth to believers by means of his truthful word.[93] The word of truth here is virtually synonymous with the gospel. It stands in strong contrast to the self-deception of evil desire and the sin it produces. The word of truth is the instrument by which God implants new life in the believer. James's concern was for the unity of knowing the truth and its practical implications of doing the truth (3:21). James later warned against wandering from the truth (5:19). The Word of truth by which God gives birth to new creatures produces a harvest that he had intended since the moment of his first creating.[94] Here is a wonderful uniting of first and second creation. What God brings about in salvation was contained in the original purpose of his creation. Indeed, those saved out of lost humanity will be a firstfruits of God's saving work that reaches every component of creation.

This word of truth is like seed that produces a fruit-bearing plant. The word of truth that brought forth the first creation brings about the regeneration of human beings in anticipation of the regeneration of all of nature.[95]

---

[92] Cf. John 1:11–13; 3:3–8; Eph 1:5; Rom 12:2; 1 Cor 4:15; Titus 3:5; 1 Pet 1:3,23; 1 John 3:9; 4:1.

[93] λόγος ἀληθείας: "word of truth." Cf. the similar passage in 1 Pet 1:25; also Rom 10:8,17. The word of truth is God's means for communicating new life; see v. 21; cf. Ps 119:43; Eccl 12:10; Matt 4:4; John 6:63; 17:7–8,17; Gal 5:5; 2 Cor 6:7; Eph 1:13; Phil 2:16; Heb 10:26; 1 John 2:29. The word of truth is essentially the gospel (cf. Col 1:5). Although "gospel" is the closest meaning to "word of truth," God's creative word and commanding word were never far apart in James's thought.

[94] κτίσμα: "creation," that which is created, thus a universal frame of reference for the scope of salvation; cf. Isa 11:6ff.; 65:13; Matt 19:28; Rom 8:19–22.

[95] This is an amazing transformation of the OT idea of offering "firstfruits" to God; cf. Exod 22:29–39; Num 18:8–12; Deut 18:3; 26:2,10; Lev 27:26; Ezek 20:40.

In the Old Testament the "firstfruits"[96] of living things, including humans, were those offered to God in thanksgiving and became his special possession. Elsewhere in the New Testament firstfruits can apply to the redeemed of the Lord both presently (Rom 16:5; 1 Cor 15:20; 16:15) and eschatologically (2 Thess 2:13; Rev 14:4). The character of God has thus been fully vindicated against the charge of his being the source of temptation by reference to his redeeming purpose with human creatures.

4. The All-inclusive Doing of the Word (1:19–27)

The practical admonition to be slow to speak follows upon reverencing the word of God that gives life. What is heard in the fellowship of believers should be speech formed by the present and active word of God. Here James introduces his concern with speech, that is, the tongue that functions so prominently in his letter.

(1) Going Fast and Slow (1:19)

[19]My dear brothers, take note of this: Everyone should be quick to listen, slow to speak and slow to become angry,

1:19   There is a strong egalitarian tone in this admonition. James's "dear brothers" knew[97] that "everyone" was to practice the discipline of slow or controlled speech.[98] Later James encouraged effective and indeed quick action (2:12). Here the quickness does not refer to acting but rather to listening. Wherever wisdom is the

---

[96] ἀπαρχή: "firstfruits"; here the phrase "a kind of firstfruits." The OT prescribed six kinds to be given to God (cf. Deut 18:3; 26:2ff.; Neh 10:35; Jer 2:3; Ezek 20:40). Paul used the term to describe his first converts (Rom 16:5; 1 Cor 16:15). This term is applied to Christ as well (1 Cor 15:30); 2 Thess 2:13 is closest to James with respect to the redemption of the created order and similarly Rom 8:23; Heb 12:23; Rev 14:3. Cf. Philo's statement "a kind of firstfruits of his creatures" (*Spec. Leg.* 4, 180), referring to the Jews, i.e., a spiritual harvest; also *Wis* 13:4.

[97] The NIV "take note of this" reflects Gk. Ἴστε, which can be indicative or imperative. Some MSS read ὥστε (KJV "wherefore") in its place, which seems to be a correction for smoother reading. There also is some question whether Ἴστε refers to what precedes or what follows. Cf. Johnson, *The Letter of James*, 198–99.

[98] For the problem of hastiness in speech, cf. Prov 13:3; 15:1; 29:20.

goal, hearing will be a first virtue. Indeed, "quick" and "slow"[99] are a frequent tandem in describing qualities of response to life. Learning requires slowness; action requires quickness. In this case the requiring quickness is that which is to be learned by hearing. The required learning is in speaking, in which case wisdom is easily abandoned in favor of self-interest. Anger may not be fully controllable, but it can be checked by avoiding impetuous speech. James connected quickness or rashness of speech and a flaring of anger, an uncontrolled human emotion (cf. Mark 3:5). By practicing a cautious response to people verbally, wrathful emotions will also be put in check. This connection of quick speech and anger is quite intelligible from the interconnectedness of all human behavior as understood from biblical wisdom. The only way that peace can prevail with the "everyone" to whom the admonitions apply is to be ready listeners and slow commentators, especially in heated situations.

Contrary to some who would defend anger as the last resort for the Christian under trial, James declared they are simply wrong. Paul's approach, "in your anger do not sin" and "do not let the sun go down on your anger" (Eph 4:26; cf. Col 3:8; Prov 29:11), is comparable to "be . . . slow to become angry." Anger is dangerous even when expressed in speech. Angry speech is part of the temptation to seek vengeance and was of deep concern to both James and Paul. Is there any suggestion here of a righteous anger for believers? In Rom 12:19–21 Paul was emphatic about not taking vengeance upon enemies. "Leave room for God's wrath," he declared.

(2) Discarding Offense and Accepting the Word (1:20–21)

[20]for man's anger does not bring about the righteous life that God desires. [21]Therefore, get rid of all moral filth and the evil that is so prevalent and humbly accept the word planted in you, which can save you.

1:20 James expressed himself clearly and strongly in this

---

[99] ταχύς ("quick," "prompt") and βραδύς ("slow") are naturally related to express types of response, here in terms of hearing and becoming angry. See 3:9,14–16; 4:1–2,11; cf. Prov 10:19; 16:32; Eccl 5:1–2; Luke 12:21; Rom 16:19; 1 Thess 4:9; *Sir* 2.29; *Herm. Man.* V. 1.3.6.

verse: "The righteousness of God"[100] (*dikaiosunēn theou*, freely translated by the NIV as "the righteous life that God desires") cannot be accomplished by human anger. Only God can vindicate the righteous by his anger without becoming involved in sin. Who is not convicted by this verse? "Righteousness" also appears in 2:23 and 3:18. Whether in relationship with God (2:23) or in relationship with others (3:18), anger must be ruled out. Human anger will inhibit the wholehearted trust necessary for the relationship between the believer and God. Human anger will injure the merciful peacemaking required for the relationships among fellow believers and those outside their fellowship. Already James hinted of things to come, in "bring[ing] about"[101] that which is righteous before God. As in 1:3–4, the tight connection of doing/acting/ becoming appears here.

1:21 If anger is to be rejected as a motive for action before God and men, then the chief causes of anger must be abandoned. James uses the metaphor of taking off[102] and putting away soiled clothes. There is a practical necessity of eliminating everything that is contrary to the word of truth. Likewise Paul commended as a

---

[100] δικαιοσύνη θεοῦ: "righteousness of God," perhaps even the righteousness of God that vindicates those who are oppressed by evil men, certainly, the righteousness willed by God. Cf. OT passages such as Gen 15:6; Exod 15:13; Deut 33:19; Pss 4:2; 9:5; 119:62,121; Prov 11:21; Isa 5:7; 60:17; and NT passages such as Matt 5:6; John 16:8–10; Acts 24:25; Rom 1:17; 3:5,22; 10:3; 1 Cor 1:30; 2 Cor 5:21; Heb 5:13; 11:7,33; 1 Pet 2:5; 1 John 3:10; Rev 22:11. In all these passages the context determines the precise meaning of "righteousness," but there is always the requirement of some righteous action before God and men.

[101] ἐργάζομαι: "work," "accomplish," "bring about." What the believer is called to do by God is what he recognizes as righteous. The connection with "man" here in the generic sense makes a strong association between violent desire and its incapacity to effect anything truly good; cf. Ps 106:32,33; John 1:13; Rom 2:9–10; 4:5; 15:2; 2 Cor 7:10; 2 Pet 1:21.

[102] ἀποτίθημι: "put off" or "away," "rid oneself of," as the way of preparing the heart for action. Frequent metaphorical comparisons are found between dress and virtue; e.g., a clean garment for a banquet or little clothing for running a race (cf. Job 14:4; Zech 3:4; Matt 22:11; Rom 13:12; 2 Cor 7:1; Eph 4:22,25; Col 3:8; Heb 12:1; 1 Pet 2:1; 3:21; Rev 3:4,18). Note this is a participle, at least putting emphasis on the imperative "accept." It may suggest an assumption that by definition a believer has done so and does "lay aside" evil.

spiritual discipline ridding oneself of everything that is displeasing to God and destructive of the Christian faith. That morally detestable practices must be discarded like a garment tells something important about their nature.

However much evil practices are rooted in the memory and structure of desire within the human soul, they are effectively dealt with as activities distinct from believers themselves. All immoral and moral behaviors are practices that are acquired rather than reflective of an "orientation." Being moral is necessary, but it always involves intentional acts. This is even more the case with Christian action, for it is closely interwoven with personal faith, prayer, worship, fellowship, and the evangelistic mandate of Christ. Christian obedience is never fully habitual. It requires a daily "putting on Christ" for its realization. Even with a strong doctrine of the new life in Christ, believers are always putting on and putting off ways of living according to the will of God. What a person "wears," particularly in the expression of values, is a highly personal matter, and the attachment to certain ways are very strong.

What God calls believers to put off, however, they must put off. Otherwise the contradiction to God's righteousness produces an anger-filled human being. A concrete term for the "moral filth"[103] of sin is used here (cf. v. 27). Physical dirt and grime denote the vices of the world, that is, those traits and behaviors that are base and low. James may very well have been referring to avarice and malice[104] (the evil impulses behind the sins mentioned in 1:13; 3:8; 4:3). But since all filthiness is to be discarded, the whole range of morally degenerate behaviors are covered. With the expression "evil that is so prevalent" (lit. "the abundance of evil"), James added the idea of a residue,[105] something left over from one's life prior to conversion. James put before his readers the necessity of

---

[103] ῥυπαρία: "filth," as in the "smirch" or "stain" of avarice in its connection with the prevalence of evil; cf. "our righteousness is as filthy rags" of Isa 64:6.

[104] κακία: "evil," or "malice," also 4:4,8. Evil behavior overflows from evil residing in the heart, as in the statement "the evil man brings evil things out of the evil stored up in his heart" in Luke 6:45; cf. Gen 6:5; Prov 1:16.

[105] περισσεία: "excess," "surplus"; cf. Ps 17:4; Matt 14:20; 15:37; Rom 5:17; 1 Cor 5:8; 2 Cor 8:2; 10:15.

repentance. The evil in view here is especially that sin of malice, of doing others harm. Malicious speech is particularly evident in conflicts between believers in the church and must be guarded against. Given the context with the words "anger" and "gentleness," this seems the best sense (cf. Eph 4:31; Col 3:8).

Whether James meant that repentance can be repeated for such evil throughout a lifetime or repentance is once and for all is difficult to discern from the text. Doing evil things of course is something that is particularly painful for Christians to admit. But since it is an even greater evil to avoid admitting it, the church and its members must exercise repentance as the only antidote to behavior that contradicts its witness. Here James was calling his hearers to eliminate evil and its old causes.

But eliminating evil and its causes is never the sole or final goal of Christian instruction. There always is a positive exhortation to do the will of God as well. This positive doing begins for James with approving what God has planted[106] within the self. The "word of truth" (v. 18) that gives birth to believers is that which has been implanted. This is the effective[107] divine word ("can"=*dynamai*, "be able"), which itself works salvation.

This notable affirmation is key for developing a theology of the Word of God. The word of the text, Scripture, takes root as the saving word in the heart and mind, shaping and saving the self ("save you" is lit. "save your souls")[108] for God. In the early history of the church, the word preached was that instrument of transmission from Scripture to heart and mind. Thus the Word of Scripture and the preaching of the word convey the eternal and living Word of God, who is God. James declared that God's Word

---

[106] ἐμφύω: "rooted in," another hapax legomenon. Metaphorically the implanted Word in the believer is as a seed planted in the heart; cf. Deut 11:18; 30:14; Job 11:13–14; Jer 31:33; Matt 13:21; 15:13; Acts 20:32; Rom 13:14; 2 Cor 3:3; Eph 4:24; Col 3:10; 1 Thess 2:13; *4 Esdr* 9.31; *Barn* 1.2; 9.9; Ign. *Eph.* 17; Justin *Apol.* 2.8,13.

[107] δύναμαι: "able," as in the power or ability of the gospel to save; cf. Rom 1:16; 1 Cor 1:18; 2 Cor 6:7.

[108] ψυχή: "soul," the self that is to be saved, which includes the body, as in 2:14; 4:12; 5:15,20; cf. Heb 10:39.

saves and actually performs this greatest of all divine works. As is the case throughout this letter, the divine gifts bestow blessing both presently and eschatologically; so the saving work of the Word has both present and eschatological effect (cf. 1:12; 2:12–13; 3:1; 5:5,7).

The implanted Word must be received[109] even though it is already present within the self. The dynamic Word must be "heard" as God speaking presently to the believer. God may be heard through the preaching, rereading, or recitation of a familiar text. Receiving the word in this sense is not entirely passive but entails an active concentration on that which has already determined the faith of the believer. Through "receiving" the word again, renewal and deepening of faith can occur.

James qualified this act of receiving with the phrase "in meekness" (NIV "humbly").[110] Just as the emphasis on humility so basic to faith in our letter (v. 9) resonates deeply with the Beatitudes of Matt 5:3–5 and Jesus' self-description of 11:29, so does the call for "meek" reception of God's Word. Meekness is the opposite of anger and is the product of the gift of wisdom required of all believers. Rather than speaking, the wise believer lets the Lord speak through his Word and through the teachers of his Word who model this virtue.[111] Later (3:13) James would require that wise teachers must demonstrate their wisdom through meekness.

(3) The Liberating Mirror (1:22–25)

22Do not merely listen to the word, and so deceive yourselves. Do what it says. 23Anyone who listens to the word but does not do what it says is like a man who looks at his face in a mirror 24and, after

---

[109] δέχομαι, "accept," is here an imperative and is a basic term for active faith in the NT; cf. Matt 10:40; Luke 8:13; 10:8–10; Acts 8:14; 11:1; 17:11; Gal 4:14; 1 Cor 2:14; 2 Cor 6:1; 1 Thess 1:6; 2:13.

[110] πραΰτης: "gentleness," receiving the Word with goodwill or with receptiveness, as in 3:13; cf. Matt 5:5; Gal 5:23; 2 Tim 2:25; 1 Pet 3:15.

[111] This teachability as the purpose of meekness for both believers and teachers is reflected in many NT texts (e.g., 1 Cor 4:21; Gal 5:23; Eph 4:2; Col 3:12; 2 Tim 2:25).

looking at himself, goes away and immediately forgets what he looks like. ²⁵But the man who looks intently into the perfect law that gives freedom, and continues to do this, not forgetting what he has heard, but doing it—he will be blessed in what he does.

1:22 If the Word implanted is dynamic, working salvation, it is imperative that believers do what the Word says (the verse in Gk. reads lit., "Become doers of the word and not only hearers, deceiving yourselves"). Certainly there is a sense of development or growth here. Being doers[112] of the Word involves becoming,[113] but the force here is in being who one is because the Word is resident within. Disciples are to "receive" the Word of God by "being" believers who do what that Word requires. In 4:11 James used a similar phrase, "doer of the law" (NIV "keeping it"), which shows the interchangeableness of Word and law in Christ (cf. 1:25). This matter of being a doer (cf. 2:7; 5:14) captures James's burden for his hearers.

Disciples cannot be hearers only, like those in the parable of the sower (Matt 13:3–9) who have no rooting of the Word. The problem of self-deception[114] recurs here. Believers can act against the Word of God and sin. Yet they simply must do what it says. For James, fruit must be produced, that is, acts of mercy. Hearing, lis-

---

[112] ποιητής: "doer." This sense is somewhat lost in the imperative of the translation "do what it [the Word] says." James perhaps was hearkening back to the original giving of the law at Sinai and Israel's response, "We will do everything the LORD has said; we will obey" (Exod 24:7; cf. Deut 28:58; 29:28; Ezek 33:32; Matt 7:24; Luke 6:46; 11:28; John 13:17; Rom 2:13). Since Christ brings a new law, note Rom 8:2; 1 Cor 9:21; Gal 6:2. Note the contrast with ἀκροατής ("listener"), as in someone who attends a lecture, as distinguished from a μαθητής, a "follower" or disciple who hears and does the word of the master. These are nouns of action and ought to be highlighted in this way.

[113] γίνομαι ("become"). The sense of becoming might be better here than "be," especially since the imperative "be" is not found elsewhere in the NT. The sense of "become" suggests the correctibility and teachability that James presupposed in the writing of his letter.

[114] παραλογίζομαι: "misconstrue," in this case "deceive" oneself; cf. Gen 29:25; 31:41; Josh 9:22; 1 Sam 28:12. Col 2:4 is the only other NT passage where this word appears; there the sense of "defraud" also is present. The deception leads to a bad exchange. Mere profession is wrong and leads to a loss of blessedness.

tening to the Word of God, is right, but it can become wrong when another type of self-deception arises. Doing what Scripture says is not a question of acting quickly or slowly but acting at all. To be a hearer or to have faith only (cf. 2:24) is self-deceiving. Faith must be demonstrated (cf. 3:13), and to miss this is a fundamental flaw in understanding. No one who has called upon God for wisdom can or should think undemonstrated faith is true. James used exhortation then to point out how easily his hearers could fall from the wisdom they required to live out true faith through action. Knowledge by itself only "puffs up" (1 Cor 8:1).

1:23 James illustrated his teaching with reference to a man who looks intently at his reflection in a mirror. This analogy is a negative one, picturing those who only listen but remain inactive and therefore unresponsive. Unlike Paul's use of mirror as a metaphor in 1 Cor 13:12, where the reflected image of God is dim,[115] James's reflected image of the creature is clear. The Word of God has penetrated the creaturely world in the form of Scripture and is highly effective in revealing the true nature of that world. This revelation is most of all the case with its hearers or readers, the men and women God intends to save.

Some believers merely glance[116] into the mirror of truth without letting God's wisdom do its work on them. The "mirror" is key for understanding this section of James. In the ancient world the mirror,[117] a specially shaped piece of polished metal, was used to inspect or decorate one's body. The ancient literature is replete with

---

[115] Paul used the analogy of the mirror to convey the imperfection or incompleteness of human perception of God and his truth. Next to this is the anticipation of seeing God "face to face," where perception will be changed from dimness to absolute clarity; cf. 2 Cor 3:18; *Sir* 12:11; *Wis* 7:26. The analogy of the mirror held an honored place within the traditions of the ancient pagan philosophers and poets (Plato, *Rep.* 7; Euripedes *Hipp.* 427–30; Seneca *QNat* 1.17; Epictetus *Diss.* 2.14) and continues into the works of early Christian theologians (e.g., *PsClem.* 13.16).

[116] κατανοέω: "glance," "observe," "look at." Here as in Acts 7:31f.; Ps 93:9 the term indicates perception. Tragically, this kind of person ignores what he has perceived, resulting in a detachment from what is observed, in this case the truth about himself.

[117] ἔσοπτρον: "mirror," here standing for God's law, which reveals who we truly are over and against our self-deceived notions (see v. 26).

references to the mirror and its use as a metaphor for moral development. There is a double mistake implied here by the believer
who does not act upon the Word. First, the Word is being treated
like a mere vision, a "theory," in the sense of a detached mental
image with no connection to the external world. The Word is like a
theory, but it is a practical one that both reflects reality, that is, the
natural face, and directs the beholder to act in a certain way. The
second mistake we make regarding the Word is to ignore its message once it is received. The mere glancing at the Word without
corrective action is of little use.

1:24   Such an unconcerned quick checking and leaving, almost
to see if the Word still condemns him, is meant to convey how terribly wrong this exercise is. The abruptness of the process is intensified by the immediate forgetting of what was seen. Johnson
highlights this point quite well by the striking dialogue with such a
person: "What were you like?" "I forget."[118] By implication, the
failure of this man is that he does not recognize the necessity of
remembering, that is, of acting. Although the image of wisdom in a
great teacher also could serve as a mirror for beholding one's natural condition, the Word of God does so here.

1:25   In contrast, the believer who learns about himself and
what God requires by concentrating on the mirror of the Word will
be blessed. The sense here is of an intense looking[119] into Scripture
for the purpose of self-change. The exercise is one of careful attention to learn what is wrong and to discern what ought to be done to
correct it. This kind of continual gazing into the Word—which is
really a kind of hearing—guards against forgetting and motivates

---

[118] ἐπιλανθάνω: "forget." Although infrequently used in Scripture, forgetting
and remembering are essentially opposing values related to the ignoring and acquiring of wisdom; cf. Hermas *Vis.* 3.12.2; Johnson, *The Letter of James,* 208.

[119] παρακύπτω: "look more closely at"—by bending over, "peer;" cf. Gen 26:8;
1 Chr 16:29; Prov 7:6; Song of Songs 2:9; John 20:1; 1 Pet 1:12; *Sir* 21.23. The verb
is associated with the training in virtue connected with the analogy of the mirror.
Together with παραμένω ("continues," "remain beside"), παρακύπτω gives the
sense of intent looking into to learn what is there and to apply what is learned to the
self rather than flippant consideration without learning and applying; cf. Deut 27:26;
Luke 2:19,51; 8:15; John 8:31.

doing. Only by remembering to do what Scripture says, as one continues hearing/reading it, can one apply it to life. "Apply yourself to the Word so you may be able to apply the Word to your life" is the proper motto here. Every believer walks back into life and away from moments of hearing the Word of God in preaching or reading, but not in the same way. Through humble, attentive, and continual exposure to the Word of God the believer will find a quickness to apply it both in the midst of trials of faith and in the temptation to give in to wealth and privilege (2:2).

What James referred to as the "Word" in vv. 18,21,22,23 he calls the "law" here.[120] As the "Word" brings new life according to v. 18, so "the law" here is what sets us free[121] (lit. "the perfect law of freedom"). The combination of law and freedom points to the free obedience of the Christian life and echoes Paul's theology of freedom in Christ (cf. Rom 6:18–22; 2 Cor 3:17; Gal 2:4; 5:1,13–14; 6:2). The law is "perfect" in that it participates in the goodness of God and is essential to his gifts bestowed in wisdom to believers.

This was James's first occasion to use the word "law," and it had a special meaning with him. Law stands by itself in 2:9–11 and 4:11 but also appears as the "royal law" in 2:8 and the "law that gives freedom" in 2:12. The New Testament conveys the understanding that Christ brought a "new law," in the sense that he fulfilled and placed the law upon a new basis in himself (1 Cor 9:21). To serve him is to serve the law; to truly serve the law is therefore to serve him. The same would go for studying the law and thus to be studying him. James made a personal connection not with the life of Christ but rather with the lives of past exemplars of faith who trusted in the Lord (cf. 2:20–26; 5:10–11,16–18)

---

[120] νόμος: "law"; cf. Prov 6:23; Rom 7:14,16; 1 Tim 1:8. That James even added the important word "perfect" virtually equates it with the law of love. Cf. Gal 6:2; 1 Cor 7:10,25; 9:21; *Barn.* 2:6; Iren. *Adv. haer.* IV.34.4; 37.1; 13.2.

[121] ἐλευθερία: "freedom," is one of the most important linkages for the commonality with Paul's understanding of the new law in Christ, where the gospel is the law of liberty anticipated by the prophets' amplification of the law; cf. Jer 31:33; Exod 35:5; Deut 28:47; Pss 1:2; 40:8; Rom 3:27. James would define this notion further in 2:12, in close agreement with Paul (e.g., Gal 5:1,13–14; Rom 13:10).

and thus can be said to have trusted Christ. The law and keeping the law as testimony to the active Word that makes the believer free is in view here. The absence of a reference in James to any law other than that contained within the Ten Commandments or that which sums them up in acts of love and mercy supports such an understanding of law.

The blessing (cf. 1:12) follows closely the words of Jesus, "Blessed rather are those who hear the word of God and obey it" (Luke 11:28). In the Lord's thinking, this obedience also can apply to his own words (cf. Matt 7:24; Luke 6:47). The blessing promised here is in the doing and as a result of the doing. These two senses need not be separated. For to know what one's purpose is as a creature of God is itself blessedness. This is the result of the freedom brought by the law of God.

There is always a direct connection between receiving the gifts of God and doing the will of God according to his Word. Those who are blessed by God live in the union of truth and action, which is their joy. This knowledge is the joy of their union with God and those they have the duty to serve. In this way their blessedness is the fulfillment of God's purpose and is also the well-being of those they are to visit who are in distress (v. 27). In this compliment of the perfect generosity of God and of the whole-hearted obedience of the believer, we see real blessedness attained in relationship with God through his Word.

(4) Worthless Religion and Genuine Religion (1:26–27)

[26]If anyone considers himself religious and yet does not keep a tight rein on his tongue, he deceives himself and his religion is worthless. [27]Religion that God our Father accepts as pure and faultless is this: to look after orphans and widows in their distress and to keep oneself from being polluted by the world.

1:26 Another important turn in James's message against self-deception (1:6–7,14,16,22) is this teaching on "worthless religion."[122] One of the chief characteristics of self-deception in the Christian life is that believers can make an empty show of religious devotion.[123] Depending on how the term is modified, "religion" is used as both the characterization of a way of life that embodies bad faith and also a way of life that embodies true faith. The problem then is both the appearance and the intent of religion in James's understanding. One can seem to be religious, that is, rightly related to God, and yet in the most basic way be failing to be so.

The self-deceiving brother is religious, but the character of his religion is disreputable. Such religion has always been a problem for the church; and now at the end of the twentieth century, with so many names for Christianity and with what Christians do besmirched by those whose religious practice is empty, perhaps we can return to a healthy use of the word "religion." Religion is the external, observable qualities of the life of faith in Christ. In this very important sense, the "religion" of the Christian and the Christian community is indispensable, but only if it is true to the faith. This is what the Letter of James is all about. Talk of the accountability of believers to the Word of God and to one another in the church is, after all, talk about religious observances practiced with sincerity. The tongue becomes the test case for true religion.

The tongue must be controlled—though not stifled. The image

---

[122] The hapax legomenon θρησκός ("religious") is obviously derived from θρησκέια, "religion," which appears in the next verse and signifies a relationship with divine reality. James should not be seen here as making some kind of apologetic for the religious status of Christianity within the Gentile world. Evangelicals, on the other hand, should not see their emphasis on personal relationship with God as non-religious. The real question about religion for James was: Which is true religion and which is vain? The great problem connected with self-deception here is that what "seems" to a believer to be "religious" turns out not to be so at all; rather, it is just the opposite (cf. Acts 26:5; Col 2:18; 4 Macc 5.6, 12; Josephus Ant. 4.4.4; 5.10.1; 9.13.3; Wis 14.18, 27; 1 Clement 1.45; Eusebius Eccl. hist. 1.4). "Worthless" is the word μάταιος ("empty," "futile"). It appears again in 2:14; cf. Isa 1:10–17; 1 Cor 15:17; Titus 3:9; 1 Pet 1:18.

[123] Cf. Matt 3:9; 6:7; 26:53; Mark 6:49; Luke 8:18; 19:11; 24:37; Acts 12:9; John 5:39; 1 Cor 3:18; 8:2; 11:16; 14:37; Gal 6:3; Phil 3:4.

used here involves the harnessing[124] of a horse at the mouth. It is not that the tongue or speech is at all bad; James would later affirm it as an instrument of blessing. Unfortunately, an unrestrained tongue is a highly destructive force and an instrument of deception. A strong confessional theme underlies this chapter and indeed the entire book. What is said of God and to God is always a claim about relationship and the truth. By drawing attention to the tongue, James avoided a comparison over the quantity and quality of obedient works. Instead, confession of faith, of sin, and of need before God and others means that the control of the tongue, of speech, stands axiomatically for true religion. Control of the tongue stands for control of the whole self against temptation to indulge evil desire and to become deceptive about one's own double-mindedness. Control of the tongue also stands for persevering under trial, praying to God for wisdom, and using the tongue, indeed the entire body, for the obedience of faith.

James called the religion that goes with an uncontrolled tongue "worthless." His attention was on the practices of religion, its services and sacrifices. Worthless religion is then merely external and a virtual idolatry involving self-deception.[125]

1:27 Genuine religion is that which is (lit.) "pure and undefiled before our God and Father."[126] There is no room for human definitions here. The standards of true religion in behavior come by the Word of truth and the reception of wisdom to produce a right relationship with God. Genuine religion means that everything in the believer's life is to bear the mark of service to God. Paul's "whatever you do, do it all for the glory of God" (1 Cor 10:31) and "everything God created is good, and nothing is to be rejected if it is received with thanksgiving" (1 Tim 4:4) are applicable here. The

---

[124] χαλιναγωγέω ("to bridle," "restrain"), a rare word in Greek. Only James used it in the NT (also in 3:2; but also anticipated in 1:19. Cf. Pss 32:9; 39:1; 141:3; cf. *Herm. Man.* 12.1; Polycarp *ad. Phil.* 5.3.

[125] Cf. Acts 14:15; Rom 1:21; 8:20; Eph 4:17.

[126] παρά τῷ θεῷ: "before God," "in the eyes of God," i.e., according to God's standards as in v. 20; cf. Rom 2:13; 9:14; 1 Cor 3:19; Gal 3:11; 2 Thess 1:6; 1 Pet 2:4,20.

totality of life is brought before God and becomes an acceptable religious form for his glory. The close association between creation and God as Father of believers reminds them that their lives now originate from God and are in his hands.

God tests and blesses so that believers' religion might be "pure and faultless." This combination of terms distinguishes genuine from empty religion. Double-minded believers flirt with idolatry so that their religion is inevitably defiled and impure. Sins of omission and commission are entailed in futile religion because of the idolatrous nature of it. That which is pure in religion is everything that can be consecrated to God (cf. 1 Tim 4:5), particularly the self as well as a way of life.[127] The undefiled aspect of religion is nearly synonymous with purity, and thus there is an emphatic quality in the use of this second term. Undefiled religion reflects the divine standard itself, while its purity reflects the quality of the practice itself.

Just as God comes to the aid of those in need, those who practice true religion "look after"[128] orphans and widows, these most vulnerable members of church and society.[129] Orphans and widows are the objects of repeated appeals for righteous action to minister to the needy and helpless.[130] These exemplify the poor to whom God shows special favor (cf. 2:1–7) against the natural human preference for the wealthy. The poor must be the object of true Christian duty (2:14–16) or all claims to true faith are mean-

---

[127] Cf. Gen 7:3; 8:20; Lev 4:12; 7:19; 11:32; 15:13; Num 8:7; Deut 12:15; Luke 11:41; Rom 14:20; Titus 1:15; Heb 10:22.

[128] ἐπισκέπτομαι: "visit," "assist," which often in Scripture refers to the coming of God to deliver his people from crisis or else visiting the sick; cf. Gen 21:1; 50:24; Exod 3:16; 4:31; Josh 8:10; Ruth 1:6; 1 Sam 2:21; Zech 10:3; Matt 25:36,43; Luke 1:68,78; Acts 7:23; 15:14; *Sir* 7.35.

[129] ὀρφανός, "orphan," and χήρα, "widow." God is ascribed "father of the fatherless" and judge of the widow, who brings an extraordinarily harsh curse upon those who oppress them. In the early church elders were charged to act as the fathers of orphans; cf. Exod 22:22; Deut 26:19; Job 31:16f.; Ps 68:5; Luke 20:47; *Sir* 4:10; Pol. *ad. Phil.* 4; 6; *Herm. Man.* 8.10; Ign. *ad. Pol.* 4.

[130] Cf. Exod 22:20–21; Lev 19:9–10; Deut 10:17–19; 24:17–18; Prov 19:17; Isa 3:5; Jer 22:3; Amos 2:6–8; Hos 12:8–9; Mal 3:5.

ingless. Not to give aid to these poor ones turns out to be only the beginning of the problem, for the rich later come under the charge of being active oppressors of the poor (cf. 5:1–6). The poor are necessarily of chief concern to the church because they live under such travail.[131] The unending tribulation of grinding poverty must move believers and their churches to assist the poor in every way: economically, legally, politically. As is the case with all of Scripture, no political, economic, or legal system is advocated per se— indeed, all the options are merely worldly ones. But proper Christian aid and defense of the poor can shape their social conditions in a dramatic way, and often for the good of all.

Along with the positive content of religion, there is also the practice of its negative content: to avoid whatever pollutes[132] the self. "Keeping" pertains to religious observance and spiritual devotion to God.[133] In view of living all life before God, the world must have no hold on the believer. Instead, believers hold themselves apart from the ways of the world. The divine/human relationship that is true religion entails a stance toward the world (cf. 2:5; 3:6; 4:4) that supplies the intention for ethical action.

Religion, however pure, places the believer before God; but, having received the life-giving Word, life becomes truly and fully religious. Life is consecrated to serve God in everything. We are already before him. The question of how faith responds, which in many ways sums up our first chapter and the entire letter, has two dimensions: one is the inward life of the self; the other, life lived with others.

First, the outward-turning duty of faith focuses on persons in trouble, especially those against whom trouble falls the hardest, the orphans and widows. Jesus summarized all religion and com-

---

[131] θλίςψις: "distress," in the combined sense of grief and want; cf. Exod 4:31; Deut 4:29; Matt 13:21; 24:9; Acts 7:10; Rom 8:35.

[132] ἄσπιλος: "spotless," "unstained," from the κοσμός: "world," the first appearance of this significant word in James; see 2:5; 3:6; 4:4, the world that pollutes the self.

[133] E.g., 1 Tim 6:14; 2 Pet 3:14.

mands in terms of total love for God and for neighbor. James's definition of true religion serves similar comprehensive functions—love, loving care, will be focused most pointedly toward those in distress. The church is to be energized for this great cause in coming to the aid of such persons. James, rather than setting out a program for how each and every person is to be related to every other in the church, held that the standard of relationships is somehow rooted and shaped by outreach toward those in greatest trial. Without the church supporting them, the most needy will not be able to find the fortitude for faith by which James's first injunction, "consider it pure joy," can be followed. Orphans and widows may be outcasts to the world, but they must be enfolded into the relationships of believers. And this ministry begins by identifying those who are in distress. Out of this sign of love, the tenor of love in all the other relationships of the church will be set.

II. ALL WORKS IN LIGHT OF JUDGMENT (2:1–26)
    1. Improper Discrimination (2:1–7)
        (1) The Glorious Christ (2:1)
        (2) Distinctive Seating (2:2–4)
        (3) The Discrimination of God (2:5–7)
    2. Mercy That Fulfills the Royal Law (2:8–13)
        (1) The Excellent Deed (2:8)
        (2) Offensive at Every Point (2:9–11)
        (3) The Freedom-giving Law (2:12–13)
    3. Unjustifiable Faith (2:14–26)
        (1) The Open Question (2:14)
        (2) Need without Deed (2:15–16)
        (3) A Pronouncement of Death (2:17)
        (4) A Question of Proof (2:18–19)
        (5) Exemplars of Faith with Deeds (2:20–25)
        (6) Recapitulation: No Faith without Deeds (2:26)

II. ALL WORKS IN LIGHT OF JUDGMENT (2:1–26)

In his first chapter, James held up the necessity of acquiring wisdom. Faith must become mature. Faith must manifest itself in true religion in order to be acceptable before God. Immature faith is marked by double-mindedness and foolishness. Mature faith is necessary because of the trials believers must endure in the world. Trials come because God the Father wills to prove the faith of believers, both to himself and to themselves. When the believing church appropriates God's promised wisdom, which is the Word of God or law of God, it will be able to endure all its testings and trials.

The second chapter of James begins with a clear break from the first chapter, signaled by the warning in 2:1. This verse introduces the first of four exhortations on authentic faith. The chapter

105

divisions, then, correspond quite well to the original organization of the letter. The ending of the chapter, 2:26, seems to complete the teaching contained in the first exhortation not to show partiality. James used all his rhetorical skill in writing this section.[1] He included the techniques of diatribe: an imagined dialogue partner (2:1,5,14), rhetorical questions (2:4–5,7,14,20), hypothetical example (2:2–3,15–16), as well as biblical personages who exemplify trust in God (2:8–11,21–25). By these literary techniques James sharpened the arguments of his exhortation and clarified the disagreement over the truth of his teaching while correcting misunderstanding and error. His use of language is also a subject of great importance exegetically, since he used terms that parallel Paul's writings so closely and yet with different meanings.[2]

The chapter shows how we should live out our faith in relation to others within the church. James laid out a basic fact: faith and works must be held together. He argued for this cooperation of faith and works in three ways, and so there are three parts of the chapter. The first argument (2:1–7) contends that authentic faith does not play favorites. Although prohibiting favoritism in principle, James made most pointed reference to the rich. Could this prohibition include a favoritism toward the poor?[3] It would have been

---

[1] There is a helpful presentation of these matters in D. F. Watson, "James 2 in Light of Greco-Roman Schemes of Argumentation," *NTS* 39 (1993): 94–121; cf. J. Brinktrine, "Zu Jak 2.1," *Bib* 35 (1954): 40–42.

[2] Cf. K.-G. Eckart, "Zur Terminologie des Jakobusbriefes," *TLZ* 89 (1964): 522–26; H. Frankemölle, "Gesetz im Jakobusbrief: Zur Tradition, kontextuellen Verwendung und Rezeption eines belasteten Begriffes," in *Das Gesetz im Neuen Testament,* ed. K. Kertelge, QD 108 (Freiburg: Herder, 1986), 175–221.

[3] It is debatable whether liberation theologies show a favoritism toward the poor or whether statements defending the poor are merely expressions of political posturing. Now in the post-Cold War era, new kinds of political assistance for the poor, perhaps more democratic, will be more favorable for them than violent revolution. The work by E. Tamez presents us with a difficult dilemma (*The Scandalous Message of James: Faith without Works Is Dead* [New York: Crossroad, 1990]). Historically and exegetically the book is somewhat questionable, but as a pastoral application of the message of James it is powerful. See also the important work by P. U. Maynard-Reid, *Poverty and Wealth in James* (Maryknoll, N.Y.: Orbis, 1987). Somewhat similar difficulties are visible from a South African context in D. J. Smit, "Show no partiality . . ." *JTSA* 71 (1990): 59–68.

obscene to suggest, in James's day, that showing favoritism could ever be a problem with respect to the poor. Indeed, the giving of special gifts to the poor was considered a necessary virtue. Moral teachers in the ancient world considered it a duty to pressure their societies to give gifts to the poor, to see that just treatment took place in the courts of the land, and to defend those who had been defrauded of their wages.

The sin of favoritism is the problem of paying attention to the rich who have no physical needs while neglecting the urgent needs of the poor. James began with an example of favoritism that lays bare the damage this behavior causes. The example is so extreme that no one could possibly object to his point that a combination of favoritism and faith in Jesus is impossible. James used such extreme examples to combat the problem of self-deception throughout his letter. His choice of rhetorical and illustrative materials then confronts not just complacent believers but those who are suffering from entrenched error.

The second argument (2:8–13) develops James's understanding of the "royal law": "love your neighbor as yourself." Once again preferential treatment of the rich violates this principle. Favoritism is the sin by which the church slides into worldliness and error. When believers recognize the truth about the poor in their midst, that they are chosen by God for special blessing, the royal law can be obeyed. Without obedience to this law of love, the practice of favoritism becomes a way of standing in judgment over the law of God. Because favoritism hurts the poor, it is an ungodly mercilessness.[4]

The third argument (2:14–25) expounds the famous distinction between living faith and dead faith. Faith must "have deeds." Without good deeds the believer is not a friend of God but of the world. James's warning against faith without deeds is about gross error in Christian living, but not about final judgment. It is not about a distinction between those "in Christ" and those "outside of Christ" but about a distinction between mature and immature faith. Immature faith can become actively unwise in its disposition toward God and

---

[4] For an interesting discussion of this section cf. C. H. Felder, "Partiality and God's Law: An Exegesis of James 2:1–13, *JRT* 39 (1982–83): 51–69.

his Word. James declared that this becomes "friendship with the world" and begins to bear witness against the believer's testimony of faith in Christ. These distinctions between present error in living and the basis for final judgment and between immature and mature faith will help us as we try to discern the relationship between the teachings of James and of Paul. James focused on those who exemplified faith with mercy; Paul, on the other hand, focused on those who thought they could add to the saving work of Christ.

1. Improper Discrimination (2:1–7)

(1) The Glorious Christ (2:1)

¹My brothers, as believers in our glorious Lord Jesus Christ, don't show favoritism.

2:1 James taught the strongest possible connection between faith in the Lord Jesus Christ and impartiality.[5] God does not play favorites, yet we do (cf. 2:9), sinners that we are. The world's love shows its true nature in its lack of love for the many who suffer under desperate circumstances. Just as James earlier demonstrated the incompatibility of double-mindedness and prayer, he here showed the impossibility of combining faith and the approval of the world.

Can favoritism or partiality coexist with the glorious Christ of faith? Impossible. God does display preferential treatment, but toward the poor (2:5) with the intent to demonstrate the greatness of his grace. Special respect of persons based on their high social standing is antithetical to faith in God. Believers must never mix faith with partiality. If they do, it is just another case of double-mindedness. When favoritism dominates, the obedience of faith is compromised and undermined.

---

[5] The command is lit. "not in partiality hold the faith of our Lord Jesus Christ of glory." προσωπολημψία: "partiality," "respect/favoring of persons," based on their social standing. The term literally means "lifting up the face" and is derived from OT descriptions of favoritism such as Lev 19:15 esp.; cf. Deut 1:17; 2 Chr 19:7; Job 34:19; Ps 83:2; Mal 1:8; Luke 20:21; Acts 10:34; Rom 2:11; Gal 2:6; Eph 6:9; Col 3:25; 1 Pet 1:17; *Sir* 4.21,27; 32.12f.

The Lord Jesus Christ is the divine glory.[6] He is the one who is the light and radiance of God. A close thought connection with Paul's ascription "the Lord of glory" in Cor 2:8 can be detected here. But even the Pauline phrase does not assert what John's Gospel does with its reference to "his glory" (John 1:14). After all, if John shared the leadership of the Jerusalem church with James (Gal 2:9), then they probably also shared the same inspired understanding of Jesus. Although the glory of Christ was made clear to the disciples in his resurrection, John asserted that Jesus' glory was always apparent by faith. In this unique verse in James, Jesus is the very embodiment of the divine glory made present in the world. Like the Shekinah to the people of God in the Old Testament and the Immanuel who is Jesus, the very glory of God is embodied in the person of Christ. An interchangeability between Christ and glory is observable here. Christ is the divine Savior, and the divine glory saves the believer.

Since the glorious divine Word came embodied as the Messiah, believers do the works he has assigned to them on an equal standing with each other. This mission is one quality of their participation in the saving glory of God. If the glory of God has not remained high and removed from his people but has come among them and delivered them from death and sin, there is no room for favoritism toward the rich.[7] God calls for a certain kind of preferential treatment but only toward the poor (cf. 2:5). Those who display an evil mind-set, for example, the proud and the envious (these latter probably were James's addressees, in particular), will have to humble themselves together with the rich (cf. 1:9–11). All

---

[6] τῆς δόξης: "the glory" of God; possibly "glorious Lord" (cf. Heb 1:3). The combinations of Greek words in this verse make it notoriously difficult to translate and therefore difficult to interpret precisely. The word "glory" stands here for the Lord himself, who contains all glory in his essence. The early date of this epistle is no argument against this ascription to Jesus Christ. It is likely that biblical references to the presence of God and the divine glory among his people are the proper frame of reference for this statement; cf. Lev 26:11f.; Pss 63:2; 85:9; Zech 2:5; 6:12f.; Hag 2:7,9; Matt 22:14; 25:3; F. Mussner, "'Direkte' und 'indirekte' Christologie im Jakobusbrief," *Catholica* 24 (1970): 111–17.

[7] Cf. Exod 14:17–18; Ps 96:3; Isa 60:1; Ezek 39:21–22; Zech 2:5–11; Matt 16:27; 24:30; Titus 2:13; 1 Pet 4:13.

acts of favoritism toward the rich of this world contradict the divine glory that saves believers.

There is a strong affinity between what James wrote in this passage and Lev 19:15.[8] The command in that verse says: "Do not pervert justice; do not show partiality to the poor or favoritism to the great, but judge your neighbor fairly." Respect for the entire people of God, particularly toward the defenseless and needy, runs throughout the commands of Leviticus 19. Whenever judgments are made based on selfish gain rather than on true need or on the truth about a wrongful act, justice is perverted. Neglect of orphans and widows (cf. Jas 1:27) and the poor visitor in church (cf. 2:2) are prime examples of Christian neglect, that is, sins of omission and injustice. The Lord does not show favoritism, and neither should his people. The law of God, reclaimed by believers in Jesus,[9] has as one of its central characteristics the cultivation of godliness. But if believers fail at this point, they cannot represent the faith of Jesus. The example of crass favoritism in the following verse, a partiality that disfavors the poor, illustrates how this sin involves a corruption within the entire community of believers.[10]

(2) Distinctive Seating (2:2–4)

[2]Suppose a man comes into your meeting wearing a gold ring and fine clothes, and a poor man in shabby clothes also comes in. [3]If you show special attention to the man wearing fine clothes and say, "Here's a good seat for you," but say to the poor man, "You stand there" or "Sit on the floor by my feet," [4]have you not discriminated among yourselves and become judges with evil thoughts?

2:2 James presented a likely case of unjust discrimination to reinforce the preceding command against favoritism toward the rich. A well-dressed rich man and an unsightly poor man pay simultaneous visits to the Christian meeting (lit. "synagogue"; cf.

---

[8] L. T. Johnson brings out this affinity in greatest detail in "The Use of Leviticus 19 in the Letter of James," *JBL* 101 (1982): 391–401.

[9] This reclamation of the law is brought out in a helpful way in O. J. F. Seitz, "James and the Law," *SE* 2 (1964): 472–86.

[10] R. B. Ward's *Communal Concern of the Epistle of James* (Ph.D. diss., Harvard University, 1966) develops this social setting at length.

5:14, which uses "church," *ekklēsia*).[11] The rich man is attired with all the marks of a man of luxury[12] and ostentation.[13] His self-presentation invites public admiration and special honor. His non-verbal communication conveys an ability and willingness to dispense favors to those who please him. He requires preferential treatment, or he will move on. The visit of the rich man becomes a test of Christian faith. Unfortunately, as exposed later in James (cf. 4:13), the rich exact a very high price for their allegiance. In parable-like fashion, knowing that the images he used would easily evoke recognition of the power that wealth exerts over the common man, James told of the congregation's failure to resist the temptation of favoritism.

The other man is called poor; his clothes are shabby and grimy. The congregation is now in the uncomfortable position of seeking the favor of the rich and disregarding the neediness of this poor man. The simultaneity of the visits is a problem. The congregation had to deal with both, and they would fail to offer both an appropriate welcome. The temptation to curry the favor of the rich was simultaneously a testing of faith in God, who has valued the poor (cf. 1:3,12). In referring to the second visitor, the term James used denotes the economically poor,[14] and therefore destitute, rather than from the lowest social class. Throughout Scripture these poor are often said to fall into desperate conditions because of the injustices committed against them by wealthy and powerful oppres-

---

[11] The term also could refer to the meeting for Christian worship. This is the only place where James used the term; cf. Justin *Dial.* 134:3; Ign. *Pol.* 4:2; Ign. *Trall.* 3:1. The synagogue is recognized in the NT as the house of worship, of study of Scripture, settling of disputes, and where the poor are cared for (cf. Acts 15:21; 16:13); cf. A. C. Mitchell, *1 Corinthians 6:1–11: Group Boundaries and the Courts of Corinth* (Ph.D. diss., Yale University, 1986). It is important not to make too much of the usage of "synagogue" here. Christians as well as Jews could utilize it. There was continuity between the "Torah-based" community and the "Jesus-based" community.

[12] Cf. Luke 23:11; Acts 10:30.

[13] χρυσοδακτύλιος: "wearing gold on the finger." Such adornment to display social standing and political influence was a common practice in the ancient world; cf. Luke 15:22; cf. B. Noack, "Jakobus wider die Riechen," *ST* 18 (1964): 10–25.

[14] πτωχός: "poor"; cf. R. B. Ward, "Partiality in the Assembly: James 2:2–4," *HTR* 62 (1969): 87–97.

sors.[15] Painfully, the congregation becomes a party to the oppression of the poor. The poor man is demeaned and devalued. His treatment readies him for dissociation through disgrace. "The poor you have always with you" (Matt 26:11), which was the Lord's way of telling his disciples that they would always be ministering to the poor, has been twisted around to mean that they are a hopeless case and that they should be helped only when it's convenient. Of course, helping the poor is never convenient.

2:3 James invited his readers to imagine a situation in which they paid special attention to the well attired. He put words into the mouth of one of their spokespersons, who shamelessly offered preferred[16] seating to the rich man. To the poor man he insisted, "Sit on the floor by my feet." In all likelihood the good seat offered to the rich man included a footstool.[17] The imagery of providing comfortable elevation of feet above the filth of the floor and then assigning the poor man a place on that floor is as crass as could be. Not even a footstool was offered to the poor man. Instead, he was offered a spot that was close to the speaker but with the proviso that he take what the world regarded as his rightful, subordinate place. Throughout Scripture the Lord's defeated enemies are said figuratively to belong to this place beneath the Lord's footstool. From the perspective of the rich, the poor are easy prey and therefore easily subjugated to unjust economic relations (cf. 5:1–4). Tragically, a leading believer acted in such a way as to contribute to this oppressed condition of the poor. Instead of joining the celebration of the poor believer entering into the glory of the Lord (cf. 1:9), the spokesperson for the congregation acted as though saving faith in Christ produces no changes in social relations at all.

Taking this parable to heart is a spiritual exercise that leads to self-indictment for many Americans. The parable requires little modification to fit in contemporary culture. What is frightening is

---

[15] Cf. Pss 9:18; 10:1–18; 35:10; 37:14; 40:16–17; 109:16; Isa 3:14–15; 10:1–2; Amos 4:1; 8:4; also Matt 26:11.

[16] ἐπιβλέπω: "look at," "look with favor"; cf. 1 Kgs 7:28; Ps 24:16; Luke 1:48; 9:38.

[17] ὑποπόδιον: "footstool," here "at my feet"; cf. Exod 19:17; Ps 110:1; Luke 8:35; 10:39; Acts 22:3.

that present problems with partiality are greater perhaps than those in James's day. In contemporary Western middle-class churches, the poor rarely would be welcome to visit. But the gospel does require a change in social relations within the church. The church's role in the world is redemptive, not judicial. But among its members, there is a judicial role to be played. Paul exercised this role in relation to Peter when confronted by the latter's partiality against Gentile believers (cf. Gal 2:11–16). In the same way, partiality within the church against the poor must be combated with equal vehemence—as James himself did, so that the redemptive message may gain credence before the watching world.

2:4   What has occurred then is an act of evil discrimination[18] in that the congregation was guided by faulty standards. They favored the rich and shamed the poor who were subjugated to them. Evil thoughts of prejudicial bias against the poor had undermined the faith and joy of the church. A divisiveness had been injected into the fellowship that was like the double-mindedness condemned in the previous chapter (e.g., 1:8). All of the believers had become like evil judges[19]—James indicted them all because they condoned the divisive act.

There are two kinds of discrimination before God, the evil kind, presented here, and the righteous kind. The latter entails "discernment," which resists deceptive and double-minded thinking. Since wisdom and the law that gives freedom are both instruments of righteous discrimination, the making of such distinctions is good and fruitful. But in this passage the process of discrimination is tainted by evil. If an extraordinary act had been called for, the poor man should have been given the good seat, and the rich man should have been given the lowly position as a sign of the lordship of Christ. The practice of judging to resolve disputes within the

---

[18] διακρίνω: "make a distinction," as in 1:6; and when wisdom is present, it makes "impartial" decisions (3:17).

[19] κριτής . . . πονηρῶν: "judge . . . false"; cf. 3:6, a "world of evil." Believers become judges when they speak against their neighbor; preferring the rich against the poor makes them judges; cf. 4:11; Matt 15:19; Luke 5:21–22; Rom 1:21. The kind of thinking here expressed by διαλογισμός is often found in the NT in a context like this and thus carries negative overtones; cf. Matt 15:19; Mark 7:21; Luke 5:22; Rom 14:1; 1 Cor 3:20; Phil 2:14; 1 Tim 2:8.

church was right and proper (cf. Matt 18:15–20; 1 Cor 5:12; 1 Tim 5:19–24). Always the pressing question remains: Is the community of believers united around the principles of Christ rather than those of the perishing world?

(3) The Discrimination of God (2:5–7)

⁵Listen, my dear brothers: Has not God chosen those who are poor in the eyes of the world to be rich in faith and to inherit the kingdom he promised those who love him? ⁶But you have insulted the poor. Is it not the rich who are exploiting you? Are they not the ones who are dragging you into court? ⁷Are they not the ones who are slandering the noble name of him to whom you belong?

2:5 Just as James emphasized the command of v. 1 with the direct address "brothers," he did so here again yet more forcefully with the added imperative "listen." James was marking off a statement of truth with another rhetorical question that demands an emphatic yes. Such a statement should supersede all lesser considerations, for God's marvelous decision puts the poor at the center of his saving work. This should not be surprising because salvation reverses the effects of sin, especially those effects that leave people destitute and harassed. God has chosen[20] the poor in the eyes of the world to inherit his salvation. God will put the glories of his redeeming work on display in them. The saving work of God reverses the status of those who were most afflicted by the curse of sin.

Just as Jesus connected forgiving much and loving much (cf. Luke 7:47), James connected God's will to make the poor heirs of his kingdom with his will that they be rich in faith. James was concerned with the believers among the poor, for he connected their faith and the electing work of God: they were reaping the benefits of saving faith because God elected the poor to faith in Christ.

---

[20] ἐκλέγομαι: "choose," which is the verb of divine election to create a people for himself out of the least significant among the nations (cf. Deut 14:1–2; Matt 11:5; Luke 4:18; 18:25; 1 Cor 1:27; Eph 1:4).

The poor believers would be made wealthy in faith.[21] After all, "not many" among believers are attractive to the world (cf. 1 Cor 1:26). But the poor, because of God's decision, are prime candidates to join the company of those who love him, and they will inherit the treasures of the kingdom that cannot perish.[22] These treasures cannot be had by willful human striving but only by the will of God.

The poor are the elect heirs of the kingdom of God. James identified this prominent concept of salvation, election, with this class of humanity. Out of their poverty God brings glory in the bestowal of his heavenly riches. Poor believers are not the only ones who will be saved, but they, above all, demonstrate God's gracious saving work. Their love (cf. 1:12) is typically the most striking. Clearly not all who are poor are lovers of God. Clearly those who love God who are not poor to some degree impoverish themselves when they joyfully give their possessions away to the poor. Certainly there are those who truly love God who are not poor. But spiritual transformation of the rich will not produce the glory that will be produced by the transformation of the poor into the kingdom.

The kingdom of God is the goal of creation. The consummation of the kingdom is greater than the fall into sin to which the creation was subjected. To be heirs of God's kingdom is to become his children and to share in his nature through resurrection. So much of the exalted language of Scripture on the subject of salvation is summed up in the promise of a shared inheritance in Christ. The poor are God's prime subjects for this inheritance as the words of Jesus in Luke 6:20 declare: "Blessed are you who are poor, for yours is the kingdom of God." How then can other believers force these poor to sit at their feet like conquered victims? Instead, every effort should

---

[21] πλουσίους ἐν πίστει, "rich in faith," is what they are "elected" to—the sphere of the riches of God's grace (cf. 1 Cor 1:5; 2 Cor 9:11; Eph 2:4; 1 Tim 6:18). Cf. W. H. Wachob, *"The Rich in Faith and the Poor in Spirit": The Socio-Rhetorical Function of a Saying of Jesus in the Epistle of James* (Ph.D. diss., Emory University, 1993).

[22] κληρονόμους τῆς βασιλείας: "heirs of the kingdom"; cf. Matt 5:3; 25:34; Rom 4:13–14; 8:17; Gal 3:18; 4:1,7; Heb 6:12,17; 11:8; 1 Pet 1:4; 3:9.

be made to ennoble the poor and to rejoice in salvation together with them.

2:6 In the next two verses James posed a series of hard rhetorical questions for his hearers. These questions were bound to put the rich in a bad light as well as the Christian assembly for condoning the mistreatment of the poor. Instead of giving special honor to the poor, James asserted that his hearers had insulted[23] them. The act of shaming the poor was inseparable from the simultaneous act of honoring the rich. To act this way, the Christian assembly had to disregard the honor God has bestowed on the poor who love him. In this way the assembly had become false judges because God's standard for what should be truly honored had not been followed. But this problem was only a prelude to what the assembly should remember was their greater problem with the rich.

James's two rhetorical questions were quite direct and were meant to be answered with the affirmative. The Christian assembly also had failed to confront the rich with regard to all the ways they suspend justice and fairness by defrauding others of what is due them. The appeal concerns not what the believers could stop being done by the rich against the poor but rather what James's "middle-class" addressees were experiencing. They in fact were the ones who were being exploited[24] by the rich. They were included among those the rich were oppressing. Their small amounts of wealth had been robbed from them. The believers' own hopes for greater wealth, status, and respect were in fact a snare manipulated by the rich. So those believers who were hard-working and gainfully employed, though of humble means, should be reminded of their own plight at the hands of the rich. Thus, the local church needed to beware of making an all-too-facile equation between the blessings of God and the wealth of this world. Quite often, those who envy the rich most find themselves the most exploited by

---

[23] ἀτιμάζω: "treat without respect," having relegated the poor to a low position; cf. Prov 14:21; 22:22; Luke 20:11; Acts 5:41; 1 Cor 11:22; 1 Pet 2:17; *Sir* 10.22.

[24] καταδυναστεύω: "oppress." The rich as a class act this way. This verb appears otherwise only in Acts 10:38; cf. Amos 8:4; Mic 2:2; Matt 13:22; 19:23; 20:25; 1 Tim 6:9; *Sir* 13.3, 18; *Wis* 2.10; *Herm. Man.* 12.5.

them.[25] This was certainly James's contention here.

The second rhetorical question regards how the rich were "dragging"[26] James's hearers into court and puts still more pressure on them to consider overlooked evils in their lives. Whether or not these wealthy were Christian brothers (though 2:4 seems to include the rich man among the "yourselves" of the addressees), the readiness of the laborer and craftsman to tolerate the wickedness of the rich went too far. James could almost be paraphrased with the question: Whose side are you on, that of God and his chosen or the oppressors? Even the judges in the courts knuckled under to the evil designs of the rich. Christians were to do this no longer. James had consciously pitted the morality of defending the poor against the material advantages of favoring the rich. Failing to take up the cause of the poor is obviously a problem everywhere and in every age, and James did not allow believers to remain neutral, even less to side with the rich and powerful for personal advantage.

2:7 A third rhetorical question was posed in this verse: are not the rich blaspheming the name of the Lord? Here James was virtually affrontive, highly confrontational. It hardly matters whether it was God's own name or the name of Jesus Christ that was being slandered here. "Slander" would be more appropriately translated "blaspheme" *(blasphēmeō).*[27] Similarly the Lord declared in the revelation on the Damascus road that Paul's persecution of Christians was committed against him (cf. Acts 9:40). The name of the

---

[25] G. M. Stulac's article "Who Are 'the Rich' in James?" (*Presbyterion* 16 [1990]: 89–102) raises important questions about whether or not the rich in James were regarded as Christian. One must be cautious about posing this question since James offered no clear distinction between the rich and the Christian brothers. The brethren came from every economic status. The rich are not favored in the divine plan, and indeed the rich as a class commit injustice by their acts of neglecting and exploiting the poor. Do Christians commit these sins? This was, in fact, James's point.

[26] ἕλκω: "drag," as a violent act, whether committed against the body or by using "legal" means. James also presented the complicity of the judges in this activity (cf. Acts 16:19; 1 Cor 6:2).

[27] "Slander" when applied to people; "blaspheme," to God, and thus is a pouring of contempt on the name of God—i.e., to instill hatred for and to malign the truth about the goodness of God and his gracious purpose.

Lord, whether God the Father or Christ, signifies the mutual belonging of God and his people.[28] He is our God, and we are his people. Because the rich were attacking believers in the law courts as though they were criminals and thieves, it was as though they were attacking the Lord. In that the rich committed acts of persecution, any of the rich who were believers were no better than the unbelievers since they had sinned against the poor and had not defended them. The noble name of the Lord was besmirched by the ignoble practices that had stemmed from playing favorites with the rich. Thus to honor the rich was to dishonor Christ. Only when the rich became an example of humility could they be an instrument that glorified the Lord.

Favoritism is thus a complex sin among the people of God. It leads to division within the fellowship and offends God's determination to elevate the poor in the life of the church. Most of all, favoritism is linked with a whole series of other gross sins of the rich in the world. These sins of persecution or oppression of the poor and lower classes of society who are associated with Christian faith detract from the glory of the Lord. Theirs is the inheritance of Christ, the very kingdom of God. To the believing poor belongs the honor of that kingdom. Utmost care must be given that nothing the church does in this present age should detract from that honor.

This concern to honor the poor is the context for the rest of the arguments in this chapter, particularly those in vv. 14–26. What this context communicates is that fellowship is impossible and faith is made ridiculous when inequality of relations are tolerated within the church. The gospel of Jesus Christ requires that every effort be made to foster equal standing among the believers through praising the hope of the poor and calling the rich believers to self-abnegation in repentance. Only in this way of humbling the self can the rich "enter into the kingdom of heaven" (Matt 19:23).

---

[28] "Of him to whom you belong" is lit. "called upon you." ἐπικαλέω: "call," "name," not in the sense of believers being given a name by God (cf. Amos 9:12; Acts 15:17), rather in their possessing the name of God, who has become "their God," and their being his possession.

2. Mercy That Fulfills the Royal Law (2:8–13)

(1) The Excellent Deed (2:8)

⁸If you really keep the royal law found in Scripture, "Love your neighbor as yourself," you are doing right.

2:8 From the royal[29] or kingly law James supplied the antidote to the wrong thinking and false judgments of the rich. What James meant by "found in Scripture" (lit. "according to the Scripture") is a direct reference to Lev 19:18 as the foundation for his appeal. This royal law belongs to the heirs of the kingdom (Jas 2:5). Under this law there should be no acts of favoritism to anyone. All alike should be equal recipients of the love that is due them. Neighbor love in Scripture is directed to everyone in close proximity to each believer, without distinction. Whether or not the "neighbor" is a believer in Jesus, that one is to receive the same love. If favoritism is going to be avoided and the righteousness of God promoted, James recalled the love that serves everyone in need regardless of their religious commitments.

This citation of Scripture and its rootage in the teachings of Jesus is an important proof that James's letter is not merely a "Christianized" Jewish tractate. Following the law of God is consistent with Old Testament obedience, but Jesus in this summary way enjoined obedience on his followers. James made no reference to the massive collection of levitical laws for ritual purity and political order. As with Jesus (cf. Matt 22:39; Rom 13:9; Gal 5:14), for James neighbor love along with love for God summed up and fulfilled the whole law (cf. v. 9). James said the believers must "really

---

[29] νόμος βασιλικός: "royal law." Although the definite article is absent, this in no way obscures the meaning of the term as the law of God or of Christ (cf. 4:11). This is the chief command that entails all of God's other commands (cf. Lev 19:18, quoted by Jesus in Matt 22:39; Rom 13:8; Gal 5:14). A vast literature throughout the history of theology reflects on this love command; e.g., Justin *Apol.* I.12; Cl. Al. *Strom.* 6.164; 7.73, who associates it with the ascribing of the people of God as a "kingdom of priests" (Exod 19:6; 1 Pet 2:9); cf. F. E. Vokes, "The Ten Commandments in the New Testament and in First Century Judaism," *SE* 5 (1968): 145–54.

keep" this law.[30] They understood the royal law as fulfilling or doing God's law completely, wholly.

This point in the teaching of Jesus was meant as that supreme antidote to favoritism and hypocrisy. No one is outside the boundary of neighbor love, not even the poor and unlovely, indeed, especially not them. When this royal law of neighbor love is obeyed, no more excellent deed can be done. In this actively loving way, and in this way alone, the rich believer and the believers who enjoy life above the poverty line can overcome the stumbling blocks to their faith. When this command controls what is meant by being a "doer of the law," every other command is effectively fulfilled. The old adage that a Christian cannot "do well" without "well doing" rests on the pointedly defined royal law: "Love your neighbor as yourself." Surely Paul's meaning in Gal 5:6 correlates well here: "The only thing that counts is faith expressing itself through love."

(2) Offensive at Every Point (2:9–11)

⁹But if you show favoritism, you sin and are convicted by the law as lawbreakers. ¹⁰For whoever keeps the whole law and yet stumbles at just one point is guilty of breaking all of it. ¹¹For he who said, "Do not commit adultery," also said, "Do not murder." If you do not commit adultery but do commit murder, you have become a lawbreaker.

2:9   James now indicated what was so wrong about the world's wealth and its system of honor: to play favorites is to commit sin.[31] The continuing sense of Leviticus 19 is at work in the text. In the previous chapter sin was like a parasitic agent slowly destroying the self (1:15). Here sin is activity that offends God, the Lawgiver. But favoritism (cf. 2:1) is sin that transgresses the royal law.

Sin can be committed many ways, and committing sin in any one of the ways amounts to transgressing the whole law. To break a command of God is to fall under the condemnation of the whole

---

[30] τελέω: "accomplish," "observe" a law "fully"; this term is closely related to "perfect," "complete."

[31] ἁμαρτία: "sin," is the object of ἐργάζομαι: "work," and so, "commit sin." The verb is used only here and in 1:20, both times in a negative sense in contrast to the "do well" of the previous verse. Note the emphasis on action; cf. 1:3; Matt 7:23.

law and of the one who judges those who break even a single one of these commands. The text hearkens back to Jesus' warning against breaking even a "least" command of the law (cf. Matt 5:19). Happily, through a single supreme command the believer is enabled to fulfill the whole law. Tragically, every sin delivers the sinner into wholesale transgression of the law. The sin of favoritism does this: it turns the one who committed it into a transgressor[32] or "lawbreaker."

According to Paul's argument in Galatians, to come under the condemnation of the law at any point is to come under the condemnation of the whole law; James likewise asserted that to break one law is to be convicted[33] as a lawbreaker. The understanding of the law's nature common both to pre-New Testament Judaic thought as well as the New Testament held that the law cannot be fulfilled merely through attending to strict external practices. Torah observance must be motivated by love and mercy. On this essential point there is no difference between James and Paul. James's particular emphasis, however, was that to break the law of love through an act of favoritism was to fall under the condemnation of the law as though one were not believing in the mercy of God for salvation. Faith and neighbor love are inextricable.

2:10 Lawbreakers are those who are under obligation to keep the whole law but who have failed to do so. Implied here are two kinds of "lawkeepers": those who keep the law by faith in acts of Christian love and those who must keep the law in all of its particulars because they will be judged by the law on all its particulars. The problem of self-deception is obviously present in the second kind of "lawkeeping." The person without neighbor love assumes that the law kept in every other respect has been fulfilled. Whereas James appealed to his hearers to live "as those who are going to be judged by the law that gives freedom" (v. 12), there is another kind

---

[32] παραβάτης: "transgressor," lit. an "overstepping," is clearly a metaphor for the way of righteousness; cf. Matt 15:2f.; Rom 2:25,27; Gal 2:18; Heb 2:2; 9:15; cf. G. D. Kilpatrick, "Übertreter des Gesetzes, Jak. 2,11," *TZ* 23 (1967): 433.

[33] ἐλεγχώ: "convince," "expose," make someone acknowledge; here in the passive, "be convicted." The law is here personified as a judge; cf. Lev 19:15; John 8:9; Rom 7:7; Gal 3:24; *4 Macc* 5.33.

of judgment against the unmerciful. Of course, those who attempted to keep the law without refraining from favoritism imagined they would be approved and not judged by a standard that would condemn them.

Those who stumbled[34] under the judgment that took every sin into account (cf. Matt 12:36; Heb 2:2) had no possibility of avoiding condemnation. "Stumbling" also appears in the next chapter (3:2), where there is clearly no threat of this kind of judgment. James's basic words are unambiguous: "The entire law in all its parts is to be fulfilled."[35] No doubt Jesus fulfilled the whole law bit by bit, but he also fulfilled the law in the sense that he perfectly and impartially loved those around him (he washed even Judas's feet; cf. John 13). Jesus' example of neighbor love was essential to James's hearers' faith in Jesus (cf. 2:1), who was their required path to perfection.

But something about the sin of favoritism undermined every other claim of obedient faith. The command against favoritism, or positively, the imperative of neighbor love, especially toward the poor, so embodied the spirit of the law that to stumble on this point was to offend the law at its heart. It must never be forgotten that wisdom, the law, and love are all inseparably bound together.[36] Any separation of these three is the result of calculated self-deception that looks for man's favor rather than God's and withholds the love that is due one's neighbor.

2:11 Two extreme examples of breaking God's law are now brought forward: adultery and murder. The logical and rhetorical force of this textual movement is obvious. The "for he who said" keeps the power behind the divine word uppermost in the matter of the nature of the law. This is the judgment that takes every offense into account rather than the judgment that approves faith acting in

---

[34] πταίω: "stumble"; cf. Deut 7:25; Rom 11:11; 2 Pet 1:10. The sense here is difficult in reference to "one" (law) in that it is contrasted with "whole" rather than "many" (commandments); cf. Ign. *Pol* 2.

[35] P. J. Hartin, *James and the Q Sayings of Jesus* (Sheffield: Sheffield Academic Press, 1991), 208.

[36] Cf. Gal 5:3; *Wis* 6:5–10; 6:18–20; Augustine *Ep.* 167 and his comparison with Stoic teaching; cf. M. O. Boyle, "The Stoic Paradox of James 2:10," *NTS* 31 (1985): 611–17.

love.[37] In the human world the law of God exposes sin's true nature: every sin constitutes a state of opposition to God. Sin is never a question of breaking a single command but of violating the integrity of the whole law.

Each command is integral to the whole law. Whoever refuses the humble, righteous path of neighbor love and of the rejection of favoritism (2:8–9) comes under the law's judgment. We offend the whole through every single trespass because we are actually refusing submission to the being and person of God rather than simply the instrument itself (cf. 4:11f.). The one who has avoided adultery but commits murder is nevertheless a lawbreaker. A close connection is made throughout the prophets and the Gospels between neglecting the poor and contributing to their demise—therefore murdering them through neglect of basic needs. In 5:6 James made this connection explicit: by defrauding the poor of their wages and keeping the wealth to yourselves, "You have condemned and murdered innocent men, who were not opposing you." But there is another connection between adultery and murder. The killing and coveting of James's hearers made them "adulterous people" (4:2,4). Because of the complexity of sin, one offense entails the other offenses.

(3) The Freedom-giving Law (2:12–13)

[12]Speak and act as those who are going to be judged by the law that gives freedom, [13]because judgment without mercy will be shown to anyone who has not been merciful. Mercy triumphs over judgment!

2:12 James exhorted his hearers to speak and act[38] as those who are to be judged by a law that makes them free. Since partial-

---

[37] The judgment of every offense can be reflected in the way the origin of the law is described, e.g., 1 Tim 1:9–10, which states: "We also know that law is made not for the righteous but for lawbreakers and rebels, the ungodly and sinful, the unholy and irreligious; for those who kill their fathers or mothers, for murderers, for adulterers and perverts, for slave traders and liars and perjurers—and for whatever else is contrary to the sound doctrine."

[38] λαλέω: "speak," and ποιέω, "act," again (cf. 1:19) anticipating the argument of chap. 3 about the tongue.

ity (favoritism) is based on false judgment and turns believers into unjust judges, they needed to remember that they too would be judged. Speaking and acting are inseparably related (2:1–4; cf. 1:26–27). When the riches of the faith are told for the glory of God (v. 5), poor believers are lifted up; orphans and widows are cared for. Christians will be judged according to their consistency of speech and action.

The law of freedom does not condemn but sets free. This law sets free those who heed it when they, in turn, set free those who are oppressed by the world. Believers heed this law of freedom through including the poor and unfortunate as full members of the church of Christ. When this inclusive fellowship is the pattern of faith practiced by believers, God will use this liberating law as the standard to judge them in the sense that he will approve and commend them. The merciful judgment that acquits is the first kind of judgment hinted at in contrast to that judgment that condemns (cf. v. 9).

Belief in the final judgment is another mark of theological background for James's writing. The reality that believers stand before God in the judgment receives more and more attention as the letter progresses (3:1; 4:11f.; 5:5,9,12). In Jesus' teaching, the offer of God's forgiveness engenders forgiveness of others on the part of the one forgiven by God; for those who have believed in God's promise of mercy are to be merciful themselves. This reciprocal nature of forgiveness is the import of Jesus' commentary on the Lord's Prayer: "If you forgive men when they sin against you, your heavenly Father will also forgive you. But if you do not forgive men their sins, your Father will not forgive your sins" (Matt 6:14–15). The reciprocal nature of forgiveness is likewise at the heart of James's repetition of the liberating law of neighbor love in v. 8. Such forgiveness is surely what Paul had in mind when speaking of the liberating law of neighbor love in the power of the Spirit in Gal 5:14. For Paul it was the Spirit who established this law of love above the law in all its ritual details. For James it was the anticipation of God's merciful judgment approving those who act out of impartial love that established this law as that which frees. To do otherwise than fulfill this law of love through acts of mercy is to act as unmerciful judges (cf. v. 4) against those who have not opposed them.

2:13 James described the nature of the second kind of judgment that condemns for every offense as "judgment without mercy."[39] To anyone who has not "acted mercifully,"[40] no mercy will be shown. To those who show mercy, that kind of merciless judgment is swallowed up, as it were, by mercy. What was declared in the previous verse is based on the principle in this verse. Love and mercy define the "law of freedom." Rejecting this liberating law means falling under judgment of the whole law.

A play on words is evident: judgment without mercy on those who have shown no mercy. James supplied the opposite case from the words of Jesus' beatitude that promises mercy to the merciful (Matt 5:7). As in the parable of the unmerciful servant who was shown mercy but did not show mercy to his fellow servant (cf. Matt 18:25–35), James's merciless hearers committed their acts in face of God's mercy. In Jesus' parable the act of mercy pertained to lack of money and the forgiving of debt. Receiving mercy obligates the recipient to show mercy. Although Jesus warned against performing acts of righteousness publicly for human praise, he did not mean that those acts were optional. The greatest act of mercy toward the poor—almsgiving (Matt 6:1–4)—is mandatory, as Jesus' words make clear: "When you give to the needy . . ." Jesus' command contains no conditional "if" about giving money to the needy. What becomes apparent here is the interconnectedness between fairness toward the poor, neighbor love, and the principle of receiving and showing mercy.

James's statement about impending judgment is harsh. James did not warn of punishment for murder or adultery—although unmerciful people can be said to be murderous and adulterous in some sense. The prohibition of showing favoritism (2:1) implies the problem of a hard-heartedness that will finally be rooted out by the judging function of the law of God. The importance of mercy in human relationships is so essential because mercy is a direct indi-

---

[39] κρίσις ἀνέλεος: "judgment without mercy." Cf. Rom 1:31, where Paul cataloged the sinfulness of those whom God has given over to their sin. There ἀνέλεος is translated "heartless"; cf. *Wis* 12.5; *T. Abr.* 12; 16.

[40] Cf. Josh 2:12; Ps 18:25–26; Prov 17:5; Matt 5:7; 6:2; 7:1; 13:28–35; 25:41–46; Titus 3:5; *Sir* 28:2f.; *Tob* 4:7–12; 12:9.

cator of repentance toward God. Although sinners are right to amend their ways, to cease sinning and to make restitution where necessary, nothing is comparable to showing mercy. Because Christians' sins are so often toward other people, they are dependent on others' mercy. Believers hope for mercy from others because they have received mercy from God. Amending of life and acts of restitution are far from perfect, permanent, or even adequate. More mercy is required. These acts following sin never recompense the one who has been offended. Mercy needs to be present. Failure to show mercy to those in need calls into question whether there has been any true act of repentance in face of God's mercy. Instead of liberation, the full force of the law's condemnation falls against those who break the law.

James offered a principle that is surely one of the highest in all of Scripture: mercy triumphs over judgment. In face of the judgment that is to come against each and every offense, mercy will be greater than judgment to those who have shown mercy. At this point the inseparable relation between faith and action in James is clear. Once faith understands the salvation God works, that the divine mercy has overcome[41] the divine justice, faith must include a stance of mercy toward others.

That James had not advocated some kind of legalistic faith must not be overlooked. Consistent faith is the core concern of James's teaching. Faith in God in no way causes God to be merciful. Rather, faith is made possible because God is merciful. Faith trusts in this merciful God. Only faith must conduct itself consistently with God's mercy. Trusting faith is merciful faith. In order to be genuine, the believer's faith must include mercy. Believers' sins are "always before" (cf. Ps 51:3) them, and yet mercy has triumphed over that sin. Merciful faith exhibits God's mercy in the giving of money to the poor, in helping them find full membership in the church, and in firmly exhorting rich believers to live humbly and modestly before the church and God in the world.

Whatever else James had to say about the law and the content of

---

[41] κατακαυχάομαι: "boast against," "override." Impending judgment has been overridden by some intervening force or principle, namely, mercy; cf. 3:14; Ps 101:1; Hos 6:6; Matt 9:11–13; 12:7; 23:23; Luke 7:47; Heb 6:10; 1 Pet 4:8; *Tob* 4.9.

faith is always in view of the final judgment before Christ. This judgment will be undone as we may have come to expect it in the case of merciful believers. Mercy will judge judgment. Just as atonement turns away wrath, mercy turns away condemnation. James was speaking of an end to judgment much like Paul spoke of the end of death: "Death has been swallowed up in victory" (1 Cor 15:54). Judgment is swallowed up in mercy. The victory of God will be his just judgment when everyone receives what they deserve. And yet the greater glory of God is clear when anyone is spared what he or she deserves, namely, condemnation. God will reverse his judgment in every case where merciful faith is evident. God's will to condemn will be emptied by his will to show mercy.

3. Unjustifiable Faith (2:14–26)

This third part of the overall argument of the chapter delivers the true content of faith according to James. Faith cannot be held together with favoritism. Faith must be held together with deeds of faith. Mere outward religion (1:26) must develop into a faith that acts consistently with the mercy of God. Faith that plays favorites does not evidence itself in merciful action. In this section the problem of self-deception has become acute: self-justifying speech is used to obscure the failure of faith to act. Striking examples are again pictured for James's readers. Great tension is created through the diatribe style of argumentation.

James's famous text that has seemed to so many to contradict Paul appears here. What we find, however, is not a collision with Paul at all. Any allusion to his teaching only stands against the very misreadings of the gospel that Paul stood against, for example, "Shall we go on sinning so that grace may increase?" (Rom 6:1). The dissimilarities between the issues that concerned James and those that concerned Paul are much greater than the similarities. The way in which James used special terms, such as "works," is quite different from Paul's usage. James's unique questions about the usefulness of inactive faith and the vitality of such faith were particularly his own.

Finally, James was expounding upon the nature of faith, not on the question of salvation in the end. James was emphatic about the reality of judgment, but here he was restricting his declarations to the reality of faith. Who can and who cannot justifiably claim to have faith? This justification of the claim to have faith or the unjustifiability of that claim is what is in question. Only genuine faith can stand up under trial and thereby be "perfected" as it was in the case of Abraham and Rahab. These two figures are crucial, for they represent two who resisted the wisdom of the world in favor of God's mercy. They are a "brother" and a "sister" (cf. 2:15) who serve as examples of authentic faith.

(1) The Open Question (2:14)

14What good is it, my brothers, if a man claims to have faith but has no deeds? Can such faith save him?

2:14   This verse contains a rhetorical question of the utmost gravity. James asked whether faith without deeds can be a saving faith, and he anticipated a negative answer. But throughout this part of the letter he did not answer his question directly. Why not? Perhaps the answer lies in the relationship to the other question in this verse: "What good[42] is it [a faith without deeds]?" Demonstrating the authenticity of faith is the primary focus of this section. James did not answer the ultimate question of how God will judge those with inactive or distorted faith (cf. 2:1).

The indirect interlocutor, the man who "claims to have faith," is crucial for James's argument. A person might say he or she has faith, but what is that claim without the deeds that reveal all authentic faith? Mere profession, because of sin, does not count. The faith Jesus lived and taught is at stake. Acts of mercy are the only demonstration of faith. The implied claimant does not say, "I have no deeds"; rather to James and any other observers, none are in evidence. James's deeds of faith are not at all what Paul meant by "works of the law." The question James placed before his hearers is very different from the issues before Paul. James was concerned with the demonstration of faith in Jesus through works of

---

[42] ὄφελος: "advantage," "use," is employed in a startling way in the text; cf. Job 15:3; Matt 16:26; 1 Cor 14:6; *Sir* 20:20; 41:14.

mercy. Paul was concerned with justification through Christ alone and not by ritual works of the law, such as circumcision, apart from faith in Christ.

The question of whether inactive faith can save requires a negative answer. But this answer does not mean that active faith is that which saves. Only God's mercy triumphs over judgment (v. 13). James already had stated in the previous chapter that only the implanted Word is able to save (1:21). The Word must be accepted, however, by those who are prepared to do it and not merely hear it (1:22–25). God alone is able to save and to destroy (4:12), but there must be the activity of faith that participates in the saving work of the Word of God (cf. 5:15,20). Similarly, in his confrontation with the leaders of the Jews over their standing as Abraham's descendants, Jesus exhorted, "If you were Abraham's children . . . then you would do the things Abraham did" (John 8:39).[43]

The question about the destiny of the inactive believer must be carefully answered. Only God is able to save. Only those who do the Word make valid claims to be believers. God will not show mercy in the judgment to those who have been unmerciful. But neither profession of faith nor deeds of faith actually "save" anyone; only God saves. It is thus much more advisable to emphasize what James emphasized: faith without deeds is good to no one. He was not implying that the deeds of faith are effective for salvation. Rather, the deeds of faith demonstrate the validity of the claim to be a believer; without them the claim is empty or "dead"—but more importantly, without deeds the needy do not receive help.

(2) Need without Deed (2:15–16)

[15]**Suppose a brother or sister is without clothes and daily food. [16]If one of you says to him, "Go, I wish you well; keep warm and well fed," but does nothing about his physical needs, what good is it?**

2:15 Much like the example of the poor man visiting the local church (2:2–3) is that of the brother or sister who is lacking food

---

[43] There were a great many disputes within Judaism over the relation between faith and works; cf. *2 Apoc Bar* 14.12; 51.7; *4 Ezra* 7.77; 8.32–36.

and clothing.[44] Within the fellowship of believers are those who
lack the necessities of daily life. These members of the church are
easily overlooked because of their constant neediness. The context
for the encounter is not limited to a particular assembly of Christians. A fellow Christian is simply encountered who is needy. What
is to be done in this encounter is all-important. What was at stake
for James's hearers was much akin to what was at issue in John's
first epistle: "If anyone has material possessions and sees his
brother in need but has no pity on him, how can the love of God be
in him? Dear children, let us not love with words or tongue but
with actions and in truth" (1 John 3:17–18). Also evident here is
the close connection between mercy (pity) and helpful actions for
the poor.

2:16   Now James shifted the focus of his address from the indirect interlocutor to his audience: "If one of you says . . ." This redi-
rection of the referent makes James's message all the more
confrontational. In the face of the needy, believers with the ability
to help reduced themselves to mere well-wishers. To the person in
misery, James's fellow believers were saying, "Have a nice day!"
The statement, "Go, I wish you well," or more literally, "Go in
peace,"[45] in the ancient world was sincere only when it accompanied some demonstrative act such as giving a gift or alms. In nor-
mal relationships between "haves" and "have-nots," the needy
person is given the gift and the accompanying verbal blessing,
without begrudging them the gift (cf. 1:5; "without finding fault").

The striking parallel between the needs of the poor for food and
clothing and the need of the believer to be saved by or to acquire
wisdom from God is apparent (the same verb, *leipō,* "lack," is used
here and in 1:4). The poor need more than mere words; so does the
believer who needs the saving act and wisdom of God. A word of
blessing without an act of blessing is like the promise of salvation

---

[44] γυμνός, "naked," may not mean unclothed but inadequately clothed, such as
only having on an undergarment; cf. 1 Sam 19:24; Job 22:6; Isa 58:7; Amos 2:16;
Matt 25:36.

[45] εἰρήνη, "peace," as a blessing when it accompanied some offer of blessing; cf.
Judg 18:6; 1 Sam 1:17; 20:42; 2 Sam 15:9; Mark 5:34; Luke 7:50; Acts 16:36; *Tob*
12.5.

without the saving act of God in Christ.

The second word of "blessing" is self-indicting. Not a traditional wish but just as hollow when not accompanied by acts of mercy is "Keep warm and well fed." The believer knows precisely what the brothers or sisters are lacking and makes no provision for them. In contrast to Jesus' declaration that the righteous "clothed me" (Matt 25:36), here believers were not doing so. Is there any righteousness in you? Would you not care for Jesus if you saw him this way? Clearly, this element of disciples' spirituality is not present; the care for the needy rendered by the believer should flow from the grace received from God. The tense of the verb here suggests either that someone nearby should hear the order and feed and clothe the poor or that the poor should take care of themselves. Whichever of these options is meant—more likely the former—the comfort of the insensitive believer has taken precedence over the need (lit. "the necessities of the body") of the poor fellow believer.

James put the insensitive, inactive believer on the side of the unjust, unrighteous rich who have neither mercy nor compassion. James doubtless believed his hearers had the capacity to supply what was needed for the poor and yet hard-heartedly were withholding the necessities of life. In the contemporary situation, this verse accuses all rich Christians, or even moderately well-off Christians who withhold what is good and necessary for life from the poor around them and most of all among the poor within the Christian family. Christians should cultivate some sort of almsgiving in their personal and church financial practices.

At the end of this verse James returned to his first question of the section: What good is it—this faith that does nothing, that helps no one in physical need? Just as the role of judge assumed by believers caught up in favoritism is unjust, inactive faith is obviously empty. James did not reiterate the question of salvation that stands naggingly in the background. Nevertheless, the uselessness of a faith and the certainty of judgment that will weigh the claims of faith according to deeds is ominous. The glory of the Lord (2:1,7) that ought to be visible in the life of believers is instead brought into disrepute by their inaction.

(3) A Pronouncement of Death (2:17)

¹⁷In the same way, faith by itself, if it is not accompanied by action, is dead.

2:17   In the same way that a word of blessing amounts to nothing without the act of blessing, faith without action is dead. James called this "faith by itself,"⁴⁶ meaning mere profession of religious belief apart from merciful acts. This solitary faith James so assertively presented is classified by having no deeds. But something internal to faith is being stated here. Faith that does not contain within it the will or spring of action appropriate to faith is dead.⁴⁷ In a very real sense, what emerges here is an individualistic faith that negates true faith and is therefore lifeless. The problem of self-deception within the believer could not have more catastrophic effects. Self-centeredness, rather than Christ-centeredness, is the dominant reality in such a faith. Can this be at all true faith? Faith that does not contain within itself a readiness to help, to show mercy, cannot be a faith in the mercy of God. Paul likewise exhorted, "Examine yourselves to see whether you are in the faith; test yourselves. Do you not realize that Christ Jesus is in you—unless, of course, you fail the test? And I trust that you will discover that we have not failed the test. Now we pray to God that you will not do anything wrong" (2 Cor 13:5–7).

James's deadness has a striking parallel in another Pauline text, where the metaphor is applied to sin: "Apart from law, sin is dead" (Rom 7:8). The presence of the law apart from Christ stimulates sin. The antidote to this thriving sin is life through the body of Christ, for then the believer can die to the law (v. 4). James's statement implies that true faith stimulates action. Active faith is alive; inactive faith is not. The classic axiom "salvation by faith alone, yet not alone" is appropriate here. Without merciful works, faith is a solitary faith, and such faith is lifeless. Does a dead or solitary faith—"faith by itself"—mean no salvation? James was no longer

---

⁴⁶ καθ᾽ ἑαυτήν: "by itself," on its own" (cf. Acts 28:16) is at the end of the sentence.

⁴⁷ νεκρά: "dead." Without action faith is lifeless, i.e., useless (cf. John 15:4; Heb 6:1; 9:14; *Herm. Sim.* 9, 21, 2).

speaking of the "claim" to have faith from v. 14. He was now speaking of actual faith. Thus James could make a comparison with the "faith" of demons in v. 19. But he did not comment on the final judgment of this faith. Such faith is dead, that is, useless, and makes any claim to being a believer illegitimate.

Ambiguous faith is part of the problem James was confronting. Double-mindedness and self-deception among believers is a state of religious lukewarmness at best. But deadness of faith is not the same as Paul's "you were dead in your transgressions and sins" (Eph 2:1). James's use of the term "dead" prepares for the special metaphor of the spirit of the body in v. 26. In pastoral fashion James was trying to stimulate his hearers to the life of faith.

(4) A Question of Proof (2:18–19)

> **[18]But someone will say, "You have faith; I have deeds."**
>
> **Show me your faith without deeds, and I will show you my faith by what I do. [19]You believe that there is one God. Good! Even the demons believe that—and shudder.**

2:18 James introduces the voice of an interlocutor. This "person" speaks in support of the community James was confronting. This "someone" is quoting an aphorism as if to settle the matter of the self-sufficiency of a faith even if it fails to act. The interlocutor is not speaking then directly to James but as a leader among the hearers of James. Distribution of labor is how he solved the problem. What perhaps is implied here is something like, "No one should act unmercifully; but some of us do the deeds of mercy, and others among us encourage them." This is a sign of the kind of clergy-laity split so often observable in lax Christianity: "Our pastor evangelizes and visits the needy as he should," implying that the necessary actions of the believers have been done through the pastor.[48] This disavowal of personal responsibility to act mercifully is a terribly misguided way of thinking but is characteristic of believers who are self-deceived.

But living faith cannot be disjoined from deeds. This truth is

---

[48] This is a notoriously difficult passage to translate because of the lack of punctuation in the Greek text; cf. Johnson, *James,* 240.

James's point. So James spoke to the interlocutor anyway, as if the latter were the one with inactive faith. The people of God cannot be divided into two camps of those believers who are merely "hearers" and those who "do the Word." But both camps professing faith have a kind of faith, and one of these kinds is lifeless. So James challenged the inactive believer in an ironic way to show him his faith.[49] This demonstration of faith of course cannot be done, for only by deeds can humans "show" anything about themselves. A claim to faith without works cannot be compared to a claim of faith with works. Later wisdom and understanding are said to be demonstrable along these lines (3:13). But a lifeless faith cannot be shown to be alive. The claim of faith is empty where there is no action, and thus no proof of faith is possible.

2:19   James equated faith without works with mere assent to the truth of God's existence. But this kind of "faith" has nothing to show for itself, no personal trust, no pursuit of wisdom; indeed, such faith is almost stereotypically the religious mask of hypocrisy. James did not fault the cognitive content of this belief. "Well done!" he wrote.[50] But this praise is surely ironic as well. Only those who are keeping the "royal law" of neighbor love can be said to be active in "well doing" (v. 8). Whether this mention of the oneness of God is a direct reference to Old Testament faith here ("The LORD is one," Deut 6:4; the "Shema" or "Hear, O Israel) or a more general monotheistic confession rooted in the New Testament (e.g., Mark 12:29; 1 Cor 8:4–6), James was unambiguous about the paltry faith of which they boasted. Such a faith benefits no one (v. 14) and thus runs contrary to God's purposes for believers in him. The profession of one God is good so far as it goes, but it does not go far at all.

Even the demons[51] possess this kind of faith. This claim, per-

---

[49] δείκνυμι: "show," part of the rhetorical form of the argument; the senses of "show" and "prove" are closely related; cf. Matt 7:16–17; Rom 3:28; Heb 11.

[50] καλῶς ποιεῖς: "you do well" (to believe). This phrase in itself is not ironical; cf. Mark 7:9; 12:32; John 4:17; 2 Cor 11:4; rather, James's contexts suggest irony.

[51] δαιμόνιον: "demon," "evil spirit"; those beings intermediate between the human and the divine who possess persons to cause sickness and derangement; cf. Matt 7:22; 10:8; Luke 4:41; 8:2.

haps, is an allusion to demons' role as influences in the creation of false religion, what Paul described as "doctrines of demons" (1 Tim 4:10). They could be said to perform miracles and receive worship through the practice of idolatry.[52] James's reference to "demonic faith" can hardly be complimentary. The demons also have monotheistic belief. They know of the reality of God, but they are still malevolent. Many believe that which is true about the Deity, but orthodoxy may have no effect on the evil activities of their lives. The only effect on the demons is that they "shudder"[53] at the thought of God's existence and his power over them. James was perhaps asking these hearers indirectly, "Do you fear the Lord more than the demons?" Indeed, later James would commend a kind of "spiritual exercise" by which inactive, hypocritical believers can appropriate the fear of the Lord and amend their lives (4:7–10). Believers should be doing more than shuddering, just as they should be doing more than merely professing belief. One can hardly miss the contrast between the demons' "fear and trembling" and that entailed in "work[ing] out your salvation" (Phil 2:12). If believers do not fear the Lord, they will have to realize that even these few words of great truth—the confession of God's oneness—can be part of the perversity of mere words that only puff us up and cause great evil (cf. Jas 1:22; 3:5).

(5) Exemplars of Faith with Deeds (2:20–25)

[20]You foolish man, do you want evidence that faith without deeds is useless? [21]Was not our ancestor Abraham considered righteous for what he did when he offered his son Isaac on the altar? [22]You see that his faith and his actions were working together, and his faith was made complete by what he did. [23]And the scripture was fulfilled that says, "Abraham believed God, and it was credited to him as righteousness," and he was called God's friend. [24]You see that a person is justified by what he does and not by faith alone.

[25]In the same way, was not even Rahab the prostitute considered

---

[52] Cf. Rev 16:14; Deut 32:17; Ps 95:5; 1 Cor 10:20–21; *Sib. Or.* 1.22.

[53] φρίσσω: "shudder" from fear; cf. Dan 7:15. In the ancient Christian literature the demons are said to shudder with fear at the prospect of their being exorcised; cf. Cl. Al. *Strom.* 5, 25, 1; Justin *Dial.* 49.8.

righteous for what she did when she gave lodging to the spies and sent them off in a different direction?

2:20 The diatribe form of address to the imaginary interlocutor continues in this verse. James asked a question (lit. "Do you wish to know?" Cf. 4:4 for a similar "Don't you know . . ."[54]) that continues the harsh attack he launched against any rationale for faith without deeds (cf. v. 18). As if the comparison with demonic faith is not enough, the positive example of Abraham and Rahab in the next verses will suffice. Indeed, James called this dialogue partner a "foolish man."[55] There is a reason faith without deeds is useless, and it is rooted in the very character of the person. This is extremely important for understanding James's argumentation throughout this section of his letter. To lack understanding is to think and act foolishly. The believer who lacks understanding knows that he should "ask God" (1:5) for his gift of wisdom. All the more, then, the believer who thinks wrongly about the nature of faith is foolish in that he willfully ignores or perverts the truth that he already knows. From James's perspective the very essence of faith was at stake since the favoritism, so readily committed by Christian churches of James's time and our time, has such destructive effects as described in the preceding verses of this chapter.

The problem is that there is no such thing as inactive faith. Claims that such a thing as mere faith exists are bogus and dangerously self-deceptive. We must understand this not only in terms of James's argument but also in terms of Paul's argument in Rom 3:28: "We maintain that a man is justified by faith apart from observing the law." The difference between the two apostles is clear. For Paul the goal was justification; for James the goal was usefulness. In the context of Paul's letter faith must not be allowed to boast in its own works in the judgment (v. 27). In the context of

---

[54] θέλεις δὲ γνῶσαι: "do you wish to know?" "do you want convincing?" is translated by the NIV "do you want evidence?" properly conveying the sense of a demand for proof.

[55] κενός: "foolish," "senseless," "empty," together with "man" becomes, "You insane fellow!" For how this term can be used derisively of human beings, cf. Judg 9:4; 11:3; Job 27:12; Philo *Spec. Leg.* 1.311; Epict. *Diss.* 4.4.25; *Herm. Man.* 12.4.5; *Did.* 2.5; Poly 6.3.

James's letter faith must not be allowed to boast in self-sufficiency
(cf. 2:7; 3:14). For James mere faith was an empty boast that
masked great evil. Faith is trust in God alone, but it must be whole-
hearted and produce good deeds based on the mercy of God. Faith
without deeds is a hoax of the double-minded. It can and surely
must be discussed because it is not honest about what it is actually
doing, such as playing favorites and withholding mercy. Faith is
always active, either producing good deeds in agreement with God
or in producing evil deeds in deceptive contradiction of him.

2:21 The example of Abraham is brought before James's audience not merely as an exemplar of faith but as "our father" (*patēr* is
lit. "father").[56] Does this ascription indicate a Jewish-Christian
audience of James? What belonged to the descendants of Abraham
belonged to James's addressees; this much can be asserted. That
Abraham exemplifies the necessity of deeds with faith but is not
described in terms of anything else suggests that Jewish or Gentile
identity is not at issue. James probably had absorbed the new teaching that began with John the Baptist: "Produce fruit in keeping with
repentance. And do not think you can say to yourselves, 'We have
Abraham as our father.' I tell you that out of these stones God can
raise up children for Abraham" (Matt 3:8–9).

In one of the most caustic passages of the New Testament (John
8:31–59), Jesus is recounted as teaching two groups of Jewish leaders, those who believed in him and those who did not. The former
are said to believe in accordance with Abraham's faith and are his
true children; the latter are not. There ensues a dispute over patri-
mony that fluctuates among the names of Abraham, God, and the
devil. The case that Jesus made requires acceptance of his testimony in order to maintain congruity with the true fatherhood of
Abraham. The opportunity of an "adoption" into the family of

---

[56] πατήρ: "father," here in a figurative sense and thus applicable also to Gentiles
who have believed in Jesus Christ as Lord (1:1). The NIV translates the word "ancestor," apparently to advance the case for a strictly Jewish audience. See Gen 17:4–5;
Matt 3:8; John 7:33–34; Luke 16:24; Rom 4:1,12,16; *Sir* 44:19; *1 Clem* 31:2;
W. Baird, "Abraham in the New Testament," *Int* 42 (1988): 367–79; R. Longenecker,
"The 'Faith of Abraham' Theme in Paul, James, and Hebrews: A Study in the Circumstantial Nature of New Testament Teaching," *JETS* 20 (1977): 203–12.

Abraham by faith becomes a reality. Because of this Paul stated in Gal 3:7: "Understand, then, that those who believe are children of Abraham." This is not to say that the physical descendants of Abraham have been displaced by these Gentile "adoptees," in spite of the early Christian polemics against Judaism. Exegesis of Romans 9–11 makes the case forcefully for the perpetual role of the Jews, "the natural branches" (Rom 11:24) of Abraham, in the redemptive plan of God.[57] Paul was aware already of the potential for hostility toward the Jews within the church but would not allow for any mistake about the place of ethnic Israel in the divine economy:

> As far as the gospel is concerned, they are enemies on your account; but as far as election is concerned, they are loved on account of the patriarch, for God's gifts and his call are irrevocable. Just as you who were at one time disobedient to God have now received mercy as a result of their disobedience, so they too have now become disobedient in order that they too may now receive mercy as a result of God's mercy to you. For God has bound all men over to disobedience so that he may have mercy on them all. Rom 11:28–32

Abraham is then both exemplar and father to all believers whether of Jewish or Gentile background. Ethnic background is not at all the issue in James but rather the religious malady of useless faith.

God regarded Abraham as righteous[58] for offering up his son Isaac (cf. Gen 22:1–18; although Abraham was counted as righteous first in Gen 15:6). Of course, although Abraham offered Isaac up as a sacrifice on an altar, the boy did not become a sacrifice. We might ask, then, in what sense this deed was "useful"? Abraham obeyed the command of God that tested him by an extraordinary

---

[57] Cf. R. Bell, *Provoked to Jealousy* (Tübingen: Mohr, 1994); J. S. Siker, *Disinheriting the Jews: Abraham in Early Christian Controversy* (Louisville: Westminster, 1991).

[58] δικαιόω: "acquit, pronounce, and treat as righteous." God can be "proved right," can also "make free/pure." Because of the many nuances to which this verb is subjected throughout the Greek texts of the Bible, context is essential for determining its precise meaning in each case. It cannot be said to have a single meaning that must be imposed upon every passage. For a glimpse of this variety of meaning whether in the active or passive sense, cf. Gen 44:16; 2 Sam 15:4; Pss 72:13; 81:3; Isa 45:25; Matt 11:19; 12:37; Luke 7:29; 10:29; 8:14; Acts 13:38–39; Rom 2:16–17; 3:4; 4:5; 5:1,9; 1 Cor 6:11; 1 Tim 3:16.

trial. Nowhere does Scripture actually expound upon the nature of the divine request for the sacrifice of Isaac. One reason, perhaps, is that as a founding event in the life of Israel it is meant to explain many other events and principles in Scripture. It is a story about what God does not want as much as about what he wants. Unlike the other gods of the nations, the God of Abraham wants true faith, not the death of sons. James's understanding has a close parallel in the epistle to the Hebrews (11:17–19):

> By faith Abraham, when God tested him, offered Isaac as a sacrifice. He who had received the promises was about to sacrifice his one and only son, even though God had said to him, "It is through Isaac that your offspring will be reckoned." Abraham reasoned that God could raise the dead, and figuratively speaking, he did receive Isaac back from death.

Much in the passage accords with themes central to James's message, such as enduring trials as God's testing of faith (1:2–4), which is the way in which God induces deeds. These deeds of trusting and humble obedience demonstrate the evidence of genuine faith. Indeed, Heb 12:1–13 exhorts believers to accept this testing from God as evidence that they are true sons of God and—from James's perspective—of Abraham as well. Abraham's act was useful then to God by which Abraham became the first proven son of his mercy.

2:22 As if drawing close to his conversation partner, James's address in the second person called him to "see" (cf. v. 20 with "you know") the truth about Abraham's deed: his faith was made complete by his actions, or literally, "his faith works."[59] James wanted it known that without action, faith cannot be complete. Without action there will be no perseverance (cf. 1:3), and without sustained perseverance faith will not become complete.[60] There is an important

---

[59] The decision by the translators of the NIV to translate ἐργά as "actions" (deeds) in order to avoid the confusion of taking James to mean the same things by "works" as Paul did means some loss of form in this phrase.

[60] James did not develop this along the lines of Matt 10:22; 24:13: "He who stands firm to the end will be saved." Completed or perfected faith then is not meant to convey God's saving work but perhaps something along the lines of Jesus' "being made perfect" through his obedience as taught by Heb 2:10; 5:9; 7:28 and which carries over into believers' destinies in 10:1,14; 11:40.

connection between deeds that complete faith and perseverance itself. Abraham's actions were his perseverance in faith. Perseverance completes faith by demonstrating the genuineness of faith (cf. 4:10–11). Thus, although usefulness is a standard by which faith is measured, so is perseverance through testing. Perseverance, of course, is connected to the former standard because it is "useful" to God and the believer in that it demonstrates true relationship.

2:23 Unique in James, we have in this verse a reference to the fulfillment[61] of Scripture. This connection arises from the relation between the statement from Gen 15:6 that Abraham's faith was reckoned as his righteousness by God and the actual birth of his son Isaac twenty-five years later. This is part of a shorthand review of Abraham's faith in God: a glancing back to the beginning of Abraham's walk of faith with God and God's acceptance of him, the waiting for the promised child, the evidence of his friendship with God and—from the previous verse—the completion of his faith in offering up Isaac. The fulfillment text is quoted by Paul as well in Rom 4:3, which frames an entire context in order to convey much more teaching on the significance of Abraham. It includes the statement, "Against all hope, Abraham in hope believed and so became the father of many nations" (Rom 4:18).

Of course the difference of perspective between Paul and James rests in this: James looked to the Abraham story to show how genuine faith operates; Paul looked to the Abraham story to show how God is predisposed to forgive sinners. At the heart of the difference between the "works" James was advocating and those that Paul was combatting by relativizing the act of circumcision (Rom 4:10–12) were the conditions under which righteousness was "credited" to Abraham. Abraham was justified by trusting the promise of God, not his act of circumcision. The lack of any reference to circumcision in James is highly significant. Circumcision signified for Paul

---

[61] πληρόω: "fulfill," by actions, prophecy, obligation, promise, law, request, purpose, desire, hope, duty, fate, destiny. Here it is passive; cf. 1 Kgs 2:27; 2 Chr 36:21; Matt 1:22; 2:15,17,23; 4:14; 8:17; 12:17; 13:35; 21:4; 26:54,56; 27:9; Mark 14:49; 15:28; Luke 1:20; 4:21; 21:22; John 12:38; 13:18; 15:25; 17:12; 19:24; Acts 1:16; 3:18; 13:27. Note how the entire life of Christ is a fulfillment of OT prophecy and is thus one of the special attributes that make a NT Gospel what it is.

the kind of relation to activities whereby his fellow countrymen justified themselves, indeed, found resources for religious boasting (4:2). Paul was vehement in his rejection of this kind of observance of the law (4:13), which damaged the divine/human relation in faith. Abraham was God's example of how boasting in the command of God and act of man had missed what was intended for faith, that "the promise comes by faith" (4:16). Thus close inspection of the ways in which Abraham's story illustrates the messages of James and Paul differently helps us allow their distinctive messages to be heard.

James summed up what he had to say about the example of Abraham by citing a choice title for him within the Old Testament: "God's friend" (cf. 2 Chr 20:7; Isa 41:8). Abraham had been drawn into God's deliberations about how he would judge the sinful cities of the plain. Abraham had asked his divine Visitor about punishing the righteous along with the unrighteous: "Will not the Judge of all the earth do right?" (Gen 18:25). In the covenant conversation between Abraham and the Lord, the Lord included him in every way. Abraham could not have been but amazed and wholly satisfied that God had heard his plea and engaged his questions. God had made Abraham his friend. Abraham as friend of God became the true exemplar of faith, for to be a believer one must commune with God in friendship. As James later argued, believers must renounce the pride that typifies "friendship with the world" (4:4–5) and humbly accept the will of God in order to enjoy friendship with God.

2:24 James shifted to the plural form of the second person "you." Not the hypothetical interlocutor but his actual audience now participated in the principle he had been driving at throughout this section. The claim of faith requires its demonstration in action. Abraham's righteousness was made manifest by the obedient offering of his son (v. 21). We noted earlier how important "showing" the genuineness of faith was for James, and this was his understanding of how believers are "justified."

Many find a verbal parallel here with Paul in Rom 3:28. Was James counteracting either Paul or misreadings of Paul? One must be cautious about the canonical availability of Paul's writings as we read James. Nothing in this verse, however, directs us to the person of Paul or some definite passage in his corpus. For Paul faith that trusts the word of God saves. This was his understanding of "faith alone." This simple faith is the point of entry "into Christ." But for James the overarching concern was with demonstration. Given that so much can be done within the church out of "bad faith," what is meant by "faith" must be clarified by deeds. For James "faith alone" was a crass avoidance of the necessity of demonstrating faith. In view of the judgment to come (Rom 4:12–13; 5:5,9), only those whose faith has been demonstrated to be genuine can hope to be saved. "Faith by itself" (Jas 2:17) demonstrates its deadness in that it shows no vitality. Vital faith is that which God considers righteous. This is visible in the lives of the two exemplars in this passage: Abraham and now Rahab.

2:25 James turned to the example of "Rahab the prostitute"[62] to underscore his emphasis on vital, useful faith (vv. 17–20). She was a "famous sinner" in contrast to "father Abraham" (v. 21). Joshua 2:1–21 tells the story of hospitality in crisis.[63] She mercifully hid the Israelite spies from her own countrymen and cared for their needs before the destruction of Jericho. She exemplifies faith in that she recognized the truth of God in his works of delivering Israel, and she demonstrated that faith. It is for this that she is remembered also in the list of the faithful in Heb 11:31.

(6) Recapitulation: No Faith without Deeds (2:26)

26As the body without the spirit is dead, so faith without deeds is dead.

2:26 Before moving on, James rehearsed the main point of this part of the letter he had started in 2:17. By way of recapitulating the principle that "faith by itself, if it is not accompanied by action, is dead," James presented the imagery of a corpse. Without

---

[62] πόρνη: "prostitute," "harlot," ranked with taxcollectors among the lowest class of people; cf. Josh 6:17,23,25; Prov 29:3; Matt 21:31–32; Luke 15:30; 1 Cor 6:16; *T. Levi* 14:5; *Sir* 19:2; *1 Clem* 12:1, where the connection with Abraham appears. Also see A. T. Hanson, "Rahab the Harlot in Early Christian Tradition," *JSNT* 1 (1978): 53–60.

[63] Cf. the important work by D. Gushee, *The Righteous Gentiles* (Grand Rapids: Eerdmans, 1994).

the spirit[64] the body has no life.[65] Deeds animate faith as the creaturely spirit animates the body. Works do not justify the believer in God's sight but demonstrate the genuineness of faith toward others inside and outside the church; for example, their faith is "useful" as God has intended it to be. Confident of the mercy of God by faith, believers are consistent in showing mercy as the demonstration of their faith and the divine truth on which it rests.

What then is the precise meaning of "dead" (cf. 2:17) in relation to faith? If the deeds of faith are absent from the life of the believer, one can only determine that his or her faith itself is not genuine. This at least is what the evidence of their lives demonstrates. The reality may be otherwise; they may be double-minded and so mixing deeds of faith with deeds arising from evil desire (i.e., sin; cf 1:13–15). But this must be corrected. Double-mindedness does not place the salvation of the believer immediately in question, but the self-deception that goes along with double-mindedness is destructive to the truth of faith as well as the lives of others who need the care and protection of believers. Faith without its deeds, then, is like a dead body. Believers must of necessity demonstrate their faith by doing what God requires, not to secure salvation but to avoid the grave dangers of distorting the Word of God or damaging the lives of other believers and needy persons to whom they have been called to minister.

---

[64] Without the definite article πνεῦμα simply means that force or substance that animates the body. Thus the body has a soul, a heart, a conscience, etc. because it is animated by a creaturely human spirit.

[65] James's allusions to a theological anthropology, while never a free-standing topic, are apparent. Throughout the letter kernels of important anthropological truths appear.

III. THE FORMIDABLE TONGUE (3:1–12)
1. The Responsibility of Teachers (3:1)
2. The Uncontrollable Tongue (3:2–8)
   (1) Analogies of Size (3:2–5)
   (2) Analogies of Force (3:6–8)
   (3) Analogies of Incompatibility (3:9–12)

————— **III. THE FORMIDABLE TONGUE (3:1–12)** —————

The basic problem of self-deception and double-mindedness raised in chap. 1 is at the root of the problem with inactive faith confronted in chap. 2. He returned as well to the theme of the tongue, which appeared in 1:19,26. There bridling this organ and controlling one's speech are chief marks of Christian wisdom. When believers do not exercise whole-hearted faith, they fall prey to their own lusts (1:14) and begin to justify themselves and to blame God for their temptations (1:13). Such maneuvering inevitably leads to preferential treatment of the rich and merciless treatment of the poor (2:3–6). The problem of the tongue, or speech, extends throughout the rest of the letter in the warning against slandering (4:11), empty boasting (4:13), and grumbling against others in the fellowship (5:9).

In this second part of the body of James's letter is found one of the most poignant teachings on the sinful forces lodged within human nature. The tongue proves to be a source of greatness, either great good or great evil. Speech has a great affect upon its hearers, even when it is making empty claims (cf. 2:14,20). The boasts of inactive faith may prove that faith to be useless, but the tongue is active in other ways, even cursing those who frustrate selfish desires. In this portion of James the tongue is presented as the key to self-control for a virtuous life of faith. Bring the tongue under control and the whole self can be guided into well-doing. Beginning and ending this part by addressing "my brothers," James developed an argument[1] for maturity of speech and its relation to the entirety of the Christian life.

1. The Responsibility of Teachers (3:1)

¹Not many of you should presume to be teachers, my brothers, because you know that we who teach will be judged more strictly.

3:1 James clearly was preoccupied with the problem of false claims and deceit. It now was time to launch the most extensive confrontations of the entire letter. He was addressing his "brothers" in the faith and offered one of the most noteworthy bits of advice for the church in the entire New Testament. James admonished them to limit the number of teachers[2] in their midst. Self-limitations should be established. To be a teacher within the church is something for which one is recognized; it requires mastering the Scriptures and their application to faith and life. Because self-deception is something all believers are prone to and, more importantly, because of the harsh judgment against those who teach falsely, this limitation should be imposed.

The injunction in this verse, however, does not teach a double standard, that is, that the church's teachers are required to live more strictly than the other believers. All believers are to live a strict Christian life. The message here is that those who teach will be judged with greater severity. But what kind of judgment? This James did not say. He presupposed much in the understanding of his hearers. If James was again following the pattern of Jesus in the Sermon on the Mount, then what James was referring to was unforgiving judgment against the unforgiving and merciless judgment to the unmerciful. Judgment will be according to God's standard of

---

[1] The rhetorical development includes several alliterative relationships: πολλὰ; πταίομεν ἅπαντες (v. 2); μικρὸν μέλος . . . μεγάλα (v. 5); φλογίζουσα . . . φλογιζομένη (v. 6); δαμάζεται καὶ; δεδάμασται (v. 7); δαμάσαι δύναται (v. 8).

[2] A "teacher" is one who holds something of an office within the church; cf. Acts 13:1; 1 Cor 12:28f.; Eph 4:11; 2 Tim 1:11; *Did.* 15.1f.; 13:2, where a teacher is one who is paid by the church; *Herm. Vis.* 3.5.1; *Herm. Man.* 4.3.1; *Herm. Sim.* 9.15.4.

true religion when all people, believers and unbelievers alike, stand before him.

2. The Uncontrollable Tongue (3:2–8)

James presented his readers with one of the most memorable arguments regarding the source of sin within the self: the tongue. The tongue, or speech, is essential to the work of teachers, mentioned in the previous verse. In the ancient world the teacher's conduct in speech was considered an especially weighty matter. James, however, was not optimistic about controlling the tongue. The tongue has its way much like the human will without the bridle of the Word of God and the anticipation of judgment. But with these instruments, Christians will be enabled to stand accepted by God.

(1) Analogies of Size (3:2–5)

²We all stumble in many ways. If anyone is never at fault in what he says, he is a perfect man, able to keep his whole body in check.

³When we put bits into the mouths of horses to make them obey us, we can turn the whole animal. ⁴Or take ships as an example. Although they are so large and are driven by strong winds, they are steered by a very small rudder wherever the pilot wants to go. ⁵Likewise the tongue is a small part of the body, but it makes great boasts. Consider what a great forest is set on fire by a small spark.

3:2 The next statement is all-inclusive: everyone stumbles[3] (cf. 2:10); everyone sins in many ways, falling short of what is taught and required by the Lord. This statement balances the warning of the previous verse. The standard for teachers disallows their failing in the matter of speech, and yet human nature is prone to violation of God's standards. James added this confession for a dual effect: knowing that James himself stumbled in many ways puts the admonition to pursue perfection into perspective; because believers

---

[3] πταίω: "stumble," "trip," in the sense of making a mistake, being at fault, of committing sin. This verb occurs twice in this verse of someone who breaks the law of God. See also 2:10; cf. Deut 7:25; 1 Kgs 8:46; Rom 3:9–20; Philo *Leg. All.* 3.66; *1 Clem.* 51.1.

stumble in many ways, their teachers need to be particularly circumspect about their conduct, above all in the way they speak.

The next sentence in the verse is governed by the conditional "if." If there is someone who does not stumble in what he says, literally, in his "word,"[4] he or she is perfect, mature. Not speaking or not much speaking was considered a high virtue. A great deal of error and evil comes from speaking (cf. Prov 6:2). This statement comes in the form of a Christian aphorism. It redirects James's hearers to God's standard of mature, fully developed faith (cf. Jas 1:4,8,23). With respect to one's own affairs in life, if the tongue is controlled, general self-control will be the result. James asserted that controlled speech enables[5] one to guide the whole body by the maturity of faith (cf. 1:26). The power of faith to bridle the tongue conveys a power to guide[6] the activities of the body (as with the horse or ship, vv. 3–4). The sense of "guide" here is important, for it not only implies the curbing of evil action but also the directing of the body into good action.

What is the connection between speaking and doing in the "perfecting" of faith? The problem of inactive faith seen in the previous chapter was a problem of mere profession, of being "a hearer only" (cf. 1:23). Now the direction of James's argumentation shifts to the effectiveness of speech, either to guide the self into the deeds of blessing or the deeds of cursing (cf. 3:10). The other side of speaking is that actions invariably follow words. Self-deception and double-mindedness in the life of the believer at times obscures this truth, so James moved on to the concrete problem of controlling one's life for the service of God. Undoubtedly this self-control is one of the fruits of the wisdom promised to those who ask for it in faith (cf. 1:5–6). Wisdom, the knowledge and skill to do the will of God when activated by faith, brings the believer further down the

---

[4] λόγος: "word," "statement," even "teaching"; cf. 2 Cor 8:7; Eph 6:19; Col 4:6; *Did.* 2:5; *T. Job* 38; *Sir* 14.1; 19.16; 25.8; 28.12–26.

[5] δυνατός: "powerful," "able"; cf. Luke 14:31; Acts 11:17; Rom 4:21; 11:23; 14:4; 2 Cor 9:8; 2 Tim 1:12; *1 Clem.* 48.5; 61.3; *Diogn.* 9.1.

[6] χαλιναγωγέω: "guide with a bit and bridle," "hold in check," both in the literal and figurative senses; cf. 1:26; 1QS 4; Philo *Somn.* 2.165; *Op M* 86; *Herm. Man.* 12.1.1.

road to perfection or completeness of faith.

3:3 The axiom of the perfect control of the body through perfect control of the tongue is now illustrated with common but pertinent imagery. A controlled tongue is like the bit[7] under the horse's tongue by which the rider controls the entire horse. Just as the rider can control the horse, the body's willfulness and appetites can be controlled. Though a horse is much larger than a human being, the rider is able to make the horse obey[8] by employing a small, simple device. The connection between turning the "whole animal" and controlling the "whole body" in the previous verse is striking. The body and its appetites were often seen in the ancient world as bestial and brutish. The physical was conceived as large and unwieldy for the self and its thoughts. But the desires of the body and the actions by which the body fulfills those desires can be directed toward other higher desires and goals. With the proper instrument the trainer or the rider can accomplish wonderful ends. What would otherwise be a beast too large for concourse with humans becomes a domesticated one, useful (cf. 2:14) to the one who masters it.

Created things of size and greatness must never be the source or object of Christian faith. Wisdom from God, however, provides the capacity for bringing usefulness out of these things, whether they be the physical body, institutions, or movements of people. Only if the Word of God is actively applied to the situation will there be the guidance required for virtuous action and beneficial results.

3:4 The bringing under control of a very large[9] object by a small but effective instrument hardly could have been better expressed than by the analogy of the ship and the rudder.[10] Against the wind an immense, rudderless vessel is uncontrollable. Out on the sea, without a mechanism for steering, the pilot would have no

---

[7] χαλινός: "bit," "bridle"; cf. Rev 14:20; Josephus *Ant.* 18.320; Philo *Agr.* 94. Note the close relation to the verb in the previous verse, "to bridle."

[8] μετάγω: "guide" (in another direction); cf. 1 Kgs 8:48; 2 Chr 36:3; Ezra 1:4. The verb is used in the passive sense in v. 4 of the rudder guiding the ship.

[9] τηλικοῦτος: "so great," "so big"; here "big as they are," applying to the size of a body; cf. 2 Cor 1:10; Heb 2:3; Rev 16:18; along with σκληρός: "hard," "harsh," of the winds that drive the massive ships; cf. Prov 27:16; Matt 11:7.

[10] πηδάλιον: "steering paddle," "rudder"; cf. Acts 27:40; for the connection between bridle and rudder see *Plut. Mor.* 33F.

way of keeping the ship on any course. The ship would be tossed and driven about like the waves that bear it along (cf. 1:6). But with the rudder, the mere will of the pilot is sufficient to direct the ship.

James pointed to the small size of the rudder. Like the small bit in the horse's mouth, the rudder, James said, is among the small-est[11] of instruments on the ship. The rudder's size is insignificant by comparison to the rest of the parts of the ship. The effectiveness of the instrument is what counts. Even in the harshest winds the boat will turn in the direction the pilot desires.[12] Of course the pilot must be someone with great training and integrity with whom the destiny of the entire ship can be entrusted. This example illustrates well a life dedicated to growth in wisdom. The tongue, representing the believer's speech, is not easily mastered. But the tongue must be mastered by acquiring the great skills of wisdom through careful and arduous study of God's Word. Only by such study can the skill to face the great issues of life be acquired. There is no other way to preserve the ship of life intact.

The activities of the body, along with its size, seem to dominate the experience of the individual. The desires and movements of the body are powerful, and yet they are actually controlled by a relatively small part. The tongue, that is, speech, is that part. The believing self within physically turns this way or that according to what the person thinks and says. The self, the tongue, and the body are one whole, and no one part is active without the others. James illustrated how they are dynamically related to each other in the fulfillment of action. "The horse" has a "bridle," and "the ship" has a "rudder." The small tongue, however, does not correspond to the bridle or the rudder but to the horse and the ship. Although the self is involved when sin is committed, the tongue is what needs to be controlled. Although the tongue is small in size, its abilities are large. Some instrument must be used to rein it and guide it. In the moral life, at first virtue seems to be a matter of controlling the body; but, in a surprising way, all comes down to controlling

---

[11] ἐλάχιστος: "very small," "insignificant"; in the NT the elative rather than superlative sense is most often used as here.

[12] ὁρμή: "impulse," "inclination," "desire," "wherever the impulse of the steersman leads him."

speech. If speech has such control over the body, however, who can control speech? This is the question James was about to answer.

3:5 The images of horses and ships, bridles and rudders show how such small things as the tongue are the real instruments of control over large things. Control is often concentrated at a single, highly significant point in the chain of action: from desire, to movement of the body, and then to fulfillment of deed. James's attention was on the effective influence of the tongue over the body through the immensity of its boasting.[13] The tongue (cf. 1:26; 3:5–6,8) is now personified as a self-conscious actor. The tongue, not the self, is the origin of action. The facts about bits and rudders illustrates the moral truth about the tongue's control of the body, for the tongue is the great lord of behavior. The tongue might rightly boast of itself, if it could. In spite of its smallness in the body, the tongue not only gives the body its chief means of communication; the body also owes its successes, whatever they are, to the effectiveness of speech. Although the boasting referred to here is not empty, speech really does control the body, a theme repeated throughout the letter. The theme of self-deception has one of its secrets exposed here. Since the believers easily forget how powerful speech is, James was intent upon alerting them. Alertness to the power of speech interrelates to alerts about mixing faith with worldly thinking and desires that undermine faith.

The second half of the verse illustrates the power of speech by comparing the tongue to a spark[14] in a forest. How deceptively small but overwhelmingly dangerous is the little spark. How great,[15] how destructive, the fire it kindles in the forest. The large horse controlled by the bit represented the power of desire moved one way or the other by the effectiveness of a small instrument. Because of the control exerted by the tongue, its immense boastfulness must be brought under control. The comparison of the tongue

---

[13] αὐχέω: "boast," a hapax legomenon in relation to the LXX and NT; but cf. Ps 12:3; Ezek 16:50; Zeph 3:12; *Sir* 48:18; *2 Macc* 15:32.

[14] πῦρ: "fire," in the figurative sense, as in v. 6.

[15] ἡλίκος: "how great" and "how small," is repeated twice here, forming a play on words with ἡλίκην ὕλην: "great forest," almost aphoristic, "how little a fire, how great a forest."

with the spark is then more precise. This analogy was perhaps most useful for James in that he then could call the tongue a fire in the next verse. The little spark kindles a fire of great force.

This illustration is also more complex than those of bit and rudder. The spark is not a neutral metaphor; the destructive figure is unmistakable. A similar use of this example can be found in Philo: "Nothing escapes desire . . .; like a flame in the forest, it spreads abroad and consumes and destroys everything."[16] Very likely, then, James meant to say that the boasting the tongue might rightly do must be understood in light of its destructiveness in much of life.

(2) Analogies of Force (3:6–8)

⁶The tongue also is a fire, a world of evil among the parts of the body. It corrupts the whole person, sets the whole course of his life on fire, and is itself set on fire by hell.

⁷All kinds of animals, birds, reptiles and creatures of the sea are being tamed and have been tamed by man, ⁸but no man can tame the tongue. It is a restless evil, full of deadly poison.

3:6   Up to this point James's use of analogy has been indirect through simile: one thing is like another thing. Here his use of analogy becomes direct, through metaphor; one thing is another thing. The tongue is "a fire."[17]

This text is extremely difficult to translate, and there are no satisfactory indicators pointing to a resolution. A definite article in the Greek text would normally require the translation "the world of evil" as the predicate complement to "the tongue." How is the tongue the world of evil? Also problematic is the sense in which the tongue is established within the members of the body (lit. "the tongue is made among our members"). Is it the tongue's placement[18] within the body that causes the world of iniquity, or does

---

[16] Johnson (*The Letter of James,* 258) cites the striking usage by Philo, *On the Decalogue* 173.

[17] For other examples of this metaphor, cf. Ps 120:4; Prov 16:27; 26:18–22; *Sir* 5:22; 28:11.

[18] καθίστημι: "be made," "become," has the passive sense and thus something, ultimately, God has done.

the tongue's prominent position show that human beings have caused the world of iniquity by their speech? Drawing upon other biblical sources does not help in the process of translation either, since both of these senses are found in Scripture. The answer probably lies with the metaphor of fire. The little spark is the cause of the entire destructive event of a forest fire. The tongue is the point of entry for the world's greatest evils. Its boasts inspire multitudes to evil, especially the words of false teachers. Thus, whether inside or outside the church, the wickedness of the world is an immense blaze set by the little fire of the tongue.

The tongue is "the world of evil." In the ancient way of thinking, this is not a difficult phrase. The body was the microcosm of the universe. In all its complexity, the human being was a small, self-contained universe, thus the term "microcosmos." There is a double sense of microcosm here: not only the body in relation to the universe of nature but also the tongue in relation to the universe of wickedness.[19] Thus, contained within the tongue or speech are all the representations of wickedness in the world. Is a representation of evil, in words that is, the same as the evil itself? Obviously not, but the power of verbal representation is not slight; this James knew full well. Words have the power to elicit action; indeed, the activity of speech itself interprets every other human action. There is no evil act that the tongue cannot tell, let alone initiate.

In the second half of the verse, the tongue is said to direct the body, and its effects are thorough and total. It perverts[20] the whole body of the person when there is a bent toward evil. True religion keeps "oneself from being polluted by the world" (1:27), but evil speech makes this impossible. For each person the evil of the world has its motive force in the tongue. The evil spreads, however, to all of a person's outward relations.[21] Just as the course of a rich man's

---

[19] Cf. 4:4; Ps 63:9; Luke 16:8–9,11; Rom 6:16; 1 John 5:19; *Enoch* 48.7; *Herm. Man.* 12.1; Vis 2.2;

[20] σπιλόω: "stain," "defile," in a symbolic sense, as here, of spiritual and moral corruption; cf. Jude 23; *Wis* 15.4; *T. Asher* 2.7.

[21] τροχός: "wheel," "course," "round" of existence, used for the course of life; in the pagan world the wheel of fortune, benefiting some and disadvantaging others capriciously; but in the LXX, Philo, and rabbinic literature, the path or period of one's life.

life proves to be all too fragile and unstable (cf. 1:11b), the individual's way of life is all too susceptible to the qualities of his speech. The person, once self-perverted by evil speech, becomes part of the larger currents of wickedness in the world. As such, evil speech proves its true nature as an extension of hell[22] itself. In a most powerful image, the fire that is the little tongue, a little spark causing great fires, has another fire that causes it. Hell has outcroppings in this world, and one of them is evil speaking.

Three causative relations are laid out here: corrupt speech spawns corruption of the body; the corrupted body sets in motion the evil course of an entire life; the destructiveness of evil speech is derived from the destructiveness of hell. Since the tongue is the world of evil, the person of perverse speech fails to distinguish between confessing faith and hypocrisy, respect and flattery, blessing and cursing (cf. v. 10). Whoever fails this way in speech certainly will fail in actions. Evil desire (1:14–15) corrupts the body; and just as a parasite destroys a host organism, the evil tongue becomes parasitical upon the whole life of the individual and indeed the church itself. When it is bent on evil, the tongue is not only its own source of evil but derives some of its inspiration from the great demonic underground.

This connection should not be surprising since in the previous chapters to promote a profession of faith while rejecting active faith is comparable to the "faith" of demons (2:19). The destructive, lying ways of the devil were well known to the biblical writers. The truth for James was that in the destructiveness of evil speech, the destructive end of that evil was present from the beginning. The destructive force of evil speaking is comparable to the destructive force of hell.

---

[22] γεένα: "Gehenna," "Valley of the sons of Hinnom"; cf. 2 Kgs 23:10; Josh 15:8b,16b; 2 Chr 28:3; Neh 11:30; Jer 7:32; a ravine south of Jerusalem that popular Jewish piety took to be the place of future judgment. In the Gospels it is the name for "hell," where the wicked will be punished in the next world; cf. Matt 5:29; 18:9; 23:33; Mark 9:45,47; Luke 12:5. The fiery aspect correlates with Matt 5:22; 18:9; *Bab. Rosh ha-Shana* 17b; *Sib. Or.* 1.103; *2 Clem.* 54; cf. C. Milikowsky, "Which Gehenna? Retribution and Eschatology in the Synoptic Gospels and Early Jewish Texts," *NTS* 34 (1988): 238–49.

3:7 Here the focus is on taming or subduing[23] all sorts[24] of animals as in the bridling of the domesticated horse (v. 3). The point is the civilizing ability of man, who tames the wild for his own security and amusement. Human forces secure cities against the savagery of the wilderness and capture its beasts for menageries and circuses. Whether beast, bird, reptile, or creature of the sea,[25] man is atop the natural hierarchy and rules them like their lord (cf. Ps 8:6–8; Gen 1:26–28; 9:2). This superiority of human force and intelligence is a fact and must be acknowledged if it is to be used rightly. The use of animals in domestic life, the use of technology as in ships, and even the taming of wild animals all fall within the abilities and rights of the human for survival and well being. (There is no warrant given here, however, for the misuse of the environment or the mishandling of fellow creatures.)

3:8 But the tongue is not like the domesticated animal, technology, or even wild beasts. There is no force within or beside the destructive force of the individual that can subdue his own greatest force, that is, the power of speech. The negativity of James's description of the tongue is blatant here. James seems almost to have delayed this declaration until he could make a forceful enough argument for it. The tongue cannot be tamed. Every other creature can be tamed, except this one. The tongue, the power of speech, is great (v. 5a); its evil is like an unquenchable fire destroying an entire environment (v. 5b).

James then called it a "restless evil," using the word translated "unstable" in 1:8 of the double-minded man and all his ways. But what is found here is no longer that of figurative speech, even on the metaphorical level (v. 6, i.e., the tongue is a "fire"). There is no ambiguity of description here. Like the double-minded person who cannot really trust in God and invariably falls into evil, the tongue,

---

[23] δαμάζω: "subdue," "tame"; cf. Dan 2:40; Mark 5:4 from the subduing of the demon; Josephus *Ant.* 3.86; the term is applied in v. 8 directly to the tongue.

[24] φύσις: "nature," but here "natural being," "product of nature," "creature," and more precisely "species" or "kind"; cf. *3 Macc* 3:29f.; *4 Macc* 1:20; Philo *Aristot. Part. An.* 1.5.

[25] ἐνάλιος, "belonging to the sea," thus "sea creature," a hapax legomenon in biblical literature; cf. Philo *Decal.* 54.

because it is uncontrollable, does the same. People do what they do because of what they are really saying. The connection between this evil within the individual and the unstable rivalry among believers mentioned later in the chapter should also be noted (v. 16). The statement that the tongue is an evil could not call for more caution. The ethicists look for sources of evil. The body is susceptible to evil influences. Deformed desire is evil. The tongue in its restless destructiveness is evil. It tends toward anger (1:20), self-deception (v. 26), offense (2:6), quarreling (4:2), boasting and bragging (v. 16), and swearing (5:12). Such is the tendency of the tongue to indulge in evil speaking. As such, the tongue, speech, is evil in humans. Is the gift of speech in general evil? Obviously not, for James knew humans could truly speak blessing and praise (v. 9). To live with the ambiguity of speech, mixing good with bad speech, is intolerable for the wise and true believer.

The restless evil is almost bestial in its venomous ways. It is hard not to think of the serpent-tempter of the Garden of Eden whose evil words led the first man astray and poisoned his thinking with lies (Gen 3:1–5). The faculty of speech is "full of death-bearing poison,"[26] an image already commonly employed in the Old Testament for the speech of the wicked (cf. Pss 13:3; 139:4; 140:3; Rom 3:13). Given the forcefulness of the tongue, its poisonous effect makes it even more formidable and menacing. No wonder the Lord Jesus could equate the worst insults with murder (cf. Matt 5:22)! The human tongue then is like a serpent that cannot be tamed. It is not like the straight sword of speech from the mouth of the risen Lord (cf. Rev 1:16; Heb 4:12). Instead, it is a wagging, lashing, writhing, and virulent creature. Its evil gets the best of all who do not keep it in check (v. 2).

(3) Analogies of Incompatibility (3:9–12)

⁹With the tongue we praise our Lord and Father, and with it we curse men, who have been made in God's likeness. ¹⁰Out of the same mouth come praise and cursing. My brothers, this should not be.

---

[26] ἰός, "poison," used here figuratively; cf. *Herm. Sim.* 9.26.7; *Herm. Vis.* 3.9.7; *Ign. Trall.* 6.2; but note 5:3, where it means "rust."

[11]Can both fresh water and salt water flow from the same spring? [12]My brothers, can a fig tree bear olives, or a grapevine bear figs? Neither can a salt spring produce fresh water.

3:9   In vv. 9–12 the ambiguous value of speech is discussed. The capacity of the tongue both to give praise and to curse is a fundamental conflict that James was intent on identifying. This inconsistency in speech is true of every believer as James's shift to the inclusive "we" testifies (cf. v. 1). He referred to the use of speech in worship, in praise[27] that is lifted to the Lord, God the Father. This blessing is the act of speaking adoringly of God in both private prayer and in the public assembly of the faithful. To use the gift of speech to praise the Giver of every good and perfect gift (1:17) and to extol the God who befriends us (2:23) is the proper use of the tongue.

But at nearly the same moment the same tongue turns against others who have been "made in God's likeness"[28] and curses[29] them. This slight, of course, is another dimension of the insulting of persons (e.g., the poor, 2:6) while professing faith in God. In the use of speech, people are schizophrenic. Not only is the tongue's capacity for blessing and cursing deeply ambiguous but the effects are devastating. One of the most important references to human nature in the New Testament is found here, for humans are in the *imago Dei,* created in the image and likeness of God (Gen 1:26–27). Interestingly, the New Testament usually makes reference to Christ himself in this connection: he is the image of God (2 Cor 4:4; Col 1:15; etc.). It is according to him, who is the image of God incarnate, that we will be remade in the resurrection (Rom 8:29; 1 John 3:1–2; etc.). Since the earliest Christian theology there has been controversy over this fascinating doctrine of the image and likeness of God in humans. Clearly, James taught that the original

---

[27] ἐυλογέω: "speak well of," "praise," "extol," directed to God; cf. Luke 1:64; 2:28; 24:30,53; 1 Cor 14:16; *Enoch* 106.11; Josephus *Ant.* 7.380; *Sib. Or.* 4.25; *Mart. Pol.* 14.2f.

[28] ὁμοίωσις: "likeness," "resemblance," quoting Gen 1:26; cf. Josephus *Ant.* 13.67; *T. Naph.* 2.2; *1 Clem.* 33.5; *Barn.* 5.5; 6.12.

[29] καταράομαι: "to curse" someone; cf. Gen 12:3; 27:29; Luke 6:28; Philo *Fug.* 73; *Leg. All.* 3.65; Josephus *Bell.* 3.297.

stamp of the likeness of God in the human creature is still present. It is to be respected and blessed, not made the object of malediction. The human being was made for God, fashioned to know God and to reflect the attributes of God in a creaturely way. To dishonor any human being in some way dishonors God. Those who bless God out of one side of their mouths and curse their neighbors out of the other side are double-tongued in speech-acts, recalling the double-minded man in 1:6–8.

3:10 James addressed the ambiguity of speech in that it is used for good and evil, something he flatly declared "should not be." The imagery shifts slightly from the tongue to the mouth.[30] The shift in images could be expressed this way: the tongue and its speech, the mouth and its voice. The reference to the mouth anticipates the illustration of the spring in the next verse. How can that which builds up and that which tears down come from the same voice? James's relentless unfolding of the implications of double-mindedness is evident. God is praised, humans are cursed; is then such praise of God merely lip service? With such gross inconsistency, had James's listeners not fallen into the same error as the unrepentant rich who "slander the noble name of him to whom you belong?" (2:7).

James spoke gently to his addressees as "brothers." They all stumbled in many ways, but they were not to tolerate a mixture of good and evil as a way of life. God had not created them to lead a life of faith in this half-hearted way. Even if they were under great stress, believers should resist the temptation to speak evil against fellows following the example of Job, who said, "I have not allowed my mouth to sin by invoking a curse against [my enemy's] life" (Job 31:30).

3:11 The poignant illustration of the spring symbolizes productivity in a different way from the fruit tree. Like the orifice of

---

[30] Ancient literature is full of references to the mouth and its significance in the moral human life, both in its actual functions and as an image of the ambiguous "orality" of human nature. One of Aesop's fables (35) includes the statement, "Out of the same mouth you send forth warm and cold"—pertaining to warming one's hands or cooling one's food. For the mouth as the organ of speech, cf. Num 32:24; Deut 30:14; Ps 8:3; Matt 15:11,18; 21:16; Luke 4:22; 11:54; Rom 10:8; Eph 4:29.

the mouth, which produces a stream of words, this orifice of the earth produces a stream of water. In this and the following verse the examples of springs of water and fruit-bearing trees bring back the force of Jesus' teaching of truth in the fruit (cf. Matt 7:16). James asked whether a single fountain or spring ever pours forth both "fresh" (lit. "sweet," *glukus*) and "salt"[31] (lit. "bitter") water, for which the intended answer is no.[32] In James's illustration fresh water corresponds to that which is desirable, for bathing, for drinking, or for irrigation; and the salt corresponds to that which is undesirable, unfit for either need. If the spring produces salt water, it cannot produce fresh, and vice versa. The implied lesson is that the heart that speaks benediction ought not pour forth malediction (cf. Mark 7:15,20–21). For the sake of the fellowship of believers, it should probably be expressed reassuringly; if the spring produces fresh water, it will not produce salty water.

3:12   Two more illustrations—the fig tree and the grapevine—do not serve as examples in quite the same way as the spring. Instead of contrasting what is useful with what is not, the argument stems from the natural order of living things: grapevines produce grapes, not figs; and fig trees produce figs, not olives. This shift in focus is more subtle than between the illustrations of the untamed tongue and of the inconsistent tongue that is signaled by the clear statement of a principle in v. 9. There is no need to ignore this shift from what is undesirable to what is unnatural in order to secure a uniform view of the argument. Perhaps the repetition of "my brothers" in this verse signals the shift. The truth from the natural order conveys a similar message: if a person is oriented one way, that one will act accordingly. There is nothing wrong with olives or figs per se, or with anything in the created order. The question now is relative to function and use.

Another indicator that a shift occurs from what is undesirable to

---

[31] πικρός: "bitter," i.e., undrinkable, water because of the concentrated salts it contains; cf. Josephus *Bell.* 4.476; paired with the strongly contrasting γλυκύς: "sweet" for potable water. Note, however, that in returning to this illustration at the end of the next verse, the adjective there is ἁλυκός: "salty."

[32] Readers must not be distracted by the more complex use of similar imagery in Rev 3:15–16.

what is unnatural is in the change of adjectives for the undrinkable water in vv. 11–12 from "bitter" to "salty." The first usage of the image of the spring refers literally to "bitter" water, not salty. The qualifier "bitter" (v. 11) anticipates the "bitter envy" mentioned in v. 14. The word "salty" fits along with the examples of other producers from the natural order. But a "salt spring" could not produce fresh water. Back to the principle at hand, those who truly praise God do not curse their brothers. James did not refer to a thoroughly new constitution of the person but to true faith that does what is natural to it, both toward God and toward other human beings. Such faith praises and blesses.

IV. WISDOMS FROM ABOVE AND BELOW (3:13–4:10)
1. Heavenly and Hellish Wisdoms (3:13–15)
2. The Fruits of These Wisdoms (3:16–18)
3. The Truth about Conflicts (4:1–5)
   (1) Their Source in Evil Desire (4:1)
   (2) Their Outcome in Envy (4:2)
   (3) The Enmity of Friendship with the World (4:3–5)
4. On Being a Friend of God (4:6–10)
   (1) Grace for the Humble (4:6)
   (2) Exercising for Humility (4:7–10)

—— IV. WISDOMS FROM ABOVE AND BELOW (3:13–4:10) ——

Up to this point James had been focusing on human deeds and their sources within the heart. Here, while retaining that focus on deeds, he introduced insights on the transcendent sources of good and evil from which various deeds emanate. The two chief categories of reference in this entire passage are a friend of God and a friend of the world. Anticipated in the declaration that the evil of the tongue is ignited by the evil of hell (3:6), the chief question to be posed to James's hearers was, Which wisdom is guiding you, the heavenly (v. 17) or the hellish (v. 15) variety? This third part of the body of James's epistle alerted them to their interpersonal warring, to the peaceable wisdom among them, and to the source for correcting their warring desires.

This section contains four subsections. The first section (3:13–15) establishes the existence of the two wisdoms: the one from above, the heavenly, and the other from below, the demonic. The second subsection (vv. 16–18) contrasts the fruits of these wisdoms. The third subsection (4:1–5) delineates the conflicts stemming from enmity with God. The fourth subsection (vv. 6–10) outlines the letter's second spiritual exercise in self-humbling (cf.

1:9–10). Much in this section is highly sermonic, containing rhetorical questions, lists of deeds good and evil, striking imagery, epithet, and antitheses. Just as the Word of God is to be received wisely with humility (cf. 1:21), the development of wisdom and character of the wise man or wise woman is put at a premium here. How could there be any other more appropriate attitude before God, the one and only Judge?

1. Heavenly and Hellish Wisdoms (3:13–15)

[13]Who is wise and understanding among you? Let him show it by his good life, by deeds done in the humility that comes from wisdom. [14]But if you harbor bitter envy and selfish ambition in your hearts, do not boast about it or deny the truth. [15]Such "wisdom" does not come down from heaven but is earthly, unspiritual, of the devil.

3:13 In the first verse of this chapter James pointed to the important role of the *didaskalos* ("teacher") in the fellowship. Now he points to the importance of the *sophos*[1] ("wise"). The first part of the verse is one of the crucial rhetorical questions for maintaining his argument against double-mindedness throughout the letter. The man or woman of wisdom and knowledge[2] who measures up to God's standards proves to be such by attitudes and good actions. The coupling of the two words "wise and understanding" has in view the truth and its application. The objective truth is that God is gracious (cf. 4:6), and subjective application is that the wise humble themselves in obedience (cf. 4:10). Both are embodied in the wise man or woman. Wisdom knows the good and knows how to do the good. Understanding has seen how good wisdom in action is and knows why wisdom is good. Understanding knows why wis-

---

[1] σοφός: "clever," "skillful," "experienced," "wise," a virtual title for a person whose knowledge comes from God and has been shaped by the divine nature. Cf. Matt 23:34 (where Jesus declares, in condemnation of the Pharisees, "I am sending you prophets and wise men and teachers..."); Rom 16:19; 1 Cor 3:18; Eph 5:15; Philo *Migr. Abr.* 58; *Barn.* 6.10.

[2] ἐπιστήμων: "expert," "learned," "understanding." This term often is combined with "wise" (cf. Deut 1:13; 4:6; Dan 5:11; Philo *Migr. Abr.* 58) but can be used negatively of those who do not regard their dependency upon God; cf. Isa 5:21; *Barn.* 4:11.

dom is good in its well-doing because it has seen how good wisdom is in its effects on others. James was then picking up the matter of understanding faith without works that cannot show itself through a good life. Instead, as James will lay out in the following verses, faith without good deeds means a life of evil deeds. Without referring to "good works" as such, the works that are done are performed out of an expression of gentleness or mercy engendered by the wisdom of God.

Wisdom then concerns the conduct[3] of one's life. Like the word that is powerful to save implanted by God in the heart of the believer (cf. 1:18), the wisdom from above gives birth to deeds and a way of life that grows in understanding. A good life is one typified by "deeds done in the humility that comes from wisdom" (lit. "deeds in humility of wisdom"). Wisdom in the life of the believer advances in cycles. Wisdom entails understanding, which entails the demonstration (cf. 2:18) of a good life, which entails humble deeds, which entail wisdom. True wisdom constantly engenders a cycle of increasing virtue that continues throughout a lifetime. The seed of the Word of God grows within and grows up in a believer according to the standard of well-being and well-doing established for us by God.

3:14 This verse begins with the adversative "but" to point up a contrast with the values expressed in the previous verse. The character of hellish, earthly "wisdom" is now described. In this way of life no living seed of the divine Word is in evidence growing in the heart. Instead, the heart is a seedbed for "bitter envy"[4] and "selfish ambition."[5] Is there, perhaps, an allusion here to the fall of man

---

[3] ἀναστροφή: "way of life," "conduct," "behavior," which can be either good or evil. Paul often spoke of his former, i.e., pre-Christian, way of life using this term; cf. Gal 1:13; Eph 4:22. In other senses cf. 1 Tim 4:12; Heb 13:7; 1 Pet 1:18; 2:12; 3:13; 2 Pet 3:11; *Tob* 4.14; *2 Macc* 6.23.

[4] The same word πικρός, "bitter," is used in v. 11, translated "salty." On ζῆλος, "jealousy," "envy," when used in a bad sense, cf. v. 15; Eccl 4:4; Rom 13:13; 1 Cor 3:3; 2 Cor 12:20; Gal 5:20; *Sir* 30.24; 40.4; Josephus *Ant.* 14.161; *1 Clem.* 6.1ff.; 43.2; 63.2.

[5] ἐριθεία: "selfishness," "selfish ambition," a rare term, found before the NT only in Aristotle, *Polit.* 5, 3 p. 1302b, 4; 1303a, 14. There the term means the selfish and unscrupulous pursuit of political office. In the NT the added senses of "strife" and "contentiousness" may be present; cf. Rom 2:8; 2 Cor 12:20; Gal 5:20; Phil 1:17; 2:3.

(Gen 3:1–5)? Are these not the primal sins of Adam? With the reference to the abiding image of God from creation, perhaps James was still thinking of original man in the background. If respect toward persons is appropriate because it reflects respect toward God, sins toward persons find their roots in sins toward God. When the heart (cf. 4:8), that center of will and emotion, is possessed by envy, then a cruel rivalry and sinful longing for what belongs to another is always involved. Envy was the sin involving the usurpation of the knowledge of good and evil that belonged to God just as it is envy of the rich man's wealth (2:1–4) that is the root of partiality. Envy, like jealousy, focuses inordinately on another person's possessions and relationships. This desire to imitate and surpass another, even if it might mean stealing from that person, destroys relationships within the church, just as it did the original relationship with God and others.

If these deleterious attitudes were present in the hearts of his hearers, James then would enjoin them to stop boasting.[6] If not, they would be denying[7] the truth they believed in. James had pressed his point as far as he needed. Now his hearers must clear their minds and hearts for action or stop making claims that conveyed only pretentiousness. In a way, he seems to have been suggesting: "Don't even say you have faith. Don't even speak about the judgment of God as if you know it (cf. 2:12–13; 4:11–12). Don't even claim the gifts of God as if you trust him (cf. 1:7). Don't even pretend you understand the love of God because of the thoughts you harbor toward him and your neighbor" (cf. 2:8). All of this boasting would only be a lie and an offense against the truth. To make any reference to the things of God or the life of faith would itself be an empty and obscene boast.

Preaching of this kind would not be warmly received in the mod-

---

[6] κατακαυχάομαι: "boast against," "exult over" someone or something; cf. 4:16; Jer 27:11; Zech 10:12; Rom 11:18.

[7] ψεύδομαι: "lie," "tell a falsehood," normally in the absolute sense. What "lie against the truth" means is still not obvious; cf. Josh 24:27; Ps 17:45; Prov 14:5; Jer 5:12; Matt 5:11; Acts 5:3–4 (they "lied to the Holy Spirit"); Rom 9:1; 2 Cor 11:31; Gal 1:20; Col 3:9; 1 Tim 2:7; Heb 6:18; 1 John 1:6; Rev 3:9; Philo *Leg. All.* 3.124; *T. Jos.* 13.9; *1 Clem.* 27.2; *Herm Man.* 3.2; Papias 2.15.

ern church. But this harshness is precisely the point. For everyone who thinks the church and the Christian faith are to be exploited for their own personal interests, James's words cut to the quick. His rebuke must be spoken again and again because of our spectacular tendency to betray the faith by our actions.

3:15 The problems of the preceding verse do not have their source in the wisdom from above, like "every good and perfect gift" from 1:17 (cf. 1 Cor 2:6–16). The adverb "from above" found in this earlier passage is a circumlocution for heaven, or God himself. The wisdom believers are to pray continually for (1:5) is a divine gift. The character of the wise described earlier (3:13) is possessed of a wisdom that finds its source outside themselves. Just as the evil of the tongue is set aflame by the evil of hell (v. 6), the good works of the wise are enlivened by the goodness of God.

The kind of conduct produced by hearts full of "bitter envy" and "selfish ambition," however, is the opposite of the wisdom that comes from God. It rather originates from below. In a descending hierarchy of values, James identified the true nature of this other "wisdom." Contrary to the heavenly source of the first wisdom, the second is earthly.[8] The earthliness of this "wisdom" stands for philosophical or other kinds of rational approach to values that does not truly take the revealed will of God into account. As such this "knowledge" partakes of death—mortality and perishability, as was the case with the "first Adam," who was "of the earth" (cf. 1 Cor 15:37–49). This earthly "wisdom" attempts to calculate its way through the world by the "shifting shadows" of its natural lights (cf. 1:17b) and indeed by imitating them. The ineffectual prayers of earthly "wisdom" achieve nothing because they are so tied to the unstable concerns of the earth. Such wisdom certainly does not reckon according to the "law that gives freedom" (1:25). Instead, earthly wisdom is bound by material and physical concerns and will not suspend its interest in the temporal plane for the sake of the divine glory (cf. 2:1). The maxim from Prov 14:12 character-

---

[8] ἐπίγειος; "earthly," as opposed to the heavenly. Cf. Paul, who used this adjective for the body prior to resurrection, e.g., 2 Cor 5:1; *T. Jud.* 21.4; Philo *Cher.* 101; *Herm. Man.* 9.11; 11.6; 11f., 14,17,19; esp. this latter, describing the character of false prophets.

izes this "wisdom" as well as any in the Bible: "There is a way that seems right to a man, but in the end it leads to death."

This other "wisdom" is "unspiritual"[9] or soulish. Rather than appropriating the perfect gifts of God (cf. 1:17) and finding joy (v. 2) in realities to come, this "wisdom" is self-centered and oriented to personal gain. The spirituality James advocated is concrete, but it is also divinely relational. In contrast this soulish "wisdom" stands behind the boasting and self-deception so frequently condemned in the letter. Soulish (synonymous with "earthly") wisdom corresponds to a way of life. James had spoken of the rich man's way of life that quickly passes away (1:11) and the corruption of one's whole way of life by corrupt speech (3:6). As the earthliness of this wisdom expresses a way of life that is centered upon physical needs and urges, the soulishness of this wisdom further expresses a way of life centered upon the dictates of the selfish mind and heart. This is a soulishness, an unspiritual state of mind opposed to God. This is "wisdom" for a person or self that is a law unto itself, approving and disapproving in an arrogant and autonomous way. One thinks of the proverb "He who trusts in himself is a fool . . ." (Prov 28:26).

This "wisdom" is then "demonic."[10] This adjective stands as an important bridge to the next verse, which lists a number of vices present among James's hearers. When the course of one's life is so directed away from God, even when God is in one's superficial religious profession, the effects are demonic. James was not saying that devils were present within their fellowship or that demonically possessed persons were. Identifying such realities was not the purpose of his letter. Instead he was bringing to light how human interests serve satanic interests. Before presuming unbelief among James's addressees, however, recall that in the Lord's rebuke of Peter (Matt 16:16–23), Peter spoke both a revelatory word and a

---

[9] ψυχικός: "pertaining to the soul or life," consistently used in the NT for earthly, material existence as against divine reality (cf. 1 Cor 2:14; 15:44), thus the physical forces of the body and mind.

[10] δαιμονιώδης: "demonic," is a hapax legomenon in the Bible and does not appear in Greek literature before this time; but cf. 1 Cor 10:20–21; 1 Tim 4:1; *Herm. Man.* 9.11.

demonic word. Jesus, in a most painful way, corrected Peter for serving the satanic by being so very human-centered in his interests (i.e., rejecting Jesus' prophesy about his own suffering and death). The demonic is an umbrella description for both the directly satanic and all human opposition to God and his Spirit. Thus the faith that merely assents to gospel truths is on par with demonic faith (2:19b). As soon as believers act out of wrath, they are no longer serving God and so are opposed to God (1:20). The powerful evil of the tongue is influenced by hellish evil (3:6). Later James's audience would be exhorted to "resist the devil" (4:7), and thus they should take very seriously the kind of correction James was offering them.

2. Two Wisdoms and Their Harvests (3:16–18)

[16]For where you have envy and selfish ambition, there you find disorder and every evil practice.

[17]But the wisdom that comes from heaven is first of all pure; then peace-loving, considerate, submissive, full of mercy and good fruit, impartial and sincere. [18]Peacemakers who sow in peace raise a harvest of righteousness.

3:16   Misanthropic behavior characterizes a way of life based on "wisdom" that is earthly, unspiritual, and demonic. James's reasoning here was *a posteriori;* from effect one can perceive cause. Actions reflect attitudes, and this verse outlines a list of internal vices. Restlessness (3:8) and instability (1:8) of evil and double-mindedness are already familiar. Envy[11] and selfish ambition have been highlighted (v. 14) as particularly evident corrupting agents within the hearts of James's hearers. Wherever the "wisdom from below" prevails, James warned, there is "disorder"[12] (related to the word translated "unstable" in 1:8 and "restless" in 3:8) and distur-

---

[11] Cf. E. Milobenski, *Der Neid in der griechischen Philosophie* (Klassisch-Philologische Studien 29; Wiesbaden: Otto Harassowitz, 1964).

[12] ἀκαταστασία: "disorder," "unruliness," in the sense of that which causes public riots and thus can be translated "insurrection"; cf. Prov 26:28; Luke 21:9; 1 Cor 14:33; 2 Cor 12:20; *Tob* 4.13; *1 Clem.* 14.1; 3.2; 43.6; a cognate word with ἀκατάστατος: "unstable," seen in 1:8; 3:8.

bance within community. But is this situation any wonder? Church leadership commonly resorts to such wisdom for pragmatic reasons. For the sake of control, whether controlled growth or entrance into leadership, the Christian community will sacrifice the peaceable wisdom of God. Expediency is never a neutral maneuver. There are always spiritual and moral consequences. The unspirituality of worldly management, if not reigned by the wisdom from above, will dominate the church and cause it to be led into a myriad of evils.

James declared that his hearers would be led by the wisdom from below into every evil[13] practice. How extensive is James's "every?" Does anyone who harbors envy and selfish ambition become expert in evil? Put another way, when believers return to the way of demonic wisdom, they express sins that even the world has not learned. Their hypocritical sins are not like those of persons who make no pretense of biblical faith. Religious evil is a special brand that produces extraordinary sin, even its own kind of blasphemy. In Proverbs the sins of the ungodly make them into fools for whom there is little hope. But for the religious fools who are, contrary to the wisdom of God, "wise in [their] own eyes" (Prov 3:7), there is no hope. Is it any wonder James was so vehement in his warnings against self-deception? All of these vices are—to borrow from the description of heavenly wisdom—the "harvest" (v. 18) of its unrighteous attitudes.

3:17 James now cataloged the virtues of the wisdom from above. The divine wisdom is like a fountain of goodness, depicting a dynamic development of virtues. When heavenly wisdom is operative in the believer's life, one virtue is linked wonderfully to another. In this catalog virtually everything James had been saying in these three chapters is summed up.

Like other passages in the New Testament (1 Pet, Gal 5), or in the Psalms extolling the life-giving law of God (Ps 19), this wisdom is, first of all, pure.[14] The pure religion of Jas 1:27 has this

---

[13] φαῦλος: "worthless," "bad," "evil," "base," in terms of morality; cf. the LXX; John 3:20; 5:29; Rom 9:11; Titus 2:8; Josephus *Bell.* 2.163; *Sib. Or.* 3.362.

[14] ἁγνός: "pure," "holy," in the sense of sacredness, applied to whatever belongs to God; here with a moral overtone; cf. Phil 4:8, "to the pure everything is pure"; Prov 21:8; 1 Pet 3:2; *Herm. Vis.* 3, 8, 7; *1 Clem.* 21.8; 29.1; Poly 5.3; *2 Clem.* 6.9.

wisdom as the source of its purity. Purity as a fruit of heavenly wisdom recalls that purity of heart that Jesus extolled in Matt 5:8. To be pure, believers must separate themselves from the vices of earthly wisdom. Since all believers have led a life sometime according to the wisdom of the world, they will soon be exhorted to purify their hearts in 4:8. Wisdom that is pure, however, is not merely separatistic. This purity of life communicates the unsullied goodness of God. Pure wisdom does not inject that which is base and dehumanizing into relationships and conversations, nor does it compromise the goodness and blessedness of God for the sake of expediency. Pure wisdom applies itself to the love of the believers (or congregation) without showing favoritism (2:1).

That the divine wisdom is pure and purifying leads to its second dimension as peaceable[15] or "peace-loving." This fruit of wisdom—precisely counteracting the disorder caused by envy—reminds one of the blessedness of peacemaking extolled by Jesus (Matt 5:9; cf. Titus 3:2). Again, those who make peace are uncompromisingly committed to the unity of the believing fellowship. Peacemaking often means unity-protecting. But of course peacemaking extends beyond the bond of faith, as Paul exhorted: "If it is possible, as far as it depends on you, live at peace with everyone" (Rom 12:18). Peace here, of course, does not mean merely tolerance; indeed not, otherwise there would not be so much exhortation in James's teaching. What James wanted was the dispelling of rivalries and factions.

To the peaceableness of wisdom is then added the virtue of gentleness[16] or the quality of being "considerate." The maxim "A gentle answer turns away wrath" (Prov 15:1; cf. Titus 3:2; 1 Pet 2:18; 3:7) applies to everyone, for no one who is wrathful can accomplish the will of God (cf. 1:20). The gentleness of Christ the Teacher comes to mind (cf. Matt 29:11), so that whether the believer is a teacher (cf. 3:1) or the taught, the process of spreading

---

[15] εἰρηνικός: "peaceable," "peaceful;" cf. Ps 36:37; Heb 12:12; *Ep. Arist.* 273; Philo *Spec. Leg.* 1.224; *T. Gad* 6.2; *1 Clem.* 14.5.

[16] ἐπιεικής: "yielding," "gentle," "kind," part of a triple chain of alliteration with the previous Greek word and the next; cf. Esth 3:13b; 1 Tim 3:3; Titus 3:2; 1 Pet 2:18; Philo *Som.* 295; *1 Clem.* 1.2; 21.7; *Herm. Man.* 12, 4, 2.m.

the knowledge of God is not mixed with harshness and anger.

Next the virtue of submissiveness or compliance[17] is added, for wherever there is gentleness, there is also "a willingness to yield." Submissiveness is not passivity but an active mode of the will. It involves willing responsiveness to authority. One of the reasons James cautioned against a multiplication of teachers (3:1) was likely his desire to foster the submissiveness of believers and to discourage their viewing the teaching office as a means of lording it over others (cf. Mark 10:42–45). Because submissiveness is directed not only to mature leadership but also to God, great care must be taken to establish the divine standards of authority for the believing community. Of course, the authority to which submission was required was not that of those who led the community of James's addressees. Their teachers were to submit to James, especially since teachers probably were James's implied interlocutors throughout his letter (cf. 2:3,18).[18]

Beyond the active yielding that is submissiveness, heavenly wisdom is linked to the virtue of fruit-bearing faith. The wise are to produce a wealth of mercy and good fruit. Mercy can be a forgiving relation to others, not holding sins against them in a judgmental way but lovingly correcting them. Mercy is also to act generously to others, especially those in need, such as in the act of almsgiving. Just as sin impoverishes the human soul and needs to be covered through conversion and forgiveness, the poverty of the world needs to be alleviated by any and every means. This perspective of seeing spiritual poverty both in active sin and in passive neglect of those in material need was James's own, and he regarded it as essential for understanding faith (cf. 2:13–17). For James mercy and good fruit should be seen as nearly synonymous or at least related as cause (the former) and effect (the latter). To halt the activity of the tongue, which is "full of deadly poison" (3:8), believers must fill their lives with the good fruit, that is, the righteousness (v. 18) that is mercy. Later (5:7–9) James would use the analogy of the farmer

---

[17] εὐπειθής: "obedient," "compliant," a hapax legomenon in the NT; cf. *4 Macc* 12.6.

[18] Unlike the author of Hebrews, who enjoins his hearers to reverence their leaders (Heb 13:17).

who must wait until the harvest for his good fruit. An eschatological element is detectable here, for only in the judgment will the complete evidence be revealed of the goodness of what faith produces.

Reflecting the basic problem of double-mindedness, the next characteristic of heavenly wisdom is to be unwavering[19] (NIV "impartial") in the ways one relates to others. "Unwavering" connects with the final virtue of being "sincere."[20] The unwavering quality of actions indicates a purity or singleness of heart (cf. 4:8), characteristic of a person of integrity whose actions match his or her words. Coupled with sincerity, the term communicates the way of relating to others that banishes discord and uncertainty of intent, that is, no double-mindedness. All of the attitudinal and practical virtues of the wisdom from above are graced by the qualities of unswerving commitment and sincerity.

3:18 Those who are possessed of the heavenly wisdom James called "peacemakers." James's focus on peacemaking returns to the very heart of the teachings of Jesus and his standards for discipleship. By another agricultural allusion, peacemakers act like a sower who sows[21] the seed of peace. Like God, who sows the seed of the living Word (cf. Matt 13:19), believers are to sow peaceable deeds that will produce a harvest of righteousness. These acts that make for peace are the deeds of mercy, and this harvest[22] is the good fruit mentioned in the previous verse. The use of the words "produce" or "a harvest" in this connection is a marvelous image of the fruitfulness of a life of wisdom. Wisely sowing the seed of peace results in a multiplication of righteous deeds not only for the individual

---

[19] ἀδιάκριτος, "unwavering," or "impartial"; the NIV uses the latter, but the former probably is a better translation; this would reflect the sense of an antonym to διακρίνω from 1:6 and 2:4; cf. LXX Pr 25:1; Phil *Spec. Leg.* 3.57; and esp. Ign. *Eph.* 3.2; Ign. *Mag.* 15.2; Ign. *Trall.* 1.1.

[20] ἀνυπόκριτος, "genuine," "sincere," "without hypocrisy," lit. "free from insincerity"; cf. Rom 12:9; 2 Cor 6:6; 1 Tim 1:5; 2 Tim 1:5; 1 Pet 1:22; *Wis* 5:18; 18:15.

[21] Cf. Jer 4:3; Matt 13:19a; 25:24,26; Luke 19:21f.; John 4:37;

[22] καρπός, "fruit" (cf. 3:17); here "result," "outcome," "product," a rich and frequently used metaphor along these lines; cf. Prov 11:30; 13:2; Amos 6:12; Matt 7:16; 21:43; Luke 3:8; John 15:5,8,16; Rom 6:21; 15:28; Gal 5:22; Eph 5:9; Phil 1:11; Heb 12:11; *Herm. Sim.* 9.19.2; *2 Clem.* 20.3.

believer but also among the members of the entire church. A church that is rich in reconciling activities, that is, evangelism, the defense of the poor, counseling the troubled, offering hospitality to the stranger, providing shelter for the battered, sending gospel missionaries throughout the world, and many more, certainly reaps a rich harvest of righteousness. Wherever the church of Christ is doing these things, the kingdom of God is in evidence. This harvest precisely is what Jesus meant by the admonition to "seek first the kingdom of God and its righteousness" (Matt 6:33).

3. The Truth about Conflicts (4:1–5)

The chapter break falls in the middle of the third (3:13–4:10) section of the body of James's letter. This section deals with the two different kinds of wisdom and is typified by two ways of life, that is, two kinds of friendship: the one with the world and the other with God. As the section continues in the fourth chapter, James expounds these two types of spiritual friendship, penetrating deeper into the basic problems of double-mindedness and self-deception and the corrective need of active faith. In the second section of the letter, James sought to prove his point by specifying what his addressees were failing to do. Now in section three he points out the failings that were obvious in what they were doing.

(1) Their Source in Evil Desire (4:1)

[1]What causes fights and quarrels among you? Don't they come from your desires that battle within you?

4:1 Returning to his querying of his readers (cf. 3:13), James turned their attention directly upon the conflicts[23] and disputes[24] among them. Instead of peace and the fruit of righteousness, his

---

[23] πόλεμος: "armed conflict," "war," here figuratively for "strife," "quarrel," or our "conflict." This very graphic metaphor is unusual for the NT; cf. Philo *Praem.* 91; Philo *Gig.* 51; *T. Gad* 5.1; Ign. *Eph.* 13.2; *1 Clem.* 3.2; 46.5.

[24] μάχη: "fighting," "quarrels," "strife," "disputes." In biblical and extrabiblical literature this term always appears in the plural and is applied to conflicts without weapons; cf. 2 Cor 7:5; 2 Tim 2:23; Titus 3:9.

addressees were manifesting just the opposite: they were full of
mutual oppositions and attacks. Now, instead of attacking faulty
thinking and misnomers, certain doctrines and truths about God's
relationship to his people or about the nature and the content of
faith, James presupposed their mutual knowledge of particular
problems in their congregation(s).

That there were disputes and conflicts among persons over particular issues and selfish interest is well known. Human anger cannot accomplish the righteousness of God (1:20). If believers' faith
were active and bringing discipline to their speech, they would not
allow the sin of envy to have its way. As it is, they are full of the
fighting that envy—only superficially masked by the language of
faith—irresistibly produces. James wanted to deal with the root
causes of these conflicts, with the objects and subjects of their
envying. What had been a fairly concentrated discussion of the
implications of the doctrine of faith in the first three chapters has
now become a major confrontation with the realities that cannot be
hidden about the real fellowship—or lack thereof—among these
believers. The terms James used for conflict come from the language of warfare but can also be used as powerful imagery for the
destructiveness of relationships where violent attitudes have broken
out unchecked. Just as a lack of mercy was evidence of his addressees' sin of favoritism, now their active hostility toward each other
is used as evidence of their conflict with God.

James then identified the source of conflicts: their cravings
(hēdōne).[25] This term implies the very physical feelings associated
with the bodily appetites. The sense is not of the inherent evil of
desire but rather the conflict of desires that cannot all be satisfied
simultaneously or without one canceling out the other. As with the
problem of temptation earlier (1:13–14)—these conflicts can be
both internal and external. They cannot be limited to those within
the heart of each individual and thus isolated to personal moral
problems. Such are only the beginnings of the conflicts "within
you"—the "you" being a plural pronoun. The verb here, of doing

---

[25] ἡδονή: "pleasure," or here "desire," in this case for evil, as in lust; cf. v. 3;
Luke 8:14; Titus 3:3; *4 Macc* 5.23; 6.35; Philo *Agr.* 83; 84; Ign. *Trall.* 6.2; Ign. *Phild.*
2.2; Ign. *Rom.* 7.3; *Herm. Sim.* 8,8,5; 8,9,4.

battle,[26] is quite apt. James was using collective language as if he were speaking of one person, but this was the nature of their fellowship, even when it was troubled by envy and selfish ambition.

Throughout James's letter, deformed desire is shown to engender conflict wherever active faith is not exercised. The demonic is never said to be the cause of strife and evil thinking. Rather James uncovered the demonic character of human willfulness when it is not willfully submissive to the word of God. Honesty and confession of sin will be necessary if the situation is at all to be corrected. Evil desire is a reality within every human being and must be confronted. This confrontation becomes all the more difficult and painful when it is raised within the fellowship of Christians who imagine they can be free from deformed desire in this life. The best that a truly religious, devout Christian can do is to keep the body "in check" (3:2) along with the tongue. But the struggle that must be won daily, in spite of much stumbling into sin, is the one every believer fights against deformed desire. When these desires are not kept in check, the worst of them blaze out of control and usher in the worst conflicts of coveting and envy.

(2) Their Outcome in Envy (4:2)

²You want something but don't get it. You kill and covet, but you cannot have what you want. You quarrel and fight. You do not have, because you do not ask God.

4:2   Here James returned to yet another theme he introduced earlier, that of the deadly effects of evil desire in the life of sin (1:15). He identified the nature of his addressees' cravings in two ways. First, wanting what they do not have and second, coveting what they cannot obtain. These desires can and do become as dangerous as they are assuredly the causes of sin. What James emphasized with regard to the internal personal conflict of deformed desire is experienced corporately. The reaction has become utterly uncontrolled in the face of these frustrated desires, both of which

---

[26] στρατεύω: "do military service," "serve in the army," can be used positively for apostolic activity and Christian warfare (2 Cor 10:3; 1 Tim 1:18) but here of the conflicts of human passion; cf. 1 Pet 2:11; Poly 5.3.

probably parallel the twin evils of the previous chapter: envy and selfish ambition. There is nothing benign or mild about what these individuals are willing to resort to. Since passion is unbridled, murder[27] is committed. In 2:11 James quoted the prohibition of killing from the Decalogue, the Greek translation of which uses precisely this word. Within our letter, James was very pointed about the death-dealing effects of partiality toward the rich and neglect of the poor. There is a ruthlessness within the hearts of those who are bent on becoming rich, maintaining their wealth and increasing it (1 Tim 6:9). The image of the unmerciful servant probably also applies here as an example of how evil desire becomes murderous. In the parable of Jesus one servant received mercy but showed no mercy to a lesser servant who owed him much less than he had owed his master. The unmerciful servant grabbed his fellow servant by the throat and had him thrown into prison. This imprisonment would cause the loss of his family's livelihood, his nearly certain death and probably that of some of his family as well (Matt 18:21–35).

The statement connecting the frustration of not having and envying with murder needs to be taken with the utmost seriousness by every Christian. A vicious logic links the frustration of evil desire with evil acts and finally with the act of killing. For there are those who will be crushed by ruthless behavior of the landowner and the marketplace. Although the creation of new wealth in the modern free-market economy can be an incalculable benefit to the poor, it can also create new forms of poverty and death through the unchecked spirit of competition and the lack of concern for one's fellow human being. Business must be penetrated by the divine standards that demand proper care of the dependent laborers within its ranks, especially in the paying of fair wages (cf. 5:4). But conflicts over material goods and the envy that attaches to them are visible in other relationships: in divorce cases where property and children are involved and in shameful sibling rivalries over inheritances. The statistic that most murders take place between family members or intimate associates testifies to the kind of destructive

---

[27] φονεύω: "murder," "kill," as from the command, "You shall not kill" (Exod 20:15; cf. Matt 5:21; 19:18; Rom 13:9). A great many interpreters wish to soften this association with literal murder, but this reinterpretation does not fit the context.

force that envy and jealousy are. That these rivalries enter into the church and spill out again into the world around is not surprising. Rivalry always wants to supplant. A frustrated rivalry can generate an anger that wants to supplant by killing. The accusation of murder should not be softened here. The malice that can potentially arise within the human heart directs itself at times against the most unlikely victims. In light of his condemnation of the unjust rich in 5:6, "You have condemned and murdered innocent men who were not opposing you," James's charge of murder in 4:2 should be taken seriously.

Coveting[28] is another dimension of the conflicts here. Whereas envy is willing to destroy in order to gain what belongs to another, coveting is willing to steal what is not ones' own. Coveting is willingness to turn an earthly object of human desire into something of ultimate concern. This idolatry becomes a particularly heinous sin in its fixation upon the property or relationship that belongs to another. Of course, consumer advertising banks heavily on the power of covetousness in the modern world: "What does he have that I don't?" is the quintessential question of the propagandistic pseudoworld of much that passes for "sales technique." Although covetousness does not attain the destructiveness of envy, it nevertheless is a dangerous step along the road of sin.

The terrifying linkage of evil desires and their deeds could have been avoided by some with an approach that is quite simple: prayer. Prayer that is consistent with true faith will not make selfish requests. Desire-filled, envious believers do not make requests of God (cf. Phil 4:6) but instead are driven by their self-sufficiency and shame, self-sufficiency in that they do not really trust in God for his provision (cf. the doubter of 1:6) and shame in that they do not correct themselves once they become aware of how bad their attitudes really are. Only God can bestow the good gifts they need and should truly desire (cf. 1:17); but they will not ask him (cf. 1:5 the command to ask for the gift of wisdom). In this refusal to humble themselves in prayer, they only show how lacking they are in the most basic traits of Christian wisdom and how driven they are

---

[28] ζηλόω: "envy," "be full of jealousy" (although there can be a good sense of the word as in "zeal"); cf. Gen 26:14; 30:1; Acts 7:9; 17:5; 1 Cor 13:4; *2 Clem* 4.3.

by worldly wisdom (3:15). Instead of asking God, they become so insistent with one another that they quarrel and fight, trying to extract what they envy from the other.

(3) The Enmity of Friendship with the World (4:3–5)

³When you ask, you do not receive, because you ask with wrong motives, that you may spend what you get on your pleasures.
⁴You adulterous people, don't you know that friendship with the world is hatred toward God? Anyone who chooses to be a friend of the world becomes an enemy of God. ⁵Or do you think Scripture says without reason that the spirit he caused to live in us envies intensely?

4:3 The negative progression continues. As an afterthought, prayers are directed to God (lit. "you ask and you do not receive"), but not from a heart that is cleaving to him who is our greatest gift (lit. "because you ask wrongly"). Such prayers cannot lessen frustrated evil desire. No "spiritual benefit" is found under such psychological conditions from prayer. The imperative of prayer (1:5), of asking God for his provision, requires the prior knowledge of our true need. But the kind of asking practiced by some of James's addressees is futile because it asks only on selfish and envious terms (lit. "in order that you may spend/squander in your pleasures"). As such, prayer becomes evil because of what is prayed for and why. Such prayers from the tongue, that is, the "world of evil" (3:6) within the body, are entirely rejected by the one to whom they are addressed.

The evil motives from which some have dared to shape their requests have their source, again, in evil desire, that is, their "pleasures" (v. 1). In such prayers God is regarded as a mere dispensary of instruments of vice. The language of monetary exchange is brought in by James. God does not answer their prayers not only because they are evil but also because they would just spend[29] his generosity on themselves. They would, as it were, simply "cash in" whatever they could exchange his gifts with for their idea of "gain." This sort of religiosity represents the worst of pagan attitudes about deity. Indeed, such a heathen approach to God is at the heart of

---

[29] δαπανάω: "spend," here in a wasteful way; cf. Luke 15:14.

"friendship with the world" mentioned in the next verse.

4:4 Very abruptly and just as harshly as his previous denunciation "fools!" (2:20), James, in classical diatribal fashion accosted
his addressees with the charge "adulterers!" The gender of the plural noun is actually feminine, hence *adulteresses*.[30] Following the
context, this charge harkens back to a standard image of covenant
relationship between God and his people from the Old Testament.
Israel was the wife of the Lord (cf. Isa 54:4–8), and he considered
her idolatries as adulteries (cf. Jer 31:21; Hos 3:1; Ezek 23:45).
Thus, spiritual adultery is synonymous with being an "enemy"[31] of
God. Instead of being faithfully wedded, James's hearers had, by
their evil ways, turned their back on God and were having an
"affair" with the world. This dangerous condition caused them to
be opposed to God and his purposes for them. What the NIV translated "hatred," evidently as a preferred antonym to "friendship,"[32]
is literally "enmity." Didn't James's audience know this? The rhetoric of this passage, again diatribal, indicates such knowledge, for
James could presuppose their full awareness of the truth about God
and themselves regarding this matter of infidelity. The terrible mis-
direction of their friendship, which should have been with God
(2:23), proves again how self-deceived they were. The status of
unbelievers is enmity toward God and friendship with the world,
and this worldly friendship is something Christians can flirt with
(cf. Matt 6:24; 2 Tim 3:4; 1 John 2:15). James was not saying con-
clusively that his addressees were completely the "friends of the
world" rather than "friends of God." Rather, they were "adulteresses," unfaithful lovers. James was speaking generally, but his
hearers were dangerously close to this negative condition, not one
of familiarity with the world or active participation in it but rather a
personal investment in it and chief concern placed in its ways of

---

[30] For a discussion of the feminine form of the noun, cf. J. J. Schmitt, "You Adulteresses! The Image in James 4:4," *NovT* 28 (1986): 327–37.

[31] ἐχθρός: "the (personal) enemy," where God or Christ is the object of enmity:
Ps 109:1; Matt 22:44; Mark 12:36; Luke 20:43; Acts 2:35; Heb 1:13; 10:13; *1 Clem.*
36:5.

[32] φιλία: "friendship," "love," as throughout the LXX; cf. Josephus *Ant.* 12.414;
Sir 27.18; Philo *Fug.* 58; *Herm. Man.* 10,1,4.

life that do not follow the standards established by God for his people.

4:5 This next verse is notoriously difficult to translate, although there are clues throughout James's letter that will help. Although the commentators have offered numerous "solutions" to the variety of ways the passage can be punctuated and translated, the simplest and most natural reading follows.

As in the previous verse, James presented his hearers with a rhetorical question to penetrate into what they were thinking—misguided as it was! But of course their thinking was misguided because they had allowed their desires for God and their desires for the idols of the world to wrap them up in a total conflict of desire and interpersonal relations. Instead of appreciating the power of the tongue and God's requirement to bridle it, they had allowed their tongues to spew forth both blessing and cursing (3:10). Instead of pursuing the wisdom from above that counsels humility and peace, they had allowed the "wisdom" from below to dominate their aspirations (vv. 15–17). This dichotomous movement of the will back and forth between different worlds of desire and deed was what James had in mind.[33] Just how much James was influenced by rabbinic thinking on the "two inclinations" is in some dispute. If James were so influenced, then behind all of this focus on desire is the belief that the will must exert itself toward good desires or evil desires and that the righteous life under the Torah, the Old Testament law, is a matter of training oneself to choose the good. But what of this reference to "the spirit he caused to live in us" (lit. "the spirit that lives in us")?

There is really no pneumatology, that is, doctrine of the Holy Spirit, in the Epistle of James. His specific doctrinal and practical

---

[33] The literature covering many different presuppositions is vast; e.g., J. A. Findlay, "James IV. 5,6," *ExpTim* (1926): 381–82; J. Jeremias, "Jak 4:5: epipothei," *ZNW* 50 (1959): 137–38; L. T. Johnson, "James 3:13–4:10 and the Topos PERI PHTHONOU," *NovT* 25 (1983): 327–47; S. Laws, "Does Scripture Speak in Vain? A Reconsideration of James IV.5," *NTS* 20 (1973–74): 24–38; H. von Lips, *Wiesheitliche Traditionen im Neuen Testament* (Neukirchen: Neukirchener-Verlag, 1990), 427–35; J. Michl, "Der Spruch Jakobusbrief 4.5," *Neutestamentliche Aufsätze: Festschrift für J. Schmid*, ed. J. Blinzler et. al. (Regensburg: Verlag Friedrich Pustet, 1963), 167–74.

concerns evidently did not warrant such a discussion. So the verse
is probably not concerned with God either desiring his Holy Spirit
to indwell believers or what Paul called grieving the Holy Spirit
(Eph 4:30). A second interpretive option understands the Holy
Spirit as desiring believers. But both these options, while not contrary to scriptural truth at all, are not likely interpretations. The
more likely reading is based upon God as Creator and as lawgiver
and as the one who is giving new life to his dying creation.
Humans are his perishing creatures. The spirit of life that transformed the newly formed body of the first man into a "living
being" (Gen 2:7) is likely what is meant here. God is the giver of
the spirit of life; it belongs to him. Moreover, the human spirit is
not merely the vitality of the body (cf. 2:26) but also that which
communes with God on the one hand or adulterates itself with idols
on the other (cf. 1 Cor 6:17). The most natural understanding of
"spirit" then is the human spirit, which gives us life and makes us
spiritual beings.

Another important clue for understanding James's intention here
is what is meant by the phrase, "Or do you think the Scripture says
without reason . . . ?" As with other passages in which James
referred to the thinking or speaking of his readers (1:26; 2:14,18–
19; 3:1), he stood to correct them. He did this to intensify the point
he was trying to make: the spirit vivifying our natural selves tends
toward intense envying (one can translate "the spirit . . . longs jeal-
ously"). By saying this, did James accuse God of causing human
sin? No, that is our own spirit's doing. But in a world of real human
decisions and powerful temptations, without the guidance of heavenly wisdom the desires of the body will be guided by the hellish
"wisdom" (3:15) of earthly thinking. Which Scripture James was
referring to is unclear, unless he was appealing to the sense of
Scripture as a whole. It is doubtful that he was quoting missing biblical material. But the issue is difficult because of the known Scripture citation in the following verse.

Thus the sense of our text is something like this: the natural inclination of the spirit, especially when unguarded from the temptations
of the world, is to envy. Here is the simple truth about your spiritual
adultery. Without active faith, making prayerful request for wisdom
from God, you will be at the mercy of your most base desires.

Destructive envy, which is as much a relational as a personal sin, will dominate the scene even of the church and inflame all sorts of quarrels and conflicts among its members. In this particular case, then, the NIV has rendered one of the most valuable translations available. This way the interrogative that expects an affirmative answer can stand without adjustment. Yes, James's addressees had forgotten what their spirits tended toward without the "law that gives freedom" (2:12), that is, without the wisdom of God.

4. On Being a Friend of God (4:6–10)

(1) Grace for the Humble (4:6)

⁶But he gives us more grace. That is why Scripture says:

"**God opposes the proud
but gives grace to the humble.**"

4:6 In contrast to the spiritual adultery he necessarily attacked, James then cited Scripture to present the antidote. His addressees needed the gracious cure of God because he will oppose those who oppose him. This prescription was not the first word, however. Instead, he reminded his fellow believers that their spiritual sins could be overcome by God's grace.[34] The "more" grace here is like Paul's "where sin increased, grace increased all the more" (Rom 5:20). God wills the correction of his people through the continuing application of his favor. James conspicuously used the inclusive "us" here, hearkening back to the earlier expression, "We all stumble in many ways" (3:2). These many ways may even include deep descent into worldliness. But God remains generous with his gifts (cf. 1:5,17). Unlike envy with its rivalry toward all, God maintains a favorable disposition toward believing sinners.

Quoting Prov 3:34, James recalled for his audience that God is determined to resist the proud.[35] Those who wrap up their selfish-

---

[34] χάρις: "grace," "favor;" in this context, that which is eminently of God bestowed upon creatures; quoting Prov 3:34 as does 1 Pet 5:5; cf. *1 Clem* 30.2.

[35] ὑπερήφανος: "arrogant," "haughty," "proud," a very unfavorable expression, a vice; cf. Luke 1:51; Rom 1:30; 2 Tim 3:2; Josephus *Ant.* 4.224; Josephus *Bell.* 6.172; *T. Levi* 17.11; *Did.* 2.6; *1 Clem.* 30.2; 59.3; Ign *Eph.* 5.3.

ness and self-sufficiency in arrogance will receive the full measure of divine rejection. Such is the universal announcement throughout Scripture and the extrabiblical writings. Pride is frequently listed among the human vices and is closely associated with the sin of envy. Earlier in James's Letter the story of the proud rich and the envious church leaders and their followers (2:2–4) shows both God's opposition to the self-promoting rich and their self-serving welcomers as well as God's preference for the humble poor. Pride stirs up the desires of all those who have succumbed to various temptations of the heart. Pride leads to boasting. The sin of haughtiness not only tends to boast in what it has and in its own life but even boasts in what it does not have and takes credit for someone else's accomplishments. Arrogance totally obscures the faith that trusts in things unseen, hidden in God.

On the other hand, God shows favor to those who humble themselves. All of James's hearers were invited to join the ranks of the humble[36] who trust in God. The term here for the "humble" is rooted in the condition of lowliness and poverty. Biblically, God is particularly interested in reversing the hierarchies of status in the world. This is why God has "chosen those who are poor . . . to be rich in faith" (2:5). The close connection between the condition of lowliness and the virtue of poverty is reflected in the story of Saul wishing to make David his son-in-law in 1 Sam 18:23. David's simple response was, "I'm only a poor man and little known." But precisely this attitude, which he maintained in spite of gross sin throughout his life, made David a man after God's own heart, that is, favored, graced. David exemplifies what the proverb is intent to teach: God is always ready to accept those who accept him and to give them more grace. Should we sin that grace might increase? No!—but grace does more than meet the challenge of our sinful desires.

---

[36] ταπεινός: "lowly," "humble," as in those who participate in this condition virtuously; cf. Matt 11:29; *T. Gad* 5.3; *Barn.* 19.6; *Did.* 3.9. Of course the meaning is rooted in the reality of the position, lack of power and esteem of those "of low position," "poor," "lowly," "undistinguished," "of no account." The attitudinal and socioeconomic senses are joined together in grace because of God's compassion for and will to reverse status; cf. Isa 11:4; 14:32; Zeph 2:3; Luke 1:52; Rom 12:16; 2 Cor 7:6; Josephus *Bell.* 4. 365; *Barn.* 3.3.

(2) Exercising for Humility (4:7–10)

⁷Submit yourselves, then, to God. Resist the devil, and he will flee from you. ⁸Come near to God and he will come near to you. Wash your hands, you sinners, and purify your hearts, you double-minded. ⁹Grieve, mourn and wail. Change your laughter to mourning and your joy to gloom. ¹⁰Humble yourselves before the Lord, and he will lift you up.

4:7 These next four verses outline a format for spiritual exercise, in a sense a "how to" for repentance. Lapses in the corporate and personal Christian faith of James's audience now had redress in these steps of spiritual self-discipline. Without these stages of true conversion in repentance and reconciliation with God, conversion is stillborn; true humility will always be thwarted. Interestingly, James did not call for a reorientation to any human authorities, even to his own. His addressees were to convert in and through direct communion with God. The series of plural imperative verbs is stunning for its cumulative effect toward purifying faith. No doubt James understood repentance to be a lifelong practice for every believer. All fall into sins that undermine faith and relationship to God; all must return to him for the restoration of wholehearted commitment.

Repentance begins with the exhortation to submit[37] to God. The word *hypotassō*, "submit," is the opposite of the word *antitassomai*, "oppose," in the previous verse. Like the imperative to humble oneself before the Lord in v. 10, the call is to stop resisting God in anything. This call implies that James's addressees knew the will and truth of God and what it was to do it; similar is John's writing to his audience because they "do know [the truth]" (1 John 2:21). This beginning of restoration compares with the imperative to seek wisdom from God (1:4) rather than relying on one's own ability. Significantly, although there were conflicts within the community

---

[37] ὑποτάσσω: "subject oneself," "be subjected," or "subordinated," "obey," all in the absolute sense of adhering to the authority of another. It is in this context that the exhortations of the NT call its hearers to respond to earthly but God-ordained authorities, even the secular ones; here it is submission to God (cf. Ps 61:2; Rom 8:7; 1 Cor 15:28; Heb 12:9; *1 Clem* 20.1; Ign. *Eph.* 5.3).

to whom James was writing that needed immediate resolution, he appealed to them to turn to God first. His approach implies that in real submission to God there is contained the necessary mutual submission to reconcile with one another. James's was a different kind of "conflict management" than is common today. Understanding how corrupt religious practices can be because of our self-deceiving ways, leadership should never resolve conflict simply by praying for those with whom believers have conflict, even prayers with them. What James was saying was that conflicts with one another are symptomatic of conflict with God. All conflict resolution should begin by a renewed submission to God by the internal act of submission to him.

The next admonition of this verse calls the believer to put up active resistance[38] to the devil and his influence. Although humbling oneself does not cause the devil to flee, such submission to God is an important precondition for doing battle with the devil. But a defensive posture is all that is required to rout the evil one: resist him, and he will flee.[39] The word for "resist," *anthistēmi*, is different from the word for "oppose," *antitassomai*, in the previous verse that describes God's activity toward the proud. Against the devil[40] resistance is the effective attack for believers. This promise of the devil's flight bears upon our understanding of his nature and influence. The devil had been referred to only indirectly up to this point (cf. 2:19; 3:6). He is the embodiment of all that resists God and is at enmity with God (v. 4). James's discussion of the nature of temptation (1:13–15) and the Gospels' temptation narratives of Jesus (e.g., Matt 4:1–11) reveal absolute evil is never a positive

---

[38] ἀνθίστημι: "set oneself against," "oppose," "resist," "withstand," expresses well the believer's proper reaction to the devil and his influence; cf. 1 Pet 5:9; *Herm. Man.* 12,5,2.

[39] φεύγω: "flee," "seek safety in flight"; cf. *Herm. Man.* 12, 4, 7; 12, 5, 2, where evil is said to flee from the good that resists it.

[40] διάβολος: "the slanderer," "the devil," is a name constructed from a verbal idea. This is the LXX translation of הַשָּׂטָן (haśśāṭān) from Job 2:1; cf. 1 Chr 21:1; Zech 3:1–2; Matt 13:39; 25:41; Luke 4:2–3,6,13; 8:12; John 13:2; Eph 4:27; 6:11; 1 Tim 3:7; 2 Tim 2:26; Heb 2:14; 1 Pet 5:8; James is in contrast to early Christian tradition that regards the devil as a positive force, e.g., Ign. *Rom.* 5.3; *Herm. Man.* 5, 1, 3.

force. Evil cannot coerce the human will but is dependent upon it, much like a parasite. The devil is the active opponent of God and his people, but he resorts to his lying, deceptive capacities. Human creatures who believe these lies contribute their physical and mental strengths to his cause of influencing humanity for their destruction and his glory. The devil is not called the tempter within James, for temptation results from evil desire within the self (cf. 1:14). But the devil is close by the temptations and conflicts that humans cause. Nevertheless, if he is consciously resisted, in submission to God, the devil cannot fight back and must flee the attack that is our resistance to him. How do believers know that he is present? Wherever envy and selfish ambition are present in the conflicts and quarrels of the body of Christ, the devil is there.

4:8 The next step in James's spiritual exercise begins with a positive exhortation and concludes with a promise: draw near[41] to God and he will draw near to you. Nearness to God is a basic call and claim of biblical faith. The language of opposition has characterized action performed by God, us and, by implication, the devil. Now the language of approach conveys the sense of reconciling action performed by God and us. Each of the exhortations of this verse is a means of entering into intimate relation with God. A progression is detectable: from submitting to God, to a mutual drawing near, then "washing" the hands, and finally purifying of the heart. A second progression in the next verse explains what James meant by purifying the heart.

What James meant by drawing near to God is founded upon the approach of the priest to God in his temple for worship and sacrifice. Godly people approach God to perform their spiritual service. Believers come near to God by focusing attention on him in the devout uttering of his name in the knowledge of God and his promises to be with them. The believer goes to God in prayer ready to hear the will of God for service and made ready to go away from the encounter to perform that service. Part of this approach to God involves service in the presence of God, who draws near to the

---

[41] ἐγγίζω: "approach," "come near," "draw near" to God; cf. Exod 19:22; 34:30; Lev 10:3; Ps 148:14; Isa 29:13; Matt 15:8; Heb 7:19; *Jdt* 8.27 Philo *Leg. All.* 2.57; Philo *Deus. Imm.* 161.

believer. In this service the language of priestly activity is apparent, suggestive of the doctrine of the priesthood of all believers, interceding before God (cf. 1 Pet 2:5,9; also Rom 15:16; Rev 5:10; 20:6). This approach to God in service is done in view of God's approaching, his initiative in coming to his people whom he has chosen as his witnesses in the earth. The mutual drawing near of people and God is their unique privilege.

Sin is that which causes spiritual uncleanness, and it is particularly the appendages of the body that represent acts of sin. The members of the body, symbolically, are those parts that need to be "cleansed." Cleaning[42] the hands and purifying the heart both recall first the ritual purity required of worshipers and of priests at the temple and second the prophetic call to the purification of the heart. One might think that this cleansing must precede the approach to God, but such is not the case with the believers to whom James wrote. God, their Father, had already planted his Word in them, had already chosen them for the new birth (cf. 1:18). Cleansing themselves was allowing God to cleanse them. Jesus' statements upon washing of his disciples' feet, "Unless I wash you, you have no part with me" (John 13:8) and then later, "You are already clean because of the word I have spoken to you" (15:3; cf. Isa 1:16), combine the themes of washing and cleansing by the Word in a similar way. Paul's declaration that the Roman Christians should now devote the members of their bodies to doing righteousness (Rom 6:13) points to the consciousness that sins are deeds committed through the body. Now believers are to dedicate afresh their hands (and the other parts of their bodies) to the purity of true religion (1:27). They are to be aiding sinners in repentance from sin (5:20), not in committing it themselves. How could they do this restorative work if their hands were constantly acting out sin?

---

[42] καθαρίζω: "cleanse," "purify" from sin, here in the active sense of cleansing a part of oneself; cf. Matt 23:26; *Herm. Sim.* 6, 5, 2; *Herm. Vis.* 3, 9, 8. For the passive or middle sense of being cleansed by, e.g., the Spirit or the Word or of the whole self; cf. Lev 16:30; Pss 18:14; 50:4; Acts 15:9; 2 Cor 7:1; Eph 5:26; Titus 2:14; Heb 9:14 (vv. 22f. are a special case where the priestly and spiritual frames of reference merge); 10:2; *Sir* 23.10; 38.10; Josephus *Ant.* 12.286; *T. Reub.* 4.8; *Herm. Man.* 9.4, 7; 10, 3, 4; 12, 6, 5; *Herm. Sim.* 7.2; *Herm. Vis.* 2, 3, 1; 3, 2, 2; 3, 8, 11; *1 Clem.* 60.2

Instead, believers should be offering up hands of praise to God, as Paul recommended to Timothy, "without anger or disputing" (1 Tim 2:9). The hand of God has blessed believers with good gifts; now they should be offering up good gifts of a purified life to God. Sinners they are, but they are accepted by God and called into a morally pure life in relation to him.

The hand and the heart, however, must move together in a purified relation of deeds and commitment before God. Morality that flows from sincere faith requires an inner life that has been purified[43] and thus corresponds with the character of God. The heart being the center of the self, of its feeling and willing, has purity as one of its chief virtues (cf. Matt 5:8; 1 Tim 1:5). God and the heart of the believer have come together in close relation, and the one should mirror the other. The God who freely gives wisdom to all who ask gives himself. None of God's gifts can be separated from God himself. The gift and the Giver are one and the same. Believers are to draw upon this heavenly wisdom that is itself "pure" (3:17) and use it to purify their hearts of "envy and selfish ambition" (v. 14). This purification is the sole antidote for their double-mindedness, witnessed in all its partiality and contradiction to this wisdom, to that which is "impartial and sincere."

Arrestingly, believing sinners are double-minded believers. No matter what particular sins believers are struggling with, they must find repentance in order to root out so much that actually resists God in their lives. Double-mindedness is sin and produces a life that cannot do the work of God (cf. 1:20). Attacking that which pollutes the heart will remove that which divides the mind. The means for this attack against the self that leads to gracious relation with God are laid out in the next verse.

4:9 The four imperatives that follow in this verse together call for a deep transformation of attitude toward God. Nothing short of an attack upon the inner self and its hypocritical attitude will do. The exhortation to attack one's own heart begins with the call to

---

[43] ἁγνίζω: "purify," drawing upon the rituals of OT practices of atonement; cf. Exod 19:10; 2 Chr 31:17–18. Later purification becomes a figurative expression for the work of God within the life of the believer; cf. 1 Pet 1:22; 1 John 3:3; *Barn.* 5.1; 8.1.

"grieve" its wretchedness.[44] Just as humans experience the devastation of war, the heart is "wretched" because of its rebelliousness
against God.[45] God uses trials to weed out rebelliousness from the
heart of the believer. In anticipation of the outcome, however, serious believers launch a spiritual war within themselves and wreak
the devastation upon their own rebellious heart. James's call was
not to put on an external show of remorse, which Jesus condemned
in connection with fasting (Matt 6:16; fasting is commended if its
harsh effects on the body are covered/disguised) but a true grieving
over one's own sorry state of a "faith" in contradiction to God and
his Word. The spiritual exercise found earlier in Jas 1:9–10 called
for the rich to humble themselves and the poor to glory in Christ in
view of the wrongness of trusting in riches. Now all the double-
minded, tossed and torn between rich and poor, are called to humble themselves. They must launch a harsh attack upon the evil
desires of the heart instead of waiting for the misery to come upon
the unjust rich on the day of judgment (5:1). When evil desire
within the believer's heart is acknowledged and attacked, then its
condition can be truly mourned.

The grief that results is expressed through active mourning[46]
over sin. This exhortation is an expression of self-humiliation or
the humbling of the self before the Lord. Several grounds for
mourning in the Old Testament shape the New Testament understanding. First, mourning over one's own sin usually occurs when
the Word of God has exposed the truth of transgression. Second,
the mourning by God's prophets and the teachers of the law over

---

[44] ταλαιπωρέω: "be wretched," thus expressing "lament," "complain"; an NT
hapax legomenon, although it is close to the misery yet to come upon the rich in 5:1;
cognates can be found in Rom 3:16; *1 Clem* 15.6. The verb conveys the sense of
torment and affliction; cf. Ps 16:9; Isa 33:1; Philo *Flacc.* 155; *Herm. Sim.* 6, 3, 1.

[45] Cf. Jer 4:13,20; 9:18; 10:20; 12:12; Hos 10:2; Mic 2:4; Joel 1:10; Zech 11:2-
3, where great destruction from war comes upon the people of God because of their
sin against him. They are reduced beyond mere humiliation to wretchedness, something that would have been avoided if they had repented from the heart.

[46] πενθέω: "be sad," "grieve," "mourn," in direct contrast to joy. The sorrow is
for the committing of sin and over the sins of others; cf. 2 Sam 19:2; 2 Chr 35:24;
Ezra 10:6; Neh 8:9; Isa 61:2; Matt 5:4; 9:15; Mark 16:10; Luke 6:25; 1 Cor 5:2; Rev
18:15,19; *1 Esdr* 8.69; 9.2; *T. Reub.* 1.10; *Barn.* 14.9; *Gos. Pet.* 7.27.

the people's sin, especially their rebellion against God, is a prophetic act of solidarity with God's people in their coming judgment. The act of mourning for others' sins is part of intercession
for them, that they might repent and be restored to the joyful service of God. Indeed, mourning is the precise opposite of joy. Third,
mourning is the response to great loss of property or life, sometimes as the punishment for sin. Whatever the basis, in the Old Testament mourning is always stimulated by the realization of the
destructiveness of sin; whether in relation to God or in relation to
others. Mourning is also more than an internal movement of the
heart. It is external as well. Indeed, there is a close relationship
between mourning and moaning. The depths of grief inflicted upon
the heart have bodily effects, and mourning is our description of
them. But like grieving, mourning is a cognitive process that reacts
against evil desire and sin. James did not stop here, however; he
exhorted his addressees to express their mourning bodily through
wailing.

The spiritual exercise is completed when they "wail"[47] through
inducement of tears. Externalizing grief through mourning now
takes on its full expression in production of sound in loud crying
and exclamation. If the same weeping should be done already by
the unjust rich who are to anticipate their own punishment (5:1),
double-minded believers here are to do so as if their destiny were a
wretched punishment. James did not say that it is; they were, after
all, his brothers. But their sin was so deeply rooted and so destructive that they needed to release the torment of the conscience in
repentance toward God. Weeping then is the full measure of the
expression of sorrow over human sin.

James thus clarified what he meant by the three imperatives,
lament, mourn, weep: they should transform their laughter[48] into
sorrowful weeping and their joy into gloom. Here is another example of the self-deception of James's addressees. What they believed

---

[47] κλαίω: "weep," "cry" over suffering, death, or sin; cf. 5:1; Mark 16:10; Luke
6:25; John 16:20; 1 Cor 7:30; Rev 18:11,15,19; *Gos. Pet.* 7.27.

[48] γέλως: "laughter"; cf. Amos 7:9; Mic 1:10; Jer 20:7; Lam 1:7; 3:14; Josephus
Ant. 4.276; 5.239; although a hapax legomenon in this noun form, its cognate verb
is found among the beatitudes of Luke.

about themselves was precisely opposite from the truth. Thus, what had caused them to laugh should actually have caused them to cry. What had caused them to rejoice should have brought them remorse. James's imperatives are quite reminiscent of Jesus' statements in Luke: "Blessed are you who weep now, for you will laugh. . . Woe to you who laugh now, for you will mourn and weep" (Luke 6:21,25).

Reversal of thinking and acting has been a characteristic call of James's letter, and this call for reversal is perhaps felt most keenly here. James's addressees were terribly mistaken about their state. Instead of enjoying well-being, they should know that they are like those the Lord described in Revelation: "You do not realize that you are wretched, pitiful, poor, blind and naked" (Rev 3:18). Instead of making jokes James's hearers should have been making war against the passions that were at war within them (cf. 4:1). The action pointed to here is to cast oneself into a gloomy[49] state of the soul, producing a feeling of shame within and therefore of self-loathing.

What an ironic presentation of joy harkening back to the beginning of the letter (1:3)! Like the other kind of "wisdom" (cf. 3:13–15), this is another kind of joy, an earthly, demonic joy, the delight in wielding the power of wealth and winning battles of personal honor and favor. Indeed, because there were many frustrated losers from these battles among James's addressees, they were fighting and quarreling (v. 1). Such persons barely comprehended the joy in the face of the trials of faith. They would gain such comprehension as they abased themselves before the Lord in whose presence they lived. It would not do to soften or reinterpret the admonition to mourn and to be dejected. These plainly are exercises for repentance, which is threatened by self-sufficiency and self-deception.

4:10 We come to James's summation of the spiritual exercise he commended: through self-abasement God elevates the believer. James's admonition to practice a form of spiritual catharsis delineated in the previous three verses is what he meant by "humbling" the self. This humbling is the same word used in 1:9. There the per-

---

[49] κατήφεια: "gloominess," "dejection"; another hapax legomenon for the NT; cf. Philo *Spec. Leg.* 3.193; Josephus *Ant.* 13.406; 19.260.

son of humble circumstances should exult in the Lord, and here in 4:6 the Lord shows favor to those who humble themselves (cf. 1 Pet 5:6). Thus, the ones to whom James directed his message at this point were not those whose socioeconomic condition was lowly, nor yet those who would be brought low by the Lord's judgment (cf. Isa 2:11; 10:33; 13:11; Ezek 17:24; 21:31; Hos 5:5; 7:10; 14:9). Instead, they were believers who should humble themselves. The implication here is: humble yourselves now rather than fall into the Lord's humbling of the proud.

Here James's call is to abase oneself "before[50] the Lord." His earlier call was to "humbly accept the word planted in you, which can save you" (1:21). The believers of James's audience were to live their lives in response not primarily to God's words but to the presence of the Lord in their midst. These believers to whom James wrote had believed the words of the prophets and the apostles, but they had not believed in the God who provides for them and who should receive their voluntary trust. Humbling the self then is not at all a matter of convincing fellow believers of one's own sincerity or contrition. It is only a matter of relating whole-heartedly to God in recognition of his total claim upon one's life.

Unacknowledged seeking for prominence and rivalry among believers is oriented to a different kind of glory than that which belongs to God and the people he blesses. Jesus' words have a close parallel: "Whoever exalts himself will be humbled, and whoever humbles himself will be exalted" (Matt 23:12).[51] The exaltation that is promised to and encouraged of the believing poor (cf. 1:9) can also be the joy of formerly double-minded believers who have humbled themselves. If they will but follow this simple course of action, believers in every circumstance of life will find themselves to have a friendship with God (cf. 2:23; 4:4).

---

[50] ἐνώπιον: "before," in this form a preposition of relation and thus implying an action that unites two parties, either for evil or for good.

[51] Cf. Esth 1:1; 1 Sam 2:7; Job 5:11; Ezek 17:24; 21:31; Matt 18:4; Luke 1:52; 18:14.

V. THE WAY OF THE BOASTFUL (4:11–5:6)
1. Ill-speaking as Law-judging (4:11)
2. God's Singular Ability (4:12)
3. When Business Is a Spiritual Liability (4:13–17)
(1) The Irony of Boasting (4:13–14)
(2) The Norm of Human Activities (4:15)
(2) The Sinfulness of Presumption (4:16–17)
4. Judgments against the Rich (5:1–6)
(1) The Misery of Hoarding (5:1–3)
(2) The Misery of Wasting (5:4–5)
(3) The Misery of Innocent Blood (5:6)

V. THE WAY OF THE BOASTFUL (4:11–5:6)

This part of James's letter presents the great sin of boasting as the height of self-deception and a great evil. Self-congratulation is condemned just as ill-speaking, judging others, presumption, prayerlessness, and indifference to what is right and to the judgment of God. Boasting and wealth go hand in hand throughout this section and unite its various segments. Just when the reader might have been ready for an exposition of the meaning of the Lord's exaltation of the humble believer, James launched into his final attack on self-exaltation and indifference to mercy as that which nourishes evil within the church and the lives of needy people. The last part of this section (5:1–6) shows the importance of the trajectory of James's thought: the final and justified judgment of the wicked. James was determined to demonstrate the evil of those who what ought to be done but sinfully fail to do it (4:17). As before (1:7,11; 2:3,6; 3:14; 4:3), the rich who live in total disregard of God's standard of mercy and the many believers who envy them are guilty of knowing God's will but not doing it.

1. Ill-speaking as Law-judging (4:11)

[11]Brothers, do not slander one another. Anyone who speaks against his brother or judges him speaks against the law and judges it. When you judge the law, you are not keeping it, but sitting in judgment on it.

4:11 James made a shift here from calling his readers "adulterous people" to "brothers." They were, of course, both; but if they would repent of their spiritual "adulteries," which had so deeply concerned James, they could now hear a basic principle: "Do not slander,[1] defame, or otherwise speak against one another. The verb *katalaleō* occurs three times in this verse, although it is translated "slander" once and "speak against" the other times. Slander was considered a vice in the ancient world, and by interjecting it here, James pronounced a judgment on their behavior that perhaps they had not expected. Some readers had exchanged the rulership of God and his wisdom for the rulership of their appetites (vv. 3–4) while maintaining that they were living in accord with the faith, so slander could be expected. Evil speaking is a part of several lists of vices in the New Testament (e.g., Rom 1:30; 2 Cor 12:20; 1 Pet 2:1; 2:12; 3:16). How is it that brothers could slander each other? The command against slander becomes an exposé of an evil that is already a part of the very mixed behavior of these Christians.

James continued with an explanation of the evil reality hidden within acts of slander. "Brother" is repeated in the elucidation of this act of unlove. Behind the slander—behind the back of the person being slandered—is an act of condemnation. Instead of the divine measure of judgment in the word of God, the slanderer establishes his or her own measure and finds a brother lacking, worthy of rejection. Judging makes a presumptive statement about the destiny of persons or their works as a whole that really only God can make. Judging is an act that only the all-seeing, all-knowing God can perform. Only God, who knows the secrets of the heart, can judge that heart. Only God, who sees what is done in

---

[1] καταλαλέω: "speak against," "speak evil of," "defame," "slander"; cf. Pss 77:19; 100:5; 1 Pet 2:12; Philo *Leg. All.* 2.66f. (commenting on Num 12:8) and 2.78 (commenting on Num 21:7); *T. Iss.* 3.4; *T. Gad* 5.4; *Herm. Man.* 2.2; *1 Clem.* 35.8.

secret, can judge these things long before they come to light. Finally God will bring them to light without the aid of any creature, and then he will judge justly. Because of ignorance and their own many sins, persons are absolutely incompetent to judge. Indeed, James here reinforced what is clear everywhere in Scripture—that the authority to judge has not been given to persons. People have, rather, the authority to preach the gospel and to announce the forgiveness of sins and indeed to forgive sins that have been committed against them personally. But people do not have a right to judge those who have sinned, making an open claim to know God's final judgment about them.[2]

There is more to slandering a person than judging them, but James focused on this connection in order to reveal another one: in slandering another, believers slander the law of God; when believers judge another, they judge God's law. James worked out a careful logic here. Believers should accept the law of God, but this law requires them to exercise mercy toward others since they have received and are putting their hopes on the mercy of God (cf. 2:13). Slander, then, offends not only the brother and constitutes judgment against him but also offends the law and constitutes judgment against it. In both cases the slanderers have placed themselves in a superior position. They are putting themselves in the place of God, whose mercy they themselves require. James showed how the little digs of the tongue turn out to be far more weighty than the believer naturally supposes (cf. 3:5–6). Those who have the problem of saying they believe but act in contradictory ways also end up undermining even the religious effectiveness of their speech. If the law is God's chosen instrument of judgment, then usurping this role is holding oneself in rival judgment with God's judgment.

In order to reinforce this last point, James contrasted the one who judges the law with one who does the law. The last clause is literally, "You are not doers of the law but judges." This reference recalls the earlier dictum about being (lit.) "doers of the Word" and

---

[2] Of course, the church must humbly but firmly discipline its members for gross sin and false teaching. But this is not the issue here There must be a humility about judgment in order for there to be a firmness in discipline.

not merely "hearers" (1:22–23). The insight that believers can become judges of the law hearkens back to 2:8–12. They should "speak and act as those who are going to be judged by the law that gives freedom" (2:12) through mercy and not place themselves above the law by placing themselves above others through their sin of slander. Just as they offend the whole law when they offend the royal law of neighbor love (2:8), they become judges of the whole law through a single act of judgment. This position of judge is not theirs or any others' as shown in the next verse.

2. God's Singular Ability (4:12)

¹²There is only one Lawgiver and Judge, the one who is able to save and destroy. But you—who are you to judge your neighbor?

4:12 James pointed out to his audience that God alone is the lawgiver,[3] echoing the earlier affirmation that there is but one God (2:19; cf. also Jesus' declaration that "there is only One who is good" in Matt 19:17). Only he who gave the law is qualified to judge based upon the law, for this law of God is the instrument of God's will by which some will be saved[4] and some will be destroyed.[5] Earlier (1:21) James had ascribed this saving capacity to the Word of God. God alone possesses the right to save and destroy (cf. Matt 12:4; and also 8:25; 16:25; Luke 6:9; 19:10). God's prerogative of judgment, whether to grant life or to condemn, is why judging is prohibited for believers. Biblical judgment is eternal judgment and should not be confused with human judgments of a proximate or penultimate nature. Divine judgment affects the eternal destiny of those who are judged. The destiny of

---

[3] νομοθέτης: "lawgiver," an NT hapax legomenon; in the LXX the noun is used only in reference to God and then only once (Ps 9:21); the verb is more common and also is used exclusively for God's actions (Exod 24:12; Pss 24:8; 26:11; 83:7; 119:33,102,104); but cf. Josephus *Ant.* 1.95; see also Heb 7:11; 8:6.

[4] Cf. Deut 33:29; Judg 2:16; 3:9; 6:14; 1 Sam 4:3; Pss 3:8; 7:11; 16:7; 71:13; Isa 19:20; 33:2; 60:16; Jer 15:20; 26:27; Dan 6:21; Mic 6:9; Zeph 3:17; *Sir* 2.11.

[5] His destructive work is applied even against his people Israel; cf. Exod 19:24; Lev 17:10; 20:3; 26:41; Num 14:12; Deut 2:12; Josh 24:10; Pss 5:7; 145:4; Isa 1:25; 13:11; Jer 25:10; Ezek 25:7; 29:8; *Wis* 18.5.

the soul, its future life or destruction,[6] is dependent entirely upon the mode of the divine disposition toward the sinner in mercy or wrath.

How could any human creature then exercise such judgment? God's judgment is not moral judgment of the conscience but the final judgment of the obedient and disobedient, the merciful and the unmerciful. Like the act of creation by the one God, only God can make a judgment by which he eternally saves or destroys the human creature. Had they not realized that in their judging they were presuming to play God? Judging one's brother in Christ or one's neighbor can only be questionable in the most negative sense. The believer has no part in the divine determination relative to the destiny of creatures. As Paul wrote: "Who are you, O man, to talk back to God?" (Rom 9:20) or "Who are you to judge someone else's servant?" (Rom 14:4). Indeed, as in Romans, the warning in James is probably not about seeking revenge but not judging those to whom God will grant salvation. Paul continued in the same verse: "To his own master he stands or falls. And he will stand, for the Lord is able to make him stand." This parallel is extremely important for understanding the context of this prohibition.

Because self-deceived Christians are so prone to sinful rivalries and conflict, they must realize that such inevitably leads to a judgmental disposition. Those who are judging are often indifferent to the abysmal condition of their own faith. Like their boasting and bragging (v. 16), these believers have set themselves up as "judges with evil thoughts" (2:4), whose speech has become filled with language no better than cursing (3:10). Is it any wonder that James warned them against presuming to be teachers (3:1) when they had already presumed to usurp God's role as judge? The juxtaposition of this section, which warns against the presumption and pride of

---

[6] ἀπόλλυμι: "ruin," "destroy," esp. "kill," "put to death." Unlike the reflexive sense of 1:11, God is here the actor behind the verb, and thus it refers to eternal destruction; cf. Matt 10:28; Mark 1:24; Luke 4:34; Rom 14:15; *Sir* 10.3; *1 Macc* 2.37; Josephus *C Ap.* 1.122; *Herm. Sim.* 9.26.3–4,7; *Barn.* 20.1. The idea of annihilationism, that the destruction of the sinner is a once-for-all moment of passage into nonexistence, is foreign to the Bible; regrettably, the unrepentant sinner must endure the wrath of God unremittingly in the resurrected body in hell.

setting oneself up as a judge, and the previous section, which exhorts the believer to humility, could not be more poignant.

3. When Business Is a Spiritual Liability (4:13–17)

(1) The Irony of Boasting (4:13–14)

[13]Now listen, you who say, "Today or tomorrow we will go to this or that city, spend a year there, carry on business and make money." [14]Why, you do not even know what will happen tomorrow. What is your life? You are a mist that appears for a little while and then vanishes.

4:13 James continued his attack against presumption by focusing on the successful businessmen of his day. As in the address to the rich in 5:1, James exclaimed (lit.): "Come now!" In this case, according to the capacity of speech to reveal the disposition of the heart (cf. 2:3,14,16; 3:9,14), James could be understood in this way: "Think about what you are saying." His addressees should take note of all of their statements about the future of their money-making ambitions. James's hypothetical example hangs on the stereotypical attitudes of the overconfident business dealer. To express this James used a series of future indicative verbs: "We will go to this or that city, spend a year there, carry on business[7] and make money."[8] They were, of course, oblivious to the presumptiveness of predicting their own future. Instead, they were caught up in their "winning" formula: the timing, the journey to a financial center, the securing of a temporary residence there, the possession of sufficient time to do business, and the expectation to turn a profit. But the divine will had been left out of this formula entirely, just as it was left out of the compulsion to judge others in the previous verse. Time and space belong only to God, and thus all the features necessary for human action are dependent upon him. In this case James's deluded addressees thought and spoke as though the whole busi-

---

[7] ἐμπορεύομαι: "carry on business"; cf. Ezek 27:13; interestingly, in 2 Pet 2:3 this verb indicates the exploitation of believers under the influence of false teachers.

[8] κερδαίνω: "gain," here "make a profit"; cf. Matt 16:26; 25:16–17,20,22; Luke 9:25; 2 Clem 6.2.

ness enterprise required only self-assuredness for control of circumstances and the achievement of the desired ends.

4:14 James struck at this presumption by questioning their view of time and human life within it. Having spoken as though they had control over their own destinies and knew the outcomes of a year of days, James reminded them of their ignorance even of tomorrow. The irony of boasting believers is dramatic here. They did not know anything about their future experience. This boast served for James as another example of self-deception to be replaced by knowledge according to God's standards (cf. 1:2–3,6–7,13–14,16,19,26; 3:1,14; 4:4–5). Their ignorance, of course, was rooted not only in their immature faith but in their very nature as human creatures.

James moved to his powerful metaphor for the fragility and shortness of life.[9] "What is your life?" he asked and then answered, "You are a mist."[10] The metaphor of mist is quantitative rather than qualitative. Mists do not last long in Palestine. Their form is transitory. They appear with the dew and quickly dissipate. But this evaporation is a fitting way to refer to the ephemeral attribute of human life that James has already observed in 1:10–11 in the case of the rich. No one knows the times of his or her own life. Without trust in God, these believers become nearly indistinguishable from the wicked, who take no account of God. These basic truths must be rehearsed. Just as the truth of God and his sole lordship are necessary correctives to human autonomy, so also is this truth about the transitory nature of humans.[11]

(2) The Norm of Human Activities (4:15)

15Instead, you ought to say, "If it is the Lord's will, we will live and do this or that."

4:15 In view of what James's hearers had been reminded of,

---

[9] Cf. Ps 38:6; Prov 27:1; *Sir* 11.18.

[10] ἀτμίς: "mist," "vapor"; typically of what passes away; cf. Eccl 1:2; Acts 2:19. Evildoers, according to the Apocrypha, are like mists or smoke that will quickly pass away; cf. *1 Enoch* 97.8–0; *4 Ezra* 7:61; *1 Clem.* 17.6, where mist is typical of nothingness.

[11] Cf. Job 7:7; Pss 39:5; 102:3; 144:4; Isa 2:22.

they should have spoken without presumption of God's will. There is one norm by which the life of faith is lived out in the world: "If God wills."[12] This phrase is a common New Testament expression and is the expression of trust in God for his ordering of every realm of human life.[13] Jesus came to do his Father's will; this he enjoined upon his disciples; and doing this will, even for those doing business, is enjoined by James. James clearly was reflecting one of the primary themes of his letter: trusting God evidenced in speech and action shaped by his will. Thus the second part of the conditional phrase (the so-called *conditio Jacobaea*) is also important: "If . . . [then], we will live and do this or that."

Does this statement also point to James's earlier warnings about being merely hearers and not doers of the Word? And does it recall that faith must express itself actively as contrasted with some kind of "faith alone" heresy?[14] The unity of the letter suggests that there

---

[12] θέλω: "wish," "will," here, of God's purpose and decision; cf. Acts 18:21; Rom 9:16; 1 Cor 4:15; 12:18; 15:38; Josephus *Ant.* 7. 373; *1 Clem.* 21.9; 27.5.

[13] Cf. Matt 7:21; 12:50; 18:14; 21:31; 26:42; Luke 22:42; John 4:34; 5:30; Rom 12:2; 1 Cor 1:1; Heb 10:36.

[14] Cf. the important essay by M. Hengel, "Der Jakobusbrief als antipaulinische Polemik," in *Tradition and Interpretation in the New Testament* (Festschrift for E. E. Ellis), G. F. Hawthorne with O. Betz, eds. (Grand Rapids: Eerdmans, 1987), 249–78. In this piece of "conjectural scholarship" (p. 252), Hengel amasses a wealth of observations to defend the thesis that James indirectly attacked Paul, or at least an extreme reading of Paul by some Gentile Christians. For his argument he focused on 4:13–16 and its context of the ways of "great businesspeople." He pointed out that the language of business from this passage conspicuously corresponds to some of the words Paul used for his missionary journeys. If the occasion for James's letter was the apprehension of Paul at Jerusalem as a result of his counsel to Paul, then this verbal connection is perhaps significant. Is there a connection between James's uncompromising polemic against the rich and the fact that wealthy believers sponsored Paul's missionary journeys and activities? I certainly cannot reproduce Hengel's arguments here. They are interesting and illuminating but remain conjecture at best. Just as Hengel recognizes that James concluded his letter with reconciling words, he offered, in view of Hengel's argument, an arrestingly reconciling word right at this point by calling the businesspeople to make their plans in reverent acknowledgment of and dependence on God's benevolence. See also Hengel's other important essay, "Jakobus der Herrenbruder-der erste 'Papst'?" in *Glaube und Eschatologie: Festschr. für Werner Georg Kümmel zum 80. Geburtstag,* E. Grässer u. Otto Merk, eds. (Tübingen: Mohr, 1985), 71–104.

is a connection, but the connection with James's polemic against the rich is more significant. The significance is surprising perhaps, for here, in this single verse, James supplied a reconciling word. If only the rich, the businessmen large and small, would trust their enterprises to the Lord! This would satisfy the requirement of faith: mature speech and action demonstrate the genuineness and humility of faith even in the plans of business. They should remember that if "every good and perfect gift" comes from God, then so does every good outcome of a human purpose.

This entire passage is one of the most important biblical sources for a Christian ethic of business. There is nothing evil or wrong per se about anything God has made and put at our disposal. But God is not at our disposal. Neither are his standards for faith. Nothing in a person's life lies outside of faith and the good deeds that must flow from faith (cf. v. 17). Life is lived, but only if God wills, just as assuredly as deeds are done only if God wills. Their actions had been based on the earlier stated problem: "You do not have, because you do not ask God" (v. 2). What kind of faith was theirs? They did not make their plans in a devout way, acknowledging God in all their plans and expectations. The question of an active versus a permissive will of God is not at issue here. No believer should test God by acting apart from the norm of faith. Indeed, if believers will say, "God willing," their prayers will result in their receiving from God (v. 3).

(3) The Sinfulness of Presumption (4:16–17)

16As it is, you boast and brag. All such boasting is evil. 17Anyone, then, who knows the good he ought to do and doesn't do it, sins.

4:16 Boasting has a place in the Christian life—if it is done in view of the work of God (cf. 1:9). But such is not the case with the believers James was confronting (cf. 2:13; 3:14). Instead of confessing their dependence on the will of God, their arrogance[15]

---

[15] ἀλαζονεία: "pretension," "arrogance," in word and deed, so here (lit.) "you boast in your in arrogance"; cf. *Wis* 5:8; *4 Macc* 1:26; 2.15; 8.19; *T. Jos.* 17.8; Philo *Virt.* 162ff.; Josephus *Ant.* 6.179; 1 14.111; *1 Clem.* 21.5; 13.1; 16.2; 35.5; *Herm. Man.* 6.2.5; *Did.* 5.1.

erupted and overflowed with bragging. More precisely, to brag here means to manifest the pretense of the self-creation and sole causation of one's own well-being. The condemnation of pretense is similar in 1 John 2:16 (cf. Job 28:8; Prov 21:24; Hab 2:5; Rom 1:30; 2 Tim 3:2) within the context of loving the world (cf. Jas 4:4) rather than God and taking pride in one's possessions. Extrabiblical literature is also replete with condemnations of this presumptive attitude. The relation between "friendship with the world" and pretense should not be missed here. After all, the worldly power of speech is all about boasting and its heart attitude of pretentiousness. This spiritual fact is extremely difficult to grasp for American believers who are so tempted to participate in the celebration of "the self-made man."

James wanted the believers to have absolutely nothing to do with boasting and arrogance. All self-referential statements of certainty about the future are wickedness. In such statements there is no willingness to yield to God's will; worst of all the temptation is to make pronouncements that claim the sure knowledge of God's will for the future to one's own benefit. Thus, James was quite strict. Not only did James prohibit boasting in possessions but persons must not even boast in their plans for the future. Such boasting stems from a prayerless, prideful, and pretentious way of life. James declared: What else is this but wickedness?

4:17 James summed up by a reference to a fundamental principle of faith. At first the verse may seem detached from what came immediately prior to it, but James has connected it (with "then" or "therefore"). The good that believers know they must do involves confessing dependence upon God's will in everything they do. Is there not a close relation here with Paul's principle "everything that does not come from faith is sin" (Rom 14:23)? That which is of faith is virtually synonymous with that which is the good because of the gift of God (cf. 1:17–18).

The problem of disconnecting what one does from what one knows is another expression of the double-mindedness and inactive faith so rife within James's audience (cf. 1:22–27; 2:14–26). Because they were believers and had heard the Word of God, they knew the good;[16] but because they had not received it with meekness and humility, they contradicted what they knew and committed sin. This principle was, in all likelihood, well known to James's hearers. But they probably had not expected it to be cited in this connection. The principle of doing only what one knows to be good begins with placing all of the intentions of the heart before God. Only this doing what is good can be whole-hearted trust in God.

4. Judgments against the Rich (5:1–6)

Of all the New Testament passages about the sins of the rich, Jas 5:1–6 stands out. One would have to go to the Old Testament prophets' condemnations for comparable judgments against the wealthy among the people of God (e.g., Hosea, Amos, Micah, Joel, Habakkuk, Zephaniah). How could Christians have fallen into such a state? But James already had shown how friendship with the world is a constant temptation for believers who do not resist the deeper temptation of envy. Envy creates its own worldview by which a person will justify any action in order to secure more wealth. The worldview created by envy will rationalize the evil consequences of any act in view of selfish interest. The picture here is horrific and cannot be regarded as merely a warning. Although James made no declaration about the hopelessness of the unjust rich, he offered no hope either. They were committed to their evil ways, and God had committed himself to oppose them.

(1) The Misery of Hoarding (5:1–3)

¹Now listen, you rich people, weep and wail because of the misery that is coming upon you. ²Your wealth has rotted, and moths have eaten your clothes. ³Your gold and silver are corroded. Their corrosion will testify against you and eat your flesh like fire. You have hoarded wealth in the last days.

---

[16] καλός: "morally good," "noble," "praiseworthy," "contributing to salvation," in the sense that here is the essential evidence of salvation; cf. Matt 5:16; 26:10; Mark 14:6; John 10:32f.; 1 Tim 5:10; 6:18; Titus 2:7; esp. Gal 6:9; Rom 7:18; 12:17.

5:1   James returned to the sins of the rich once more (cf. 1:10–
11; 2:3–6). As in 4:13, "Now listen" (or "Come now!") establishes
the sharp confrontational address James intended. At the outset this
verse declares the fact of the future condemnation of the wicked
rich. The verses that follow will lay out the crimes that stand
against them. James displayed rage against the rich because of their
outrageous acts against the poor. Only certain passages in the Gospels anticipate the kind of condemnations leveled here against the
rich (e.g., Matt 19:23–24; Mark 10:25; Luke 1:53; 6:24; 16:19–31;
21:1–4). What James said is much harsher than the classic warning
of 1 Tim 6:10 against the love of money.

The prophecy of 2 Tim 3:15 does warn of "terrible days" to
come in which people will fall into gross wickedness of every kind,
including the love of money, "having the form of godliness but
denying its power. Have nothing to do with them." This warning is
close to James, who addresses them now simply as "O rich ones"
(hoi plousioi) rather than "brothers." Whatever appearance these
people had that suggested Christian faith, their actions were so
worldly and so destructive that the truth about them could only produce righteous indignation. Like Paul and John, James was willing
to speak to believers as if they were not believers, for their actions
toward their brothers contradicted their own faith (cf. vv. 4–6). The
declaration of judgment is real. But what does this declaration
mean if James still regarded them as believers, though compromised? Were they in danger of missing salvation? No. But real
believers do not act in the ways listed below.

The call for them to "weep and wail"[17] uses the language of humbling oneself found in 4:9. Sinners who have heard the prophetic
word of judgment should mourn and weep over their sin now
instead of waiting for the judgment that will afflict them with greater
weeping. Then instead of self-induced sorrow, the sorrows of judgment will be inflicted upon them. The former weeping is performed
by the believer who lives in faithful relation to God. In spite of sin
this believer can hear the Word of God and respond positively.

---

[17] ὀλολύζω: "wail," "cry out" in joy or pain, a participle defining the kind of
weeping appropriate to their approaching end. Note this word's character of ono-
matopoeia; the verb is a hapax legomenon of the NT.

In this section grievous sins against poor laborers are recounted. In the economy of God, those oppressors who caused such abuse would be judged. Yet these oppressors were exhorted to weep, here also, prior to judgment. Is this a third type of weeping? Does this call to weep mean that the possibility of repentance is hidden within the declaration of impending judgment? It is difficult to say. Miseries (wretchedness, distress, trouble, much worse than the disregarded and ill-treated poor experience in this life) are coming for these unrepentant sinners. Do they claim to have faith in God? This prophetic word will prove that faith or lack of it. For those lacking faith that comes from humility toward God, this revelation of God's will includes the foretelling of their judgment.[18] If there is faith, there is yet time, though a very short time from James's perspective, for some to repent and do the works of true faith.

5:2 The truth about greed and selfish hoarding of wealth is presented in this verse. James earlier illustrated the perishability of wealth with the simile of the wildflower quickly scorched by the desert sun (1:10–11). Here James turned to the degrading influence wealth has for all who place their confidence in it rather than God. The wealth of these rich believers is vividly portrayed as having rotted[19] and their clothing as having become moth-eaten.[20] It was not so much that the treasures themselves were in this condition[21] but that the manner in which believers were holding them already evidenced decay. The one who has known God and experienced the eternal realities of the spiritual world can sense in the opulent treasures of this world the underlying corruption. In the world a characteristic value of treasures is their relative durability, but James warned his audience of the falsity of this notion. The end of each

---

[18] Noting the prophetic mode of James's address in this section, cf. P. J. Hartin, "Exegesis and Proclamation: 'Come now, you rich, weep and wail . . .' (James 5:1–6)," *JTSA* 84 (1993): 57–63.

[19] σήπω: "cause to rot," "decay," a perfect tense. Cf. Job 19:20; 33:21; Ps 37:6; *Sir* 14.19; of things that become degraded, e.g., a vine producing rotten fruit because it lies on the ground, cf. *Herm. Sim.* 2.3; also, Philo *Aet. Mund.* 125; Josephus *Ap.* 2.143; *Bell.* 6.164; *Diog.* 2.2, 4; *1 Clem.* 25.3.

[20] σητόβρωτος: "moth-eaten," another NT hapax legomenon; cf. Job 13:28.

[21] But see M. Mayordomo-Marin, "Jak 5,2.3a: Zukünftiges Gericht oder gegenwärtiger Zustand?" *ZNW* 83 (1992): 132–37.

life and the final judgment show that the person and the possessions are not durable. Trusting in wealth because it supposedly
"retains its value" is trusting in a charade. The rituals of amassing
wealth and curating precious objects are really a dance of death.
Trusting in wealth is then a damaging and degrading attitude.[22]
Speaking with the voice of a prophet, James proclaimed the nearness of judgment from the signs of corruption already in evidence.

The deceptiveness of riches is dangerous for the soul because it
will endanger so many others. Is there a connection between the
"fine clothes" of the rich in 2:2 and the moth-eaten clothes of this
verse? All of the wealthy believers need to take heed from this
verse and then to see how each of them have treated those who are
in their employ or any to whom they owe just wages (cf. 5:4). All
wealth is perishable; none of it will survive the judgment; when
wealth is the result of withholding wages, its perishability is a
warning of its hoarders' destruction. James had already seen the
connection and was warning rich believers in the harshest way.

5:3 In the judgment, gold and silver will become tarnished or
"corroded" (*katioō,* another perfect tense here vividly describing
the future as a present reality). Commonly used metals such as iron
or bronze corrode; and when they do, they are no longer useful, as
in the case of cooking utensils. James prophesied that gold and silver will lose their value as investments because what is impossible—their corrosion—will come to pass; God's judgment will
make it a reality.

Gold and silver would corrode precisely because the rich oppressors valued them for not corroding. God's judgment would physically empty them of value. God would use their most precious
investments against the wealthy. Rather than acting justly with their
wealth to secure the well-being of their laborers and their families,
they had invested it in "frozen" assets that would nevertheless burn
in the judgment to come. Is it possible that the phrase "testimony
against you"[23] could contain any hope of repentance and salvation?

---

[22] Cf. Matt 13:22; Mark 4:19; Luke 8:14; 12:21; 1 Tim 6:9.

[23] μαρτύριον: "that which serves as testimony," "proof," "testimony." Cf. Matt
8:4; 10:18; 24:14; Mark 1:44; 6:11; 13:9; Luke 5:14; 9:5; 21:13 for the way in which
the outcome of certain actions "speak against" someone because of God's relation to
them. Every sin is known by God even when hidden.

The rich who had been dragging believers into court (2:6) were the ones who would appear in the court of the Lord. The "corrosion" (*ios,* "rust," translated "poison" in 3:8 and Rom 3:13) on their hoarded gold and silver would be made to "testify" against the rich oppressors in James's version of a covenant lawsuit. The rust is personified. The rich had willfully refused to listen to the voice of justice calling for fair wages; now the rust was given a voice declaring their guilt.[24] Thus, instead of paying wages, the gold and silver would be paid to the rust. The hoarded wealth would help pay for the trial against them.[25] Again, there was hope for repentance because the judgment was not yet here; nevertheless, to borrow a metaphor from the testimony of John the Baptist, "The ax is already at the root of the trees . . ." (cf. Luke 3:9).

The personified rust is active in another way. Having ruined the hoarded gold and silver (perhaps even consuming the metals entirely as rust eventually does), the rust continues its destruction by turning upon the wealthy themselves in the day of judgment. The rust is transformed from a witness of guilt into an instrument of wrath. Having acquired a voice, the rust also acquires a mouth by which to "consume"[26] the bodies of the unjust rich.[27] In the same way that fire can be personified and said to "eat" what it burns up, the rust or poison will "eat" their flesh. In the natural world rust only degrades common metals. But God's judgment on the unjust rich consumes not only the wealth they trusted to buy security but also the rich themselves. The power of speech is great

---

[24] One imagines it "testifying" with the word, "I have ruined these metals that should have been paid to your workers." Notice how voices will be given to the voiceless in the day of judgment; indeed, these voices are already audible to the ears of the Lord and his faithful: the rust speaks, v. 3; the wages cry out; the harvesters cry out, v. 4.

[25] One can detect here how the early church could interpret the atonement of Christ as a "ransom" paid to deliver sinners from the devil and evil forces.

[26] ἐσθίω: "eat," here figuratively "consume," "devour"; cf. "fire, which is about to consume the adversaries" (Hb. 10:27; Isa 10:17; 26:11; 30:27). In the Greek the connection with fire personified is most ancient (cf. Homer *Iliad* 23, 182).

[27] This text becomes one of the most significant references for understanding hell by the early and medieval Christians. For an important study on how the believer was seen to overcome this threat, cf. C. W. Bynum, *The Resurrection of the Body in Western Christianity, 200–1336* (New York: Columbia University, 1995).

because it is always connected with activities that control the course of life, sometimes in hellish fashion (cf. 3:6,15). The misery of divine judgment is said to be brought about indirectly by a natural force—rust—radically intensified by God's power. Since these precious metals had been utilized in a way inappropriate to them, hoarding as a source of security rather than paid out in just wages or in alms, their "rust" would be conferred with extraordinary power to destroy as a metaphor for hell. If death cannot hold the dead who are to arise to blessedness, no vault can hold the money or the lives of those who have trusted in their wealth rather than God. At the resurrection such ones will break out and will be cast into the place of punishment.

As it turns out, this passage is essentially eschatological. There is a possible connection here with the rich fool of Luke 12:13–21 who "stores up things for himself but is not rich toward God" (v. 21). This one had imagined that his life was about securing his own well-being only and not creating a flourishing environment about him in which the well-being of others and the praise of God was evident. The Lukan parable concerns personal eschatology— this man's appointment with death (cf. Jas 1:11); it does not carry the same prophetic charge that James's passage does. Indeed, even the figurative use of storing up "treasures in heaven" (Matt 6:20) meant for Luke the performing of present godly actions in view of the eschatological reward of heaven. There was for James, perhaps, also the scandal of stored wealth in the end times. James charged, "You have hoarded[28] wealth in the last days," likely referring to the eschatological testimony of the rust against the wealthy who were quite literally hoarding wealth, something no believer in God should do. Wealth was then robbed of its usefulness in paying the wages of the laborers. The prophets of the Old Testament repeatedly denounced the wealthy in their selfishness and self-deceiving

---

[28] θησαυρίζω: "store up," "gather," "save," here in the quite literal sense; cf. Ps 38:7; Matt 6:19; 2 Cor 12:14. The figurative sense often applies to storing treasure in heaven rather than the literal storing of earthly wealth (cf. Matt 6:20; *Tob* 4:9; *Ps Sol* 9:5); and yet the figurative sense applies also to wrath (Prov 1:18; Rom 2:5; *Tob* 4:9) as well as to an activity of God for heaven and earth (2 Pet 3:7; *4 Macc* 4.3; Philo *Sacr. Abel.* 62; Philo *Deus. Imm.* 156).

belief in the security of riches.[29] In the New Testament the same indictment is transformed in view of God's readiness to bring an end to the present world system; thus these are "the last days."[30] The indictment of hoarding wealth has a reliable witness, the rust that turned to consume this wealth. Why should it not continue its consuming activity upon the guilty? They had hoarded wealth in the last days, and now they had been warned, for in the economy of God this wealth had contracted a corrosive infestation that would destroy both it and its holders.

(2) The Misery of the Innocent (5:4–6)

⁴Look! The wages you failed to pay the workmen who mowed your fields are crying out against you. The cries of the harvesters have reached the ears of the Lord Almighty. ⁵You have lived on earth in luxury and self-indulgence. You have fattened yourselves in the day of slaughter. ⁶You have condemned and murdered innocent men, who were not opposing you.

5:4 With the imperative "Look!" (cf. 3:4–5; 5:7,9,11), James directed the attention of the unjust rich to evidence against them here and now. If somehow the eschatological outlook of the previous verse was veiled, it is very apparent in the case of those who worked[31] for the wealthy and went unpaid. This economic oppression was particularly urgent because many of the field laborers of the ancient world were transients (as they are today) and often were in need of special compassion because of their foreign status.[32] The wages[33] that were due, however, never passed out of the vault of the wealthy. The biblical view of economic justice holds here: "Do not defraud your neighbor or rob him. Do not hold back the wages

---

[29] Cf. Isa 2:2; Jer 23:20; Ezek 38:16; Dan 2:28; Hos 3:5; Mic 4:1.

[30] Cf. John 6:39–44; 11:24; Act 2:17; 2 Tim 3:1; Heb 1:2; 1 Pet 1:5,20; 2 Pet 3:3; 1 John 2:18; Jude 18.

[31] ἐργάτης: "workman," "laborer," esp. in agriculture; cf. Matt 9:37; Luke 10:2; *Wis* 17:6; Philo *Agr.* 5.

[32] Cf. A. S. Geyser, "The Letter of James and the Social Condition of His Addressees," *Neot* 9 (1975): 25–33.

[33] μισθός: "pay," "wages"; also "reward" or "punishment." Cf. Matt 20:8; Luke 10:7; John 4:36; Acts 1:18; 2 Pet 2:15; *Wis* 10:17; *2 Clem.* 19.1; *Barn.* 1.5; 21.3.

of a hired man overnight" (Lev 19:13).[34] In this biblical view prof-
its and benefits to the property owners beyond their own basic livelihood were secondary to the necessary wages of persons who
labored for them. Instead of heeding the Old Testament call to "act
justly" (Mic 6:8), the wealthy had kept (*apostereō,* lit. "stolen")[35]
the wages that were due these workers. Holders of great wealth can
speak cavalierly about deferred payments, their "need" to wait for
another increment of interest, or alternative "compensations"; but
for those whose very survival depends on receiving their wages at
day's end, such financial plans are no solution.

Now, just as the personified rust on precious metals had a voice
and a say, the wages have a voice as well. The wages utter their cry
of accusation against the unjust rich. The laborers who had
mowed[36] the fields of grain for rich landowners had wages in the
vaults of the wealthy, but the first cry of complaint was by the
wages themselves. The field work had been done, but the work of
properly managing wages was not done. It is as if the wages had
begun crying:[37] "You are holding us against our will; we belong to
others!" The picture here is of precious goods that have been hidden away but which will join in the list of witnesses against the
unjust rich in the judgment. In a world of work, the wages were
disallowed from performing their "labor" of buying bread for the
needy laborers. In a world of the unjust rich, any believers among
them—indeed all of them—should hear the words of James that are
much like that of the prophet Malachi:

> "So I will come near to you for judgment. I will be quick to testify
> against sorcerers, adulterers and perjurers, against those who
> defraud [the same verb, *apostereō,* used by James] laborers of their
> wages, who oppress the widows and the fatherless, and deprive

---

[34] The import of Leviticus again makes itself felt in this whole section, and I am
indebted to the very fine work of Johnson, *The Letter of James,* 301–2.

[35] ἀποστερέω: "steal," "rob," "defraud," "withhold"; cf. Mark 10:19; 1 Cor 6:7–
8; 7:5; Neh 9:20; *2 Esdr* 19.20.

[36] ἀμάω: "mow"; used frequently in the LXX; cf. Josephus *Ant.* 4.231.

[37] To God, just as he had heard cries from his people in their times of captivity
and distress (cf. Exod 5:8; Num 11:2; Judg 3:9; 6:7; Pss 3:5; 21:3; Isa 19:20; Mic
3:4).

aliens of justice, but do not fear me," says the LORD Almighty. (Mal 3:5)[38]

That withholding wages is a sin is hardly astonishing, but that it is listed among the worst of those known to Israel and is now condemned so harshly in the New Testament may be surprising to economically comfortable Christians.

The cries increase—now the voices of the harvesters themselves are heard. The wages were crying out, so to speak, in frustration. Now the voices of agony were raised by those who had cut and gathered the grain during the long, hot day. This sound was the cry[39] that the Lord hears. Like that of Abel's blood (Gen 4:10) and of the oppressed Israelites in Egypt (Exod 2:23), it is a cry of distress and suffering. Perhaps the wealthy had not heard these cries, but the Lord had heard them. Or perhaps the rich had discounted their workers' cries, but to the Lord those cries touched his heart and moved him to action.

God had heard, that is, he knew all of this tragic situation, both the suffering and who had caused it. God, the Lord "Sabaoth"[40]—a title most reminiscent of Old Testament devotion, is best translated "Lord of the Armies." In the life of Israel, this address characterized God as the one who moves to deliver his people. Now this Lord and his forces will come to defend the oppressed among his people on the last day.[41]

In the modern world much wealth is amassed by profit from interest, as well as by finding ways to control the value of real property. There are clear benefits to a society from the investment of wealth that creates new wealth. But the rich must exercise personal frugality. They must further exercise the greatest of care, for this type of business creates two great problems. (1) Those who do business outside of the direct relations between proprietor and average worker lose their connection to the ethics of maintaining decent wages. (2) Those who do business largely based upon deferred pay-

---

[38] Cf. Exod 23:9–11; Lev 6:4; 19:35; Deut 24:10–16; *T. Job* 12.1–4.

[39] βοή: "cry," "shout"; cf. *2 Macc* 4:22; Josephus *Bell.* 4.306; 310; *Ant.* 8.339.

[40] Σαβαώθ: "Sabaoth," plural form of "army"; typically found in the expression "the Lord of Hosts"; cf. Isa 6:3; Rom 9:29; *1 Clem* 34.6.

[41] Cf. Jer 22:13; *1 Enoch* 47.1; 97.5.

ment lose the sense of urgency relative to the well-being of wage-earning people. Within the circle of the Christian community, a clear voice must constantly call the wealthy to greater responsibility for the well-being of the average laborer. The skills necessary to create wealth, powerful as they are, must be guided by Christian wisdom. Likewise, ministers who labor among all the people of God must maintain their independence from undue influence by any group in order to foster responsible relationships among all. The goal of long-term economic culture shaped by biblical principles is a community shaped by real colaboring in Christ.

5:5 James's third indictment was against the heartlessness of the rich. Their callousness was rooted in their self-centered pleasure and luxury at the expense of their laborers. Self-indulgence,[42] reveling in earthly pleasures, was universally condemned by all the sages of the ancient world. Its offensiveness here stems not only from the unseemliness of self-indulgence but more from the indifference to others' needs and sufferings that a life of pleasure always entails. Living luxuriously was regarded by the ancient moralists as a source of moral laxity and indecision in precisely those situations in which ethical firmness is required. All Christians are to resist revelry and to move out from a satisfied life to encounter the lives of those who barely survive so that they too might achieve a level of well-being.

All of this self-directedness, overindulgence of the appetites, and pleasure taking amounts to special preparations for destruction. These wealthy ones had fattened themselves (lit. their "hearts"; cf. 1:26; 3:14; 4:8; 5:8) for the slaughter. The concept that the judgment will be like a great slaughtering of animals is a frequent Old Testament apocalyptic image (Isa 34:2; 65:12; Jer 15:3; 19:6; 32:34; Zech 11:4). Indeed, the oppressive rich, like senseless sheep, will be slaughtered. Whether the sheep was slaughtered for a meal

---

[42] James used two synonyms here (note KJV, "Ye have lived in pleasure on the earth and been wanton") τρυφάω: "lead a life of luxury" or "self-indulgence," "revel," carouse," as hapax legomenon in the NT (cf. Neh 9:25; Isa 66:11; *Sir* 14.4; Josephus *Ant.* 4.167; 7.133; *T. Jos.* 9.2; *Herm. Sim.* 6.4.1f.; 6.5.3–5) and σπαταλάω: "live luxuriously," or "voluptuously," "in indulgence" (cf. Ezek 16:49; 1 Tim 5:6; *Sir* 21.15; *Barn.* 10.3).

or for sacrifice, the best was sought out and overfed in order to make the meal that much larger and richer or the sacrifice that much more pleasant to God. Thus the self-indulgence also had a utility, but not as the rich had imagined: it had served their own self-destruction. Instead of making sure that a hungry brother or sister was indeed "well fed" (2:16), the rich "fattened" themselves; soon they would find that their own bodies would "feed" the all-consuming wrath of "the day of slaughter."[43] Based on the unsightly dismemberment of human bodies common in warfare, this metaphor of butchery for the ancients suggested the preparation of meat for a great victory feast at the end of battle. The slaughter of the battle can then be regarded as a preliminary part of the celebration and, therefore, the "glory" of war—from the victor's perspective. In this case the enemy turned out to be the unjust rich, something already alluded to in James (cf. 2:6).

This section of James should send tremors through many American Christians, for the culture in which we live is fundamentally oriented toward leisure. Whether people say they live to "play" or that they "worship the game," all such living represents a massive investment of one's worldly possessions primarily for pleasure. Some may swoon, "Too much of a good thing is wonderful," but there are always real evils involved with such a self-indulgent attitude and this motivation for living. These selfish tendencies in every culture must be fiercely assaulted with the Word of God in order to expose their gross sinfulness and harm to others.

5:6 The question of the guilt of the unjust rich is decided by James in this verse, declaring the final ground for the punishment of the rich on the last day: they have "condemned and murdered innocent men." The laborers whose Christian character had restrained them from rebelliousness are innocent of any crime, certainly of any against the rich. But rather than being rewarded for their worthwhile labor they supplied to the rich, these day laborers had been made to suffer for applying their faith to their work. Such

---

[43] σφαγή: "slaughter," "bring to be slain," figuratively in the context of war, a massacre or bloodbath, which will characterize the Day of Judgment; Ps 43:23; Isa 53:7; Jer 12:3; Zech 11:4,7; Acts 8:32; Rom 8:36; Josephus *Ant.* 1.102; 7.39; *Barn.* 8.2; *1 Clem.* 16.7.

suffering is the basic reason God has elected the poor to be rich in his grace (cf. 2:5). God selects the poor and converts them to serve as a sign of his glory, nullifying what the world has taken for glory and wealth (cf. 1 Cor 1:28–29).

But these working poor are the very ones that the rich had condemned,[44] these poor, who as fellow believers should have been treated with honor and respect out of duty. Instead, the rich had acted like judges of their fellow believers (in spite of James's question, "Who are you to judge your neighbor?" in 4:12). The righteous poor had become like the servant thrown into prison by his unmerciful fellow servant in Jesus' parable. In that parable both servants are debtors, and the unmerciful one is shown the greater mercy (Matt 18:21–35). The first servant, who had borrowed a vastly greater sum of money (like the rich who posses nothing but have received an extraordinarily large "loan" from God) had lived a much more luxurious life than his poor fellow servant. His greater debt had been forgiven, but the mercy he received did not transform him into a merciful person. And so the words of the rich will be used against them, much as in Jesus' teaching against the proud: "For by your words you will be acquitted, and by your words you will be condemned" (Matt 12:37). And again: "If you had known what these words mean, 'I desire mercy, not sacrifice,' you would not have condemned the innocent" (Matt 12:7). So by their own condemning words the rich were voicing their own condemnation.

James declared, however, that these rich had not only condemned the righteous but had committed acts of murder.[45] If the earlier reference to breaking the law by the sin of adultery (2:11) was at first puzzling, it was fully substantiated by revealing the idolatry of their friendship with the world (4:4). Next to the rehearsal of the commandment against adultery was that of the commandment against murder—James forcefully alluded to this in 4:2, "You kill and covet, but you cannot have what you want." The

---

[44] καταδικάζω: "condemn," "pronounce guilty"; cf. Lam 3:36; Luke 6:37; Josephus *Bell.* 4.274; *Ant.* 7.271.

[45] φονεύω: "murder," "kill"; the word is used in the LXX in the commandment of Exod 20:15, "You shall not commit murder." Cf. Prov 1:32; Matt 5:21; 19:18; 23:31,35; *Barn.* 19.5; *Did.* 2.2; *1 Clem.* 57.7; *Gosp. of Pet.* 2.5; 5.15.

connection between covetousness and murder is now brought to full light here. The suffering caused to the poor by unjustly withholding wages has caused many of their deaths. This equation of economic injustice and murder is anticipated in intertestamental Jewish literature.

> Bread is life to the destitute,
> and to deprive them of it is murder.
> To rob your neighbour of his livelihood is to kill him,
> and he who defrauds a worker of his wages sheds blood.
>
> *Sir* 34.21–22, REB

Even though the rich may have given thanks to God for their successes, their praises were proven to be a sham if they had neglected the needs of poor laborers.

The vicious connection between idolatry, mercilessness, and murder becomes part of the guiding logic of James as he sternly warned his audience.[46] God, who "opposes the proud" (4:6), here does so by slaying them because, as seen earlier, "judgment without mercy will be shown to anyone who has not been merciful" (2:13). Not to have done what they knew they should have done was sin (4:17), and God would treat the oppressive rich as he treated all of his enemies: destroying the destroyers of his people. The poor among James's hearers also should hear this promise, even those in the middle classes, so that they could develop a wiser response to the unjust rich than envying them (3:14) and coveting what was theirs; for finally what was theirs was God's judgment. The workers were right not to oppose the rich evildoers who had mistreated them (cf. Matt 5:39).[47] Their innocence then became the final indisputable piece of evidence against the rich who had brought about many of their deaths by a continual lust for more wealth.

---

[46] Cf. Deut 12:30–31; Isa 1:21–23; Jer 2:27,34; Ezek 16:49,52; Amos 5:4–6; Hab 1:16.

[47] The translation of the NIV and its theological import is followed here rather than the interpretation suggested by L. A. Schökel, who argues that the final phrase of this verse should be understood as a question: "Does not [God] oppose you?" ("James 5:2 [sic] and 4:6," *Bib* [1973]: 73–76).

VI. COMMON LIFE BEFORE THE LORD (5:7–20)
   1. Patience among Friends (5:7–11)
   2. Rejection of Oaths (5:12)
   3. Effective Prayer (5:13–18)
   4. The Ministry of Restoration (5:19–20)

VI. COMMON LIFE BEFORE THE LORD (5:7–20)

This concluding section of James is united by the theme of the brethren's present exercise of faith and their submission to James's teaching (vv. 7,9–10,12,19). All of the exhortations are meant to encourage and unite the readers as a community of Christ. Living before the Lord is also living in light of his certain coming, his Parousia. James returned to the opening theme of persevering (1:12), for believers now have very strong grounds for doing so. Their faith is always tested,[1] but they should take heart since the Lord knows all about their trials and will deliver them in his time. Job, the great example of persevering under trial, will be presented as the illustration of the patient faith believers are to emulate. And if they are patient, they will not, "above all," be rash in their use of speech (v. 12)—reinforcing another important teaching of the letter. When believers endure the trials of faith through trust in God's vindication of them, the unity of speech and active faith that James had been teaching as the only way for Christian life can usher in effective prayer, the experience of forgiveness, and the conversion of sinners. The letter then ends on a powerful missiological note, establishing his obedient hearers in the great lineage of God's witnessing people dispersed among the nations (1:1).

---

[1] Cf. E. Fry, "The Testing of Faith: A Study of the Structure of the Book of James," *BT* 29 (1978): 427–35.

1. Patience among Friends (5:7–11)

[7]Be patient, then, brothers, until the Lord's coming. See how the farmer waits for the land to yield its valuable crop and how patient he is for the autumn and spring rains. [8]You too, be patient and stand firm, because the Lord's coming is near. [9]Don't grumble against each other, brothers, or you will be judged. The Judge is standing at the door!

[10]Brothers, as an example of patience in the face of suffering, take the prophets who spoke in the name of the Lord. [11]As you know, we consider blessed those who have persevered. You have heard of Job's perseverance and have seen what the Lord finally brought about. The Lord is full of compassion and mercy.

5:7 With this verse James began the closure of his letter, returning to the initial theme of trials in the Christian life. He exhorted his Christian "brothers"[2] to be patient in the midst of suffering that is caused by injustices done to them. The conjunction *oun*, "then" or "therefore," here closely connects the call to patient waiting to the previous section by reminding his hearers of God's opposition to the unjust rich.

The sense of patience[3] in this case includes waiting and endurance until the Lord takes action on their behalf. What does it mean to be patient until the Lord's coming? It means to do what God also is doing: enduring human evil for a season. James's authoritative counsel is not revolution or a taking of justice into one's own hand. This judgment is not within their rights but God's, who will judge oppression in his time. After all, even the courts of the present time are all too influenced by the superior resources of the rich. The exhortation is something like: "Let the Lord come against your oppressors in his time, but presently, wait just as he is waiting."

---

[2] Note the radical shift in tone from "you rich" in v. 1. I disagree with arguments that place the rich outside the Christian community simply because they are not among James's addressees.

[3] μακροθυμέω ("have patience," "wait," also in v. 8; cf. Heb 6:15 and the sense of absolute dependence upon God; Job 7:16; *Sir* 2:4; *Bar* 4:25; *T. Jos.* 2.7) can refer to God's forbearing ways (Prov 19:11) and that which is at the heart of *agape* love (1 Cor 13:4). Thus it can be a Christian virtue that imitates one of the attributes of God; cf. Matt 18:26,29; 1 Thess 5:14; 2 Pet 3:9; *Sir* 18.11; 29.8; *1 Clem.* 49.5.

The Lord's coming[4] will be as judge of humanity. When Christ comes, he will reveal the opposition of God against the rich who have been unmerciful. Until then he waits, and believers also should wait.

James used the example of a farmer who must labor without knowing what the weather will bring or the degree of abundance of crops. This illustration is appropriate in that the oppressed believers of the previous section were also agrarian laborers. Again the farmer's patience was like God's (cf. John 15:1, which uses the same word, *gēorgos,* "farmer," there translated "gardener"; cf. 1 Cor 9:7–10; 2 Tim 2:6). Just as the harvest of righteousness comes from divine wisdom (cf. 3:17–18), a final harvest comes for the patient believer. This harvest will not be the destruction that awaits the wicked rich but the "valuable"[5] crop that is the heavenly reward for those who have endured faith's trials. The focus of the comparison, however, is not on the crop as representing the heavenly reward; rather the believers's patient endurance compares with the patient waiting of the simple farmer. Faith here and now is like that. The farmer waited for the precious fruit of his labor. For the farmer the final result of his faithful labor and God's gracious gifts of sun and rain was worth the wait. How much more, then, is our waiting for the Lord?

The farmer could only wait for the early and the later rains—an allusion to the climatic conditions of Palestine. The early rain causes the seed to germinate and the plants to sprout. The later rain strengthens the stalks for the production of the buds, which will make for much harvestable grain when it ripens. In both cases the farmer waited for the sake of the grain in order that the grain (lit. "fruit"; cf. 3:17) might be his at harvest time.

The eschatological frame of reference here is unmistakable: believers are called to wait on the Lord. But the illustration is also a

---

[4] παρουσία: "presence," "coming," "advent," usually of persons, esp. visiting kings, in ancient literature. In the NT the term is used of Christ in his coming as universal Judge at the end of the age (cf. Matt 24:3,27,37,39; 1 Cor 1:8; 15:23; 1 Thess 3:13; 4:15; 5:23; 2 Thess 2:1,8; 2 Pet 1:16; 3:4; 1 John 2:28).

[5] τίμιος ("valuable," "precious") can be applied to a range of objects: the blood of Jesus (1 Pet 1:19), wisdom (Prov 3:15), and faith itself (1 Pet 1:7).

word of wisdom: the *wise* farmer learns to wait patiently for the harvest. Rather than reading too much into the time of the rains in search of some tenuous eschatological sign, interpreters do much better to look to the context within James and to make a connection with the "good fruit" of heavenly wisdom from 3:17–18. The same noun, "fruit," is used in the original in both places. The framework of James is certainly eschatological, but life until the eschaton is characterized by heavenly wisdom that is to produce mature faith in every believer (cf. 1:3). From God the believer will receive "the crown of life" (1:12); but from faith the believer produces "a harvest of righteousness" (3:18). The unmerciful rich hoard their wealth according to "devilish wisdom" (cf. 3:15) and incite only "envy . . . and every evil practice" (3:16) in the double-minded who do not humbly seek God's true wisdom (cf. 1:6–8). By this self-centered kind of life, they show that they are not friends of God but of the world (4:4). In this example then James pictured the productivity of wise faith in view of the certainty of vindication and judgment to come. To wait on the coming of the Lord is to be included among his friends who imitate him by sowing the seeds of a righteous life. In the New Testament wisdom and eschatology become bound together inseparably: faith in the coming of the Lord expresses itself only in faithful obedience in the present time.

5:8 Therefore, as seen in the wisdom of the farmer, the believers must also wait patiently and, James added, "stand firm."[6] The imperative "stand firm" could be more literally translated "strengthen your hearts," meaning to confirm its faith through patient endurance. Highlighting the word "heart" also shows the overall interconnectedness of James's teaching. The great problem of the double-minded believer is the deceiving of one's own heart (1:26b). The only hope for the self-deceived is a rigorous purifying of the heart (4:8). Without the heart's being purified, it is fattened for the day of slaughter (5:5). Instead of a heart that patiently waits for the Lord by active faith, the fattened heart is filled with the self-

---

[6] στηρίζω ("establish," "support") here with the figurative sense of "confirm," "establish," "strengthen," some aspect of the self; cf. Judg 19:5; Ps 50:14; Luke 22:32; Acts 18:23; Rom 15:25; 1 Thess 3:2; 2 Thess 3:3; 1 Pet 5:10; Rev 3:2; *Sir* 3:9; 6:37; 22:16; *1 Macc* 14.14; *2 Clem.* 2.6.

centeredness and envy that are the primary characteristics of an unmerciful life.

James repeated the reference to the Lord's coming but now focused on its nearness. Because the Lord's coming was near, oppressed believers should strengthen their commitment to endure. Divine nearness is a familiar metaphor in the New Testament and can carry either a spatial sense (e.g., 4:8) or a temporal one (e.g., 5:9). Since the wider context is temporal (i.e., the "day of slaughter," 5:5), the temporal and eschatological sense is the preferred interpretation here. But the entire letter is written from the perspective that the time will be short in that we live in the last stage of redemptive history preceding the Lord's return. Those reading this text today are aware that 2000 years separate us from the original audience. The imminency of the Lord's return, therefore, referred to the necessity of constant readiness and persevering faith based upon the knowledge that he may return at any time. This larger passage tells what the nearness of the Lord signifies and how the knowledge of it strengthens the heart of the believer.

5:9 James had been speaking to his entire audience about their patiently waiting together; now they must be reminded not to grumble[7] or complain (*stenazō*, "sigh" or "groan" due to the unpleasant circumstances). This caution would limit the kind of rivalry that can flare up under difficult circumstances. James's context shows that if believers were to endure their sufferings, they would do so together. Indeed, trials are better endured with the encouragement of community than in solitude. Since believers already had to endure the attacks of the wicked wealthy, the last thing the oppressed faithful needed was attacks against each other. Quite often in the Old Testament the Israelites are said to have complained to the Lord in their suffering under the oppression of foreign powers. The foundational text for such suffering is found in Exod 2:23–24:

> During that long period, the king of Egypt died. The Israelites groaned [LXX, *katustenazō*] in their slavery and cried out, and their

---

[7] Cf. Job 30:25; Isa 59:10; Lam 1:21; Neh 3:7; Ezek 26:15; Mark 7:34; Rom 8:23; 2 Cor 5:2,4; Heb 13:17; *T. Jos.* 7.1; *Mart. Pol.* 2.2; 9.2; *Herm. Vis.* 3.9.6.

cry for help because of their slavery went up to God. God heard
their groaning *[stenagmos]* and he remembered his covenant with
Abraham, with Isaac and with Jacob. So God looked on the Israelites and was concerned about them.

In much the same way, the believers in James's day needed to
remember the Lord's concern for them and not to fail to uphold each
other in the faith. James addressed Christian "brothers"; grumbling
within the family of mature believers was entirely inappropriate. To
do so suggests that suffering has been caused by a fellow believer
and that the opposition also exists within the church, not only outside of it. Very quickly the problem of controlling the tongue has
reemerged (cf. 3:2,5). Since believers are all the recipients of mercy
(cf. 2:13), they should not complain against each other, for this constitutes an act of judging a fellow believer. As seen earlier, the attitudes of those who judge others are often so impure that their
judging is actually an act of cursing (cf. 3:10).

James warned, however, that if the cursing of a brother took
place, the one passing judgment faced the reality of answering for
careless judgmental words at God's judgment. Judging wrongly, or
the failure to control the critical tongue, was a great problem for
James's audience (cf. 2:12–13; 3:1; 4:11–12; 5:12). Humility (cf.
4:6,10) and joy before God should characterize their relations in
order to produce a solidarity in suffering injustice until the Lord
himself delivered them. Believers should not speak to each other as
if the causes of suffering arose from within their own fellowship.
James's advice was that of the words of Jesus: "Do not judge, or
you too will be judged" (Matt 7:1).

Indeed, how could believers complain in the very presence of the
divine Judge, who was standing at the door?[8] The Lord Jesus is the
judge. Did James mean the doors of the local church as though the
Lord witnesses everything that transpires within? Did James mean

---

[8] θύρα: "door," "gate"; note the plural "doors" is the form in the Gk. text and also
the possible wordplay with θερίζω ("to harvest") in v. 4. Nearness is emphasized in
this usage (cf. Mark 13:29; Acts 5:9) and should be seen as closely related to the
door to the kingdom of heaven (cf. Luke 13:24; Rev 3:8) and the door that is opened
by God to give access to his blessings (cf. Acts 14:27; 1 Cor 16:9; 2 Cor 2:12; Col
4:3); indeed, Jesus is himself the Door (cf. John 10:9).

the "door" of the present into which the Judge is about to come for final judgment? The *Apocalypse of Matthew* 24.32–33 is instructive:

> You know that the summer [lit. harvest] is near. Even so, when you see all these things, you know that it is near, right at the door.

There is an important connection between the image of the Lord's nearness—the door—and that of the harvest (cf. Jas 3:18; 5:4,7). Signs indicate the nearness of the harvest, just as the sign of the Lord's presence at the "door" indicates the nearness of his coming. Just as the coming of the Judge is the coming of judgment, so the coming of the kingdom is also the coming of the King. As in Rev 3:20, which portrays the Lord standing, knocking at "the door," in James keeping faith now and the promise of the coming eschaton are inseparable, encouraging believers that they will be delivered from their present trials. Believers should fear Christ, for he is the Judge; they should act not as those appointed for judgment but as those who know that their deliverance is near.

5:10 Again James addressed his Christian brothers affectionately, this time to reinforce all that he had been exhorting about both the reality of God's lordship and the proper attitude of faith in the present time. He now illustrated faithful endurance of trials with the positive example[9] of the prophets. James was inviting his hearers to emulate the prophets (compare Hebrews 11 or Jesus' words in Matt 5:10–12) because both believers and prophets share the experience of suffering and patience.

The Lord's prophets are worthy of imitation. Along with Job in this passage (v. 11), James provided other exemplars of godly faith throughout the letter: the man who puts the law of liberty into practice (1:22–25); Abraham and Rahab (2:20–25); and Elijah (5:17–18). These role models are the ones who have suffered trials because they were faithful in their obedience, even when God was testing them. The patient waiting demanded of the believers (v. 7) is exemplified by the prophets, who showed peerless endurance

---

[9] ὑπόδειγμα: "example," "model," "pattern," used positively of someone who is worthy of emulation; cf. John 13:15; Heb 4:11; *J. Bell.* 6.103; Philo *Rer. Div. Her.* 256; *Sir* 44:16; *2 Macc* 6:28,31; *1 Clem.* 5.1; 6.1; 46.1; 55.1.

under suffering.[10] They endured their suffering patiently as they waited for God to accomplish his purposes for Israel. This challenge of pursuing a prophet-like faith clarifies the kind of spirituality that is expected of all believers by the New Testament writings. Based on the teaching of Jesus to his disciples, every believer is to mature into the fullness of faith and potency of witness exemplified by the prophets. The receiving of the word of God in the heart (cf. 1:21) is best compared to the manner in which all the prophets received that same word. Here, because of that same word, believers are called to that same patience in suffering that the prophets evidenced rather than to complaining (v. 9).

This call to imitate the prophets is important for tying together the various themes of James. The prophets were those who understood that they must forego the benefits, even of religious success, in order to gain the promised divine benefits for those who persevere under trial (e.g., "the crown of life," 1:12). Rather than attending to the wants of the rich (2:1), the prophets were to attend to the needs of the destitute and keep themselves from the filth of the world (1:27). Since the world's wealth and good fortune inevitably entail moral filth, believers must recognize the world's enmity with God and be at enmity with it. This God-inspired enmity with the world and with quasi-religious ways of life by which some try to befriend both the world and God incurs the wrath (cf. 1:20) of the double-minded believers. Consequently, the prophets—especially Jeremiah and Ezekiel—became known for their suffering at the hands of the people of God. This connection of faithfulness to the prophetic task and suffering at the hand of coreligionists is why Jesus was the "man of sorrows." The wicked rich, and those enviously allied to them, are those who "slander the noble name" (2:7) while professing true faith (v. 18). Such a way of life inevitably leads to slandering others (4:11), expecting one's own personal success (v. 13), committing sins of omission (v. 17). The upshot of this double-minded way of life is the slaying of the innocent (5:6).

---

[10] κακοπάθεια ("suffering," "misfortune," "misery"), an NT hapax legomena. The noun can have an active meaning of "suffering" that a person endures, thus, "a strenuous effort." This latter, active sense may in fact fit James's setting best (cf. Mal 1:13; *2 Macc* 2.26f.; *4 Macc* 9.8).

In James's day as in ancient Israel, those who murdered the prophets did not recognize that the judgment foretold by the same prophets would surely come upon them. There is nothing to say other than that the faithful believers were caught up in the same divine service as the prophets and should joyfully share the same destiny of suffering and, in time, of divine vindication.

5:11 The NIV's "as you know" is an imprecise translation of the Greek *idou*, commonly rendered "behold." Nevertheless, the teaching here was an elaboration of something his readers should know, especially since James had presented earlier the message of the blessedness of perseverance (cf. the "blessing" of 1:12). In many ways endurance was James's chief virtue of faith. Whether it was their perseverance in maintaining their faith under trial or in enduring the suffering of their oppressors (v. 7) as the prophets did, this virtue is highlighted here. For this perseverance the prophets and now all believers are called "blessed." Acts 5:41 recounts that the apostles rejoiced "because they had been counted worthy of suffering disgrace for the Name." The trying conditions James referred to called them to accept their sufferings in order to be called blessed, both by their fellow believers and most of all by God.

James cited the specific example of Job[11] and therefore accorded him a place among the prophets and the blessed.[12] The reference to his addressees' having heard about Job implies that Job had been an example of patient endurance of suffering. But how is Job such an examplar in view of his great complaining? It is because Job addressed his complaints properly to God and not against others. Perhaps the most important insight on Job comes from the words of the Lord in Job 2:3, which are not taken back at any point:

---

[11] Cf. Ezek 14:14; Philo *Mut. Nom.* 48; Josephus *Ant.* 2.178; *1 Clem.* 17.3; *2 Clem.* 6.8. On the fact that this is a somewhat difficult allusion, cf. H. Fine, "The Tradition of a Patient Job," *JBL* 74 (1955): 28–32; D. H. Gard, "The Concept of Job's Character according to the Greek Translator of the Hebrew Text," *JBL* 72 (1953): 182–86; and esp. C. Haas, "Job's Perseverance in the Testament of Job," in *Studies on the Testament of Job,* ed. M. A. Knibb and P. W. van der Horst, *SNTSMS* 66 (Cambridge: University Press, 1989), 117–54.

[12] μακαρίζω: "call [or consider] blessed," "fortunate," "happy"; cf. Gen 30:13; Luke 1:48; *Sir* 11:28; Josephus *Bell.* 7.356; *1 Clem.* 1:2.

> Then the Lord said to Satan, "Have you considered by servant Job? There is no one on earth like him; he is blameless and upright, a man who fears God and shuns evil. And he still maintains his integrity, though you incited me against him to ruin him without any reason."

Here is the sobering truth about the nature of trials in the life of righteous persons, that God allows them to be tested in order to prove their faith (cf. 1:2; Heb 12:7–11). In some ways their endurance proves the Lord's boast in them and in other ways confirms to the world that God's approval rests on those who remain faithful to him in spite of the evil they suffered. This text gives insight into the basis for Job's prominence and the Lord's own word on his standing in God's sight. What else could Job be but one of the Bible's chief exemplars? The key point is that in all his trials Job maintained "his integrity," and this integrity in spite of trial is what was found most pleasing to God.

James then said that his readers had "seen what the Lord finally brought about" (lit. "and the end of the Lord you saw").[13] Likely James was referring to Job in this declaration, thus harkening back to prophetic literature and the way in which suffering can be a means to acquiring wisdom. Surprisingly, Job seems to be identified here as a prophet, perhaps because in the end he is said to have spoken "what is right" about God (Job 42:7). God even instructed him to act as intercessor on behalf of his friends so they might escape the Lord's judgment. The wise are those who know their God even in the midst of suffering, even when they must complain to the Lord over the agony of their lot. Finally, there is an end to Job's suffering, and the Lord reversed the great trial that had befallen Job by restoring to him the blessedness of family and property (Job 42:10–17). All of this end James indicated his addressees had "seen." If the reference is to what God accomplished in Job's life, then the "seeing" is the knowledge of the story they had been told. Job was already a prime example for them. James was reminding his audience of what they knew, as he had to

---

[13] This is a notoriously difficult phrase to translate, esp. the τὸ τέλος κυρίου, "the ending brought about by the Lord." Cf. R. P. Gordon, "KAI TO TELOS KYRIOU EIDETE (Jas. v. 11)," *JTS*, n.s., 26 (1975): 91–95.

do often in the letter.

James concluded this verse with the leading attribute of God and with the virtue of faith he had concentrated on throughout:[14] mercy[15] and the related quality: compassion[16] (lit. "rich in compassion"). Faith is not confessed when the believer merely states, "There is one God" (2:19); rather one also must confess the Lord's mercy and compassion. These traits identify the Lord, who blessed Job and the prophets even when they complained to him under their severe hardships. The traits are the primary attributes of God in his covenant with Israel (cf. Exod 34:6; Num 14:18; Ps 103:8); therefore James's alluding to them here reminds believers that their trials will produce in them virtues that correspond to those of their God. The reference to the outcome of Job's life is appropriate in that what had appeared to be abandonment by God or even opposition from God proved to be God's means of proving his mercy and compassion. Our endurance is used by God to prove his mercy and compassion.

2. Rejection of Oaths (5:12)

[12]**Above all, my brothers, do not swear—not by heaven or by earth or by anything else. Let your "Yes" be yes, and your "No," no, or you will be condemned.**

5:12   This final section's concern with common life before the Lord (5:7–20) continues with James introducing that which is to be remembered "above all."[17] Having made the case for perseverance without grumbling against one another, James confronted a funda-

---

[14] Cf. 1:5,13,17–18,20,27; 2:5,11,13; 3:9; 4:4,12; 5:6.

[15] οἰκτίρμων: "merciful." Although different from the ἔλεος of 2:13, both adjectives are often united and are among the supreme attributes of God connected with the establishment of his covenant with his people (cf. Ps 108:12; Lam 4:10; Luke 6:36; Rom 12:1; 2 Cor 1:3; *1 Clem.* 23.1).

[16] πολύσπλαγχνος ("sympathetic," "compassionate," "merciful") is not even found in the LXX; cf. *Herm. Man.* 4.3.5; 5.7.4; Cl. Al. *Quis Div. Salv.* 39.6; *Acts Thom.* 119.

[17] Cf. W. R. Baker, "'Above All Else': Contexts of the Call for Verbal Integrity in James 5:12," *JSNT* 54 (1994): 165–94.

mental prohibition. The repetition of "brothers" (5:7,9–10,12), along with the negative exhortation, reinforces the interconnection of this verse with the larger context. James placed the greatest of emphasis on this prohibition of oaths because of what he had stated earlier about speech: "If anyone is never at fault in what he says, he is a perfect man, able to keep his whole body in check" (3:2). Within the fellowship of believers one's conduct is largely determined by what one says. The power of the word is greatest (cf. 3:5); thus it is imperative that what is said conform to the goodness and mercy of God.

"Do not swear,"[18] James's prohibition, stands in contrast with many texts of the Old Testament and New Testament in which the wording of the oath or the attitude in taking an oath determines whether it has been taken properly. James was emphatic that these Christian "brothers" should renounce oaths altogether. Perhaps this total prohibition was because such talk is not compatible with the blessedness of true endurance. The patient believer is to be one who answers his accusers with simplicity and with confidence in the God of mercy. Again James was advocating that his addressees follow the teaching of Jesus:

> Again, you have heard that it was said to the people long ago, 'Do not break your oath, but keep the oaths you have made to the Lord.' But I tell you, Do not swear at all: either by heaven, for it is God's throne; or by the earth, for it is his footstool; or by Jerusalem, for it is the city of the Great King. And do not swear by your head, for you cannot make even one hair white or black. Simply let your 'Yes' be 'Yes,' and your 'No,' 'No'; anything beyond this comes from the evil one. (Matt 5:33–37)

Indeed, James virtually reproduced the content of this entire quote.

---

[18] Cf. Lev 5:4; Num 30:11; Zech 8:17; Matt 5:33; 14:7,9; 26:72; Mark 6:26; Luke 1:73; Acts 2:30; 2 Cor 1:15–20; Heb 6:16; *T. Jud.* 22.3; *2 Macc* 4:34; Josephus *Ant.* 3.272; 7.294; *1 Clem.* 8.2; *Justin Apol. I* 16.5; Cl Al *Strom.* 5.99.1; 7.67.5; cf. also E. Kutsch, "Eure Rede aber sei ja, ja, nein, nein," *EvT* 20 (1960): 206–17; P. S. Minear, "Yes or No: The Demand for Honesty in the Early Church," *NovT* 13 (1971): 1–13; G. Dautzenberg, "Ist das Schwurverbot Mt 5,33–37; Jak 5,12 ein Beispiel für die Torakritik Jesus?" *BZNS* 25 (1981): 47–66.

Heaven, as God's abode; earth, as his footstool; anything else, for example, Jerusalem or one's hair, all belong to the Lord and therefore cannot be called to accredit claims by the human creature. With Jesus, James was saying, in effect: All you have is your yes and your no;[19] use them; all other claims are false and dangerous. Jesus made plain that evil attaches to the false claims entailed in all such oath-taking. James came to the conclusion that this evil was condemnable.

As in other passages where he warned of God's judgment for participation in evil by their actions (2:4; 3:12–13; 4:11–12; 5:9), James here warned that their words were actions and would be counted against them when they did not conform to the faith required of them (cf. 4:17).

3. Effective Prayer (5:13–18)

[13]**Is any one of you in trouble? He should pray. Is anyone happy? Let him sing songs of praise. **[14]**Is any one of you sick? He should call the elders of the church to pray over him and anoint him with oil in the name of the Lord. **[15]**And the prayer offered in faith will make the sick person well; the Lord will raise him up. If he has sinned, he will be forgiven. **[16]**Therefore confess your sins to each other and pray for each other so that you may be healed. The prayer of a righteous man is powerful and effective.**

[17]**Elijah was a man just like us. He prayed earnestly that it would not rain, and it did not rain on the land for three and a half years. **[18]**Again he prayed, and the heavens gave rain, and the earth produced its crops.**

5:13 Instead of grumbling against each other (v. 9) or taking oaths (v. 12), the believers should pray, strengthened by the corporate life that was theirs. James's tone had become very pastoral. He asked if anyone was "in trouble" or (the better translation) "suffering" (the noun form of the same root, *kakopath*, is used in v. 10). He

---

[19] τὸ Ναί ναί . . . τὸ Οὔ οὔ is a precise repetition of the words of Jesus quoted above from Matthew's Gospel. One can only speculate about the degree of dependency of James upon Matthew. As much as any other passage within this epistle, however, this one contributes the most to the sense of close relationship.

then commended private prayer[20] as the antidote to falling into the temptation of grumbling against another believer. Their prayer must be for wisdom (1:5), and it should be whole-hearted (1:6), seeking a firm conviction for the perseverance needed to endure the suffering.

By contrast (in the manner of classic diatribe), James asked if there were any who were happy.[21] The proper response is songs of praise.[22] Happiness is a blessing of God and must be received with gratitude. Thus gladness is directed and channeled by praise to God (cf. Col 3:16). In this way someone's good fortune will not be a cause of envy but rather a joy shared with the entire fellowship.

5:14   In this and the next two verses, James's teaching on prayer and praise emphasizes the community of Christian faith. The present verse is a classic text for the power of prayer in healing and forgiveness of sins in the history of Christian interpretation.[23]

---

[20] προσεύχομαι: "pray." The usage here is the first instance of this verb in James; next is in v. 18; cf. Matt 6:5–7; 14:23; Mark 1:35; 6:46; Luke 1:10; 5:16; Acts 1:24; 6:6; 1 Cor 11:4f.; 14:14; *Mart. Pol.* 5.2; 12.3; *Herm. Vis.* 1.1.4; 3.1.6; *Sim.* 9.11.7; *Did.* 8.2.

[21] εὐθυμέω: "be cheerful," from "cheer up," "keep up one's courage." The term is difficult to define clearly in that it does not appear in the LXX. Cf. Acts 27:22, where it means to take courage; Josephus *Ant.* 18.284.

[22] ψάλλω: "sing," "sing praise," which originally meant to "pluck"; e.g., a stringed instrument but attains our usage by the time of the LXX. "Make melody" also could very well be intended here; cf. 1 Cor 14:15: "Sing praise in spiritual ecstasy" and "in full possession of one's mental faculties." Also cf. 1 Sam 16:16–23; Job 21:12; Pss 7:18; 9:12; 17:50; 26:6; 32:3; 56:8; 107:4; Rom 15:9; Eph 5:19; *Barn.* 6.16.

[23] Indeed, the Roman Catholic sacramental tradition of "extreme unction," i.e., the practice of anointing the sick as an instrument of grace, utilized this text as foundational to its doctrine. Right interpretation of this text, however, begins with its context in James rather than with the history of its interpretation or even some specific Jewish tradition. Cf. K. Condon, 'The Sacrament of Healing (Jas 5:14–15)," *Scr* 11 (1959): 33–42; H. Friesenhahn, "Zur Geschichte der Überlieferung und Exegese des Textes Bei Jak V,14f," *BZ* 24 (1938–39): 185–90; E. J. Kilmartin, "The Interpretation of James 5:14–15 in the Armenian Catena on the Catholic Epistles: Scholium 82," *Orientalia Christiana Periodica* 53 (1987): 335–64; M. Meinertz, "Die Krankensalbung Jak 5,14f.," *BZ* 20 (1932): 23–36; B. Reicke, "L'onction des malades d'après saint Jacques," *La Maison Dieu* 113 (1973): 50–56; J. Sailer, "Jak 5,14 und die Krankensalbung," *TPQ* 113 (1965): 347–53; J. Wilkinson, "Healing in the Epistle of James," *SJT* 24 (1971): 326–45.

By mentioning illness[24] (cf. v. 15), James returned to the theme of suffering (vv. 1–10). Like the problem of sin (especially sins of self-deception and envy), sickness greatly challenges faith and unity within the fellowship of believers. Just as happiness is to be shared with other believers in praises to God (v. 13), the practice of prayer for the sick must be shared as well. The temptation to show disdain for the poor (2:3), to ignore their needs for food and clothing (2:16), and to threaten their physical survival (5:4) by withholding their fair wages is the same temptation to neglect fellow believers that would leave the sick alone on their backs. Believers who are sick and infirm are to receive special attention by the whole congregation.

This verse presents a simple threefold pattern that is to be followed on behalf of the sick: first, the sick one should call the elders; second, they should anoint the sick with oil; third, they should pray over the sick for healing. James exhorted the sick to summon[25] the elders[26] of the fellowship. These persons of spiritual authority within the congregation (cf. Acts 20:17) should come to the place where the sick person resides, since the matter of sickness would affect the whole fellowship. The movement of the fellowship to the side of the sick would demonstrate that sickness is not a cause for exclusion but an opportunity for concern regarding the "physical needs" (cf. 2:16) of each member. Those who have been

---

[24] ἀσθενέω: "be weak," "powerless"; here quite literally to "be sick." Cf. Matt 25:39; Luke 4:40; 7:10; John 4:46; 11:1–3,6; Acts 9:37; Phil 2:26f.; 2 Tim 4:20.

[25] προσκαλέω: "summon," "call to oneself," "invite someone"; cf. Gen 28:1; Esth 4:5; Matt 10:1; 15:10; Mark 3:13; 15:44; Luke 7:18; 15:26; Acts 6:2; 23:17f.; Josephus *Ant.* 1.271; *T. Reub.* 4.9; *Herm. Vis.* 1.4.2; *Sim.* 5.2.2; 6; 9.7.1.

[26] Beginning with the appointment of elders by Moses (Exod 19:7; 24:1), the office became standard in Israel; cf. Lev 4:15; Num 11:16; Deut 31:9; Josh 9:2; Judg 21:16; 1 Sam 4:3; 2 Sam 17:4. References to the council of the elders of Israel are interspersed throughout the NT. Although elders in the Christian churches were established on the bases of their own doctrine, they represent something of an office with recognized authority. Cf. Acts 11:30; 14:23; 15:2,4,6,22f.; 16:4 (in Acts 15 "elder" is always coupled with "apostle" in this record of the proceedings of the first Jerusalem council); 20:17; 21:18; 1 Tim 5:17,19; Titus 1:5; 1 Pet 5:1,5; 2 John 1; 3 John 1; *1 Clem.* 44.5; 47.6; 54.2; 57.1; *2 Clem.* 17.3, 5; Ign. *Magn.* 2; 3.1; 6.1; Phil 10.2; Ign. *Pol.* 5:3; 6.1; Ign. *Trall.* 3.1; 12.2.

recognized by the local church *(ekklēsia)*[27] as its leaders (cf. 1 Tim 3:1; 5:7) represent the assembly in their act of believing prayer before the Lord. By using the term *ekklēsia,* James showed that through the elders the church maintains its embrace around even the sick who have been quarantined from the gathered community of believers. The elders are to "pray over" the sick one, for this one is afflicted with debilitating trouble (v. 13). The group of elders are to draw very close in faith to the sick one so that the prayer might be uttered directly over her or him. Touching the body of the sick with oil in the name of Jesus and joining their voices in prayer above the body of the sick person is in view here. This prayer could include the act of each elder prostrating himself over the sick person. Elijah in v. 17 is the exemplar of that faith James had in mind. The famous story of Elijah's healing the son of the widow of Zarephath includes this action:

> Then he stretched himself out on the boy three times and cried to the LORD, "O LORD my God, let this boy's life return to him!"
> The LORD heard Elijah's cry, and the boy's life returned to him, and he lived. (1 Kgs 17:21–22)

Is this the kind of "praying over" that James meant? It certainly cannot be ruled out as the way the church should utter "powerful and effective" (cf. 5:16) prayer for the sick. Certainly, physical touch upon the sick person is in view both in this act of praying and in the anointing with oil. Rather than withdrawing from the sick like someone who is in "friendship with the world" (4:4), the elders should pray as those who receive "more grace" from God (4:6), who "gives generously to all without finding fault" (1:5). Praying as a group in such close proximity to the sick person intensifies and makes efficacious their faith for the healing.

The anointing with oil[28] is not merely a kind of home remedy. As it is applied, the name of the Lord Jesus (cf. 1:1) is to be

---

[27] ἐκκλησία: "assembly" of people; the physical gathering of believers in the local sense; cf. Deut 4:10; 9:10; 18:16; 31:30; Acts 15:22; 1 Cor 11:18; 14:4,34; Phil 4:15.

[28] ἐλάιον: "olive oil," as used in cooking, in lamps, and in treating wounds; cf. Isa 1:6; Mark 6:13; Luke 10:34; Josephus *Ant.* 17.172; *T. Sol.* 18.34; *2 Enoch* 22.8–9; *T. Adam* 1.7.

invoked. Olive oil, according to Old Testament and Jewish understanding, was prized for its nurturing of human well-being and for its healing properties. In Jesus' and his disciples' ministry, olive oil was utilized in their healings of the sick when combined with the preaching of repentance:

> They went out and preached that people should repent. They drove out many demons and anointed many sick people with oil and healed them. . . . for Jesus' name had become well known. (Mark 6:12–14)

The connection between the act of anointing[29] and of calling on the name of the Lord (Mark added the call to repentance) shows that although James never directly related sin and sickness as cause and effect, he indirectly related them in that sickness and sin make persons suffer and in that God can save from the effects of either (e.g., 5:6,10, and esp. 16). The name of Jesus the Lord is the all-embracing name and foundation for this act of faith in which there is healing and in which there will be judgment against the wicked.

In 5:10 James declared that the prophets had spoken in this name and in 2:7 that these believers belonged to him whose name was being slandered by the unmerciful rich. Paul testified that his fellow believers were "assembled in the name of our Lord Jesus and I am with you in spirit, and the power of our Lord Jesus is present" (1 Cor 5:4).[30] That power associated with the name of the Lord is fundamental in the New Testament and is directly associated with the prayer of faith itself (Jas 5:15).

5:15   The prayer[31] of faith (cf. 1:6), not the prayer with "wrong motives" (4:3), will heal the sick. The faithful prayer of the gathered believers, united by the plea of the sick member and the authority of the elders, has real effectiveness. The Gospels

---

[29] ἀλείφω: "anoint" with oil as a home remedy for illnesses; cf. M. Meinertz, "Die Krankensalbung von Jk 5:14f," *BZ* 20 (1932): 23–36.

[30] Baptism, healing, and exorcism all took place, according to Acts, in the name of the Lord Jesus; cf. 2:38; 3:6; 4:10; 8:16; 10:48; 15:26; 19:13; 21:13.

[31] εὐχή: "prayer," not "oath" (cf. Lev 22:29) because this is committed as an act of faith; cf. Philo *Sacr. A.C.* 53; Josephus *Bell.* 7.155; *Ant.* 15.5; *T. 12 Patr.*; *Mart. Pol.* 15.1; Pol. *Phil.* 7.2.

emphasize the connection between the prayer of faith and healing.[32] The word for healing here, translated "make well," is *sōzō*,
"save." It is used in the Synoptics for either spiritual salvation or
physical healing.[33] "Save" in a spiritual sense has appeared in Jas
1:21 as the effect of "the word planted in you" and has appeared in
2:14 in the debate about whether faith without deeds can save. In
the present verse healing of the sick is meant, but close connection
between the physical and the spiritual should be noted. This statement recalls the words of Jesus, for instance, to the woman who
had been subject to bleeding for twelve years: "Take heart, daughter . . . your faith has healed [using *sōzō*] you" (Matt 9:22). In our
verse, however, the instrument of healing is prayer rather than
faith—though not without faith.

Then James elaborated by stating that the Lord would "raise" the
person up. This choice of verb *(egeirō)* is remarkable because it
does not repeat the word meaning "save/heal," which had just been
used, but rather brings in another word with the same kind of dual
meaning. "Raise up" refers to an act of God in the present, as in
healing one who is bedridden, or an act of God in the eschaton, as
in resurrection. Jesus' healing of the synagogue ruler Jairus's
daughter is an example of this raising: "Little girl, I say to you, get
up!" (Mark 5:41)—a restoration of life. The connection between
being raised up miraculously from the bed of sickness and the resurrection is also poignantly presented in Martha's confession at the
tomb of her brother Lazarus (John 11:27).

But what is the connection between sin and sickness? Some
texts do indicate a very close one,[34] especially Paul's statement in
1 Cor 11:29–30:

> Anyone who eats and drinks without recognizing the body of the
> Lord eats and drinks judgment on himself. That is why many among
> you are weak and sick, and a number of you have fallen asleep.

---

[32] Cf. Mark 5:34; 10:52; Luke 7:50; 8:48; 17:19; 18:42; Acts 3:16; 4:9–10; 14:9;
15:9,11; 16:31.

[33] On the use of σῴζω of physical healing see Matt 9:21–22; Mark 3:4;
5:23,28,34; 6:56; 10:52; Luke 8:36,50; 18:42; John 11:12; Acts 4:9; 14:9.

[34] E.g., Deut 28; 30; Job 8:1–22; 11:6; 22:1–30; Prov 3:28–35; 13:13–23; 23:19–
21.

Other texts,[35] however, do not, such as John's quotation of Jesus:

> As he went along, he saw a man blind from birth. His disciples asked him, "Rabbi, who sinned, this man or his parents, that he was born blind?"
>
> "Neither this man nor his parents sinned," said Jesus, "but this happened so that the work of God might be displayed in his life."
>
> John 9:1–3

James stated the case conditionally: "If he has sinned . . ." Sin can be an element in the problem of sickness but is not necessarily so. When the prayer of faith is prayed over the believer, both sin and sickness are committed to the power of God to heal and to forgive.

In the final verse of the letter, the provision for sin will be a "covering," but here it is forgiveness.[36] In coming together for prayer with the sick believer, perhaps the confession of some sin takes place. This sin too will be forgiven. The Lord who raises the dead will forgive. Perhaps the closest text to this idea is found in Mark 2:8–10, where the forgiveness of sins and healing demonstrate Jesus' authority:

> "Why are you thinking these things? Which is easier: to say to the paralytic, 'Your sins are forgiven,' or to say, 'Get up, take your mat and walk'? But that you may know that the Son of Man has authority to forgive sins . . ." He said to the paralytic, "I tell you, get up, take your mat and go home."

James reflected Jesus' goal, the forgiveness of sinners and, only secondarily, their physical healing. The literal translation of "sinned" here would be "become a doer of sins"—a striking contrast to the earlier "doer of the word" (cf. 1:22). Not everyone is sick because of sin; not everyone who is sick has unforgiven sin, but there are some of both. The Lord is willing to forgive those who humbly confess their sin (just as surely as he is willing to

---

[35] E.g., Job 9:13–21; 13:18–14:22; 29:1–30:31; Eccl 3:16–22; 5:12–17; 6:1–9; 7:15.

[36] ἀφίημι: "cancel," "remit," "pardon," here esp. "forgive" in the passive tense and of persons; cf. Lev 4:20,26,31,35; 19:22; Num 15:25f.; Isa 22:14; 33:24; Matt 18:21,35; Luke 12:10; 17:3f.; 23:34; John 20:23.

bestow wisdom on those who humbly request it; cf. 1:5). Where healing of the body is needed, there will be healing; where forgiveness is needed, there will be the forgiving of the sin.

But what about the healing that does not come? Have sins been unforgiven? Comparison with other New Testament texts reveals that in this life the Lord's primary work is the forgiveness of sins. James, however, stated confidently that God will heal through the prayer of faith. He made no comment, however, about a prayer that does not result in healing. With a text like this interpreters ought not read into it any conclusions that are not explicitly stated. The straightforward teaching then is confidence in the efficacy of prayer. The result of prayer is always dependent on the will of God to heal in a particular case. Such healing points to resurrection and reconciliation with God and is never an end in itself. Healing then is a sign of the complete saving work of God: the demise of sin and death and the restoration of the body on the last day. Of course, not every believer receives the healing requested, and not every believer is healed in the same way as another. But all healing stimulates hope in the God who will one day remove all causes of sickness and death.

5:16 "Therefore," James continued, the entire fellowship of believers should be characterized by mutual confessing[37] of sin. The confession of sin entails humble honesty about the fact of having committed sin, not a public retelling of the details of the act. This way of confessing sin can be detected in the classic text of Old Testament confession, Psalm 51. Curiously, the subtitle adds the detail: "When the prophet Nathan came to him after David had committed adultery with Bathsheba." But this superscription is not a part of the psalm itself. Many employ this psalm in private confession without recognizing that it is a "public" testimony to the people of God. The psalm could even function as an aid to fulfilling the imperative of James's counsel.

Texts are important for what they include and do not include. In following this verse, it is appropriate to name a sin but no more.

---

[37] ἐξομολογέω: here "confess," "admit;" cf. Pss 7:18; 117:9; Matt 3:6; Mark 1:5; Acts 19:18; Josephus *Bell.* 1.625; 8.129; and 8.256; *Herm. Vis.* 3.1.5,6; *Did.* 4.14; *1 Clem.* 51.3; *Barn.* 19.12; *2 Clem.* 8.3.

Following David one might confess the personal suffering caused by an unspecified sin; indeed, how "sick" it had made the person (cf. Ps 51:8). When confessing sin, there is no room for reliving it in the retelling. There should not be anything sensational about the mutual confessing of sin, nothing that feeds sinful desire (cf. 1:14). Confession should entail only humble acknowledgment of the act of sin and the joy of release from the offensiveness of those acts. Along with active correction of those who fall into sin among believers, Paul surely had mutual confession in mind as he counseled how to carry out the law of Christ:

> Brothers, if someone is caught in a sin, you who are spiritual should restore him gently. But watch yourself, or you also may be tempted. Carry each other's burdens, and in this way you will fulfill the law of Christ. (Gal 6:1–2)

Although believers bear one another's burdens, nothing in confession should spawn temptation and sinful acts.

Mutual confession leads to mutual prayer. The prayer of faith (cf. v. 15) is not exclusively a prerogative of the office of elder but is a shared responsibility among the members of the church. The believers are to intercede for one another, both in the greatest matter of ministry, that confession that appropriates forgiveness, and also in the great matter of healing sickness. This mutual intercession is a prime New Testament example of the evangelical doctrine of the priesthood of all believers (cf. 1 Pet 2:4–5). Along with the sacrifice of praise that arises from the worship of the whole body of Christ, the mutual interceding of believers one for the other(s) is a priestly function. A number of biblical references to healing[38] are spiritual in nature, but this probably was not the case here. The same kind of prayer over the sick was being offered for one another. Faithful prayer is the sole means of healing in this verse— oil is not mentioned here as it was earlier. The same confident faith for healing should be evident throughout the fellowship of believers.

James asserted the important relation between the virtue of righ-

---

[38] ἰάομαι: "cure," "heal"; cf. 2 Chr 30:20; Isa 6:10; 47:19; Matt 13:15; Heb 12:13; 1 Pet 2:24; *Herm. Sim.* 9.23.

teousness and the quality of prayer for all believers. The essence of biblical righteousness is dependence upon God in all one's dealings.[39] To be righteous is to live a life centered upon the word of God; not sinlessness but mercy (cf. 2:13) typifies this life. Indeed, since it is the prayer for others that is being discussed, the righteous are the ones who intercede not so much on behalf of themselves but in obedience to God and for others. This was characteristic of the exemplars Job (v. 11; cf. Job 1:5) and Elijah (v. 17). The prayer of the righteous believer is both powerful and effective.[40] These two terms have overlapping meaning, together connoting the potency of prayer to accomplish the purposes of God.[41] Just as Jesus taught that his disciples would suffer for the sake of righteousness in fulfilling their prophetic task (cf. Matt 5:11–12), James called his audience to the same righteousness in the face of suffering. The reference to healing does not include a special gift (cf. 1 Cor 12:9); rather, healing is simply a part of the intercessory role to which believers are called. The question of the assurance of healing must be balanced with the will of God in each case. As C. Hodge wrote,

> It cannot be supposed that God has subjected Himself in the government of the world, or in the dispensation of his gifts, to the shortsighted wisdom of men, by promising, without condition, to do whatever they ask. No rational man could wish this to be the case.[42]

He then asserted that the condition expressed in 1 John 5:14 is everywhere else implied: "This is the confidence we have in approaching God: that if we ask anything according to his will, he hears us." It was the divine will in Elijah's case that drought and rain should be limited to a certain time (see vv. 17–18). This is also the case with every event of healing. The intercessor must trust the will of God.

5:17 The prophet Elijah, with his power and effective faith, is the final exemplar of faith in James's epistle. And yet, "Elijah was a

---

[39] Cf. Pss 1:5–6; 2:12; 7:9; 32:1; 33:16; 96:18; Prov 4:18; 10:6; 12:3.

[40] ἐνεργέομαι: "be at work," "be effective"; probably should be taken in the middle voice; cf. Rom 7:5; Gal 2:8; 5:6; 2 Cor 1:6; 4:12; 1 Thess 2:13; Eph 3:20; Col 1:29; 2 Thess 2:7; *1 Clem.* 60.1.

[41] In Greek they are both verbs, one finite and the other a participle. More lit. we could translate, "The prayer of a righteous person, being effective, can do much."

[42] C. Hodge, *Systematic Theology* (Grand Rapids: Eerdmans, 1940), 3:704.

man just like[43] us." Following on his career as a prophet of Israel, Elijah received extraordinary honor in late prophetic and intertestamental writing that became the basis for the expectation that he would return at the opening of the Messianic Age.[44] Although James was about to recount the greatest exploit of Elijah's faithful praying (cf. 1 Kgs 17–18), he was no less an example to every believer. The healing of a lame man in Lystra by Barnabas and Paul occasioned their pleading with the populace not to exalt them, for they were "only men, human like you" (Acts 14:15). However great the results of his prayer, this great effect did not change his essential nature as a mere man, a simple believer.

The form of prayer James encouraged, praying over the sick (v. 14), was used by Elijah for the healing of the son of the Zarephath woman. Here in James the incident of Elijah's fervent praying[45] for nearly four years[46] of drought is recounted.

> Now Elijah the Tishbite, from Tishbe in Gilead, said to Ahab, "As the LORD, the God of Israel, lives, whom I serve, there will be neither dew nor rain in the next few years except at my word."
> (1 Kgs 17:1)

This event has an eschatological dimension in James. God's lordship over the elements and the nations is the same dominion that ordains the prophet to be his instrument of punishment and fulfillment.[47]

---

[43] ὁμοιοπαθής: "with the same nature," as in having the same circumstances, feelings, and experiences in life; cf. Acts 14:15; *Wis* 7.3; *4 Macc* 12:13; Philo *Conf. Ling.* 7. Of course, there are many ways in which Elijah's experiences are also very different from those of other believers.

[44] Cf. Mal 3:22–23; Matt 11:14; 16:14; 17:1–12 (and parallels); Luke 1:17; John 1:21; *Sir* 48.1–4; *2 Esdr* 7.109.

[45] The duplication in προσευχῇ προσηύξατο (lit. "he prayed with a prayer") is a semitizing construction to convey intensity of action; cf. Deut 7:26; Josh 24:10; Isa 30:19; Luke 22:15; John 3:29; Acts 4:17; 5:28; 23:14; 2 Pet 3:3.

[46] Cf. Luke 4:25, where the time frame was also considered three and a half years for the famine initiated by Elijah's prayers.

[47] Cf. the statement regarding the two witnesses, who are like Moses and Elijah, in Rev 11:6: "These men have power to shut up the sky so that it will not rain during the time they are prophesying; and they have power to turn the waters into blood and to strike the earth with every kind of plague as often as they want." Note that such power is viewed there as extraordinary.

Elijah's bold assertion "except at my word" is surely part of what James understood by fervency in prayer.

The Kings account of Elijah's encounter with Ahab does not refer to Elijah's prayer unless the phrase "whom I serve" stands for his prayer indirectly. The kind of prayer Elijah prayed to stop the rain probably was like what he uttered at the end of the three-and-a-half-year drought (cf. Luke 4:25). In 1 Kgs 18:1 the Lord informed Elijah that he would cause the rain to fall again for his people. Elijah, fulfilling the prophetic function of mediation, was led to the moment of prayer for rain in a way that demonstrates the sole lordship of God. Throughout this chapter of 1 Kings another theme that is crucial for understanding James appears, namely, double-mindedness. The problem for many believers in the day of revelation of the judgment of God will be their divided loyalties to the world and to their Lord. This double-mindedness is why Elijah uttered the words: "'How long will you waver between two opinions? If the LORD is God, follow him; but if Baal is God, follow him.' But the people said nothing" (1 Kgs 18:21).

Elijah's prayer included the following: "Answer me, O LORD, answer me, so these people will know that you, O LORD, are God, and that you are turning their hearts back again" (1 Kgs 18:37). The repetition in this prayer expresses the earnestness of the prophet, along with his absolute confidence in the purposes of God for wayward Israel. And we note the intent of the prayer: not merely to demonstrate the power and truth of God but most of all to fulfill his purpose of converting Israel back to faithfulness (cf. Jas 5:19–20). The prophets of Baal, their idols, and their worldview had no rootage in truth or reality, nor does, "Anyone who chooses to be a friend of the world . . ." (4:4). Elijah was an instrument of God's lordship not over the regularities of seasonal rainfall (v. 7) but over the extraordinary regulation of the elements that are the Lord's prerogative.

5:18 The second prayer of Elijah ascended in order to reverse the effects of his first prayer that had brought drought. First Kings 18:41–42 states that Elijah not only told Ahab the king, "Go, eat and drink for there is the sound of a heavy rain" but also "Elijah climbed to the top of Carmel, bent down to the ground and put his face between his knees," showing faith that God would answer his prayer, a positive posture suggesting prayer. Elijah's prayer moved heaven because heaven had been moving Elijah.[48]

The second prayer of Elijah reversed the famine-producing effects of the first prayer. "Heaven" as an indirect way of referring to God is a common form of expression in biblical writings (cf. 1 Sam 12:17, where God answers Samuel's prayer for rain; 1 Kgs 18:1; Acts 14:7). Heaven is personified by the attribution of divine action, in this case of giving. God is always the "giver" of that which is good (cf. Jas 1:17), of grace (4:6), and even of trial that is meant to convert the sinner and the sinful people of God (1:2–3 or of famine-producing drought, as in 1 Kings). God will not answer prayers to a false god (cf. the statement "you do not have, because you do not ask God . . . you do not receive, because you ask with wrong motives," 4:2–3) but only the prayers of those who pray faithfully according to his word that saves (1:21) and heals (5:15–16). This giving that saves and heals produced the needed crops after three and a half years of famine. In another indirect construction the earth is said to accomplish divine action by producing crops. It is not that the heavens or the earth are divine but that they are part of the dynamic order of God's creation, which he faithfully maintains for all human beings (1:17; 5:7) and within which he acts to accomplish his special purposes for his people.

The example of Elijah illustrates everything about James's plea for a faith that rejects worldly standards of judgment in favor of divine standards. Human beings are not the masters of their own fate, and faith cannot be mixed with delusions of human autonomy, as the double-minded among James's hearers had attempted. Believers must cultivate their trust in the word of God and do what it says. In spite of deep personal or corporate struggle and strong opposition (as in the case of Elijah), they must persevere in faith (cf. 1:4; 5:11). James viewed Elijah as exemplifying any righteous believer whose prayer is heard by God. This prophet of God was given wisdom (cf. 1:5) not only to endure his trials but also to

---

[48] 1 Kgs 18:43–19:1 shows how concerned Elijah was that conversion might also come to Ahab, if not to Jezebel. He ran to Jezreel ahead of Ahab and waited. He fled into the wilderness when he realized that there had been no conversion but only the threat of his own death.

mediate the word of God to his generation. Elijah knew the will of God concerning the signs of drought and rain; this knowledge was why he prayed so fervently. By applying Scripture believers can know and should do the will of God through their own fervent praying, whether it be a matter of planning their business affairs (cf. 4:15, "You ought to say, 'If it is the Lord's will . . .'"), persevering through suffering (5:10–11), searching for healing (v. 14), or asking for forgiveness of sin (v. 15).

4. The Ministry of Restoration (5:19–20)

¹⁹My brothers, if one of you should wander from the truth and someone should bring him back, ²⁰remember this: Whoever turns a sinner from the error of his way will save him from death and cover over a multitude of sins.

5:19   Like believers who have gotten into some kind of trouble (v. 13), James's readers may "wander"[49] from the truth. The verb is a passive of *planaō,* to "deceive" or "mislead." The next verse points out that this wandering is a taking of the way of falsehood and death (cf. 1:11). The goal of faith in the Lord is maturity; but, as James indicated earlier, everyone stumbles in many ways ("we all stumble," 3:2). His statement here is quite general. Any believer could stumble and stray from God's truth. Not only this, but the believer may stray outside the restorative fellowship where mutual confession of sin secures the confidence of forgiveness and right relationship to God (v. 16). The truth from which believers wander is that which comes from the word of God that birthed them (1:18) and which they deny when they "harbor bitter envy and selfish ambition" in their hearts (3:14) while claiming to be faithful to it. The wandering from the truth here may be the wandering away from the gathered church itself. Just as the sick person cannot join in the gathering of believers (v. 14), believers who return to the way of the world avoid the fellowship of God's friends.

Just as the fellowship of believers must overcome the temptation to dissociate from the poor (2:16) and the sick, it should not leave

---

[49] Cf. Deut 22:1; Ps 119:176; Ezek 34:4; Luke 21:8; 2 Pet 2:15; Rev 18:23.

the wandering believer to his own wrong path. Just as they should practice mutual correction through confession of sin within the gathered community, they should also seek to restore (lit. "turn") the wayward brother or sister. As realistic as James was about stumbling and straying from the truth into sin, he presupposed that the church would be in a constant state of readiness to minister restoration to any who do so. Since one's own evil desires readily drag him away into sin (cf. 1:14–15), a believer should not condemn (4:11–12) but seek the wayward and bring them to effective restoration through the mercy of God (cf. 2:13). This final charge involves a ministry of bringing back, of restoration.[50] In the next verse this term will be used to indicate the turning away from evil; here it is the positive turning (returning) to the good that is found in the gifts of God. The believer who brings restoration becomes an instrument of those inexhaustible gifts to those who will listen and return to the way of truth.

5:20 The command to "remember" with which the NIV begins this verse translates the Greek word *ginōsketō*, which is a third person imperative of the verb *ginōskō*, "know," and means "let him know."[51] As James reminded his readers of the purpose of trials at the beginning of his letter (cf. "you know" in 1:3), so here in the conclusion he reminded them of the significance of a restoration ministry. These diaspora believers who were prone to wander because of doubt were to help others who had strayed into sin. Reminding believers, subject as they are to double-mindedness and self-deception, is a fundamental pedagogical task that James had set for himself and encouraged in others. The conditional "if" of the previous verse is then really about the one who brings restoration to wandering fellow believers. These are the ones—literally, "he who restores the sinner"—who should realize the significance

---

[50] Cf. Ps 79:3; Lam 5:21; Mal 2:6; Matt 13:15; Luke 1:16–17; Acts 26:18. This is another dimension of what I have suggested is functioning here under the principle of the "priesthood of all believers"; cf. v. 16.

[51] As in the opening of his letter, James exhorted these diaspora believers (1:1) who were prone to wander because of doubt to help others who have strayed into sin. Cf. T. B. Cargal, *Restoring the Diaspora: Discursive Structure and Purpose in the Epistle of James* (Atlanta: Scholars Press, 1993), 198–99.

of what they are doing in the divine economy of salvation.

Elijah is an exemplar of faith (vv. 17–18) not only because of the God-given effectiveness of his prayer on the physical environment but also, and much more, because he was an instrument of repentance. However dramatic the effectiveness of prayer, the divine intent is that sinners should be converted to God. The believer is always also a sinner (as in 4:8; cf. 4:4, where James could call them "adulterous") who needs to repent if he or she has succumbed to friendship with the world. Friendship with the world is the "error of his way,"[52] that is, a way of life that effectively denies the truth (e.g., the "practical atheism" of a prayerless and inactive "faith"). The minister of restoration exerts an active influence: he or she is said to turn the sinner away from the false path. The power of faith to serve the good purposes of God should be the norm for every active believer. The word of truth at work within the believer is not only effective to move heaven (v. 18) but also to move a fellow believer to a restored relationship with God.

Much is at stake in the sinner's need for restoration: his or her very life (lit. "he will save his soul from death").[53] The one who works to restore sinners (believer and unbeliever alike) does, effectively, what the word of God and the Lord himself do, as stated in 1:21 and 4:12. In comparison to what the word of God does in an absolute sense, the one who restores sinners turns them away from death. Death here virtually defines what is meant by the way of error, the way of the world. Believers who wander from the truth have been led into sin by their own evil desires, and the end of this process is death (cf. 1:14–15). Like Elijah, the brother who restores another lays down his own life for the sake of the other's life. The motive here is the rescue of the sinner from death, not one's own self.[54] If sickness is connected

---

[52] In the figurative sense it is a way of life out of which the sinner is turned; cf. where "way" of life can be either good or evil: Job 24:13; Ps 119:29–30; Prov 4:24; 5:6; 7:24; 8:20; 12:19; 15:25; Isa 26:7; 59:8; Matt 19:28; *Wis* 12:24.

[53] Cf. 1:21; Heb 10:39; 1 Pet 1:9,21. Paul could also use this language of a person "saving" the soul of another; e.g., Rom 11:14; 1 Cor 7:16; 1 Tim 4:16.

[54] Some have suggested, incorrectly, translating the phrase "save him" to read "save himself" in comparison with the statement of Ezek 3:21: "If you do warn the righteous man not to sin and he does not sin, he will surely live because he took warning, and you will have saved yourself."

in some way to sin (vv. 15–16), how much more is death to be connected with a way of life oriented to sinning? The word of God
implanted within the believer gives life, but it is this act of being
turned away from sinning that is a deliverance from its killing
effects. Sin slays the sinner. James's focus is on the death of the
body. He was not commenting on that which will follow the judgment of God (cf. 4:12), who will cause the destruction of the wicked.
That death is caused by human sins—"you kill and covet" (4:2)—is
quite apparent. James wanted merciful believers to rescue sinners
from the path of error, where its wanderers kill and are killed by their
sin. The frame of reference is to the "wayward among the wandering," that is, those who are among the "Dispersion" (1:1) who had
strayed onto the wrong path. James's hearers were most certainly
also "reaching out" to all in search of those poor whom God "has
chosen . . . to be rich in faith and to inherit the kingdom he has promised those who love him" (2:5).

Living for a time on the way of error has a shameful legacy: "a
multitude of sins" (5:20).[55] The future sense of the passage is an
important reminder of the eschatological dimension of James. The
one who converts the sinner not only turns him away from death
but also accomplishes the covering[56] or hiding of that transgressor's sins from the day of judgment (cf. 4:12; 5:3,5). Although
believers may have acted wickedly for a time prior to repentance,
their turning away from wickedness, their doing now what God
requires—such as caring for the poor they once had neglected (cf.
1:27; 2:14ff.) and restoring the wages of those they once had
defrauded (cf. 5:1–6)—will be shielded from the judgment that
destroys the wicked. The converting of a sinner in no sense supplies some kind of compensatory merit for the one who is instru-
mental in the conversion.[57] Nor is the amended life the basis of

---

[55] πλῆθος ἁμαρτιῶν: "multitude of sins;" cf. Ezek 28:17f.; 1 Pet 4:8; *Sir* 5.6;
Josephus *Ant.* 12.147.

[56] καλύπτω: "cover (up)," "remove from sight"; cf. Ps 84:3; Prov 10:12; 1 Pet
4:8; *1 Clem.* 49.5; *2 Clem.* 16.4.

[57] Although many in ancient Judaism and Christianity thought this way; cf., *Tob*
4.10; *Sir* 3.3; 5.14; *Const. Ap.* 7.12; *Bar* 19.10; *Did.* 4.6; *1 Clem.* 2.16; *Clem. Al.*
Paed. 3.12; Origen *Hom. in Lev.* 2.4.

one's withstanding the judgment of the Lord. Instead, restoration takes place in view of God's mercy, which triumphs over judgment (2:13), and God's requirement of the humbling of the self (4:6–10). God is predisposed to show mercy to all who humble themselves before him. Sinners are considered restored because they know that God will show them mercy. God will no longer "find fault" (1:5) with the one who is humbled, requesting his wisdom to live the life of faith he requires.

Selected Bibliography

Adamson, J. B. *James: The Man and His Message*. Grand Rapids: Eerdmans, 1989.

———. *The Epistle of James*. NICNT. Grand Rapids: Eerdmans, 1977.

Allister, D. *Sickness and Healing in the Church*. Oxford: Latimer House, 1981.

Amphoux, C. B. "Systèmes anciens de division de l'épître de Jacques et composition littèraire." *Bib* 62 (1981): 390–400.

Baird, W. "Abraham in the New Testament." *Int* 42 (1988): 367–79.

Baker, W. R. "'Above All Else': Contexts of the Call for Verbal Integrity in James 5:12." *JSNT* 54 (1994): 165–94.

———. *Personal Speech-Ethics in the Epistle of James*. WUNT 2.68. Tübingen: Mohr, 1995.

Barclay, W. *The Letters of James and Peter*. Edinburgh: St. Andrews, 1960).

Bartlett, D. L. "The Epistle of James as a Jewish-Christian Document." SBLSP 19 (1979): 173–86.

Bauckham, R. "James, 1 and 2 Peter, and Jude." In *It Is Written: Scripture Citing Scripture*. Edited by D. A. Carson and H. G. M. Williamson. Cambridge: Cambridge University, 1988, 303–17.

———. *Jude and the Relatives of Jesus in the Early Church*. Edinburgh: T & T Clark, 1990.

Beck, D. L. "The Composition of James." Ph.D. diss., Princeton Theological Seminary, 1973.

Bell, R. *Provoked to Jealousy*. Tübingen: Mohr, 1994.

Blackman, E. C. *The Epistle of James*. TBC. London: SCM, 1957.

Böhlig, A. "Zum Martyrium des Jakobus." *NovT* 5 (1962): 207–13.

Boggan, C. W. "Wealth in the Epistle of James." Ph.D. diss., The Southern Baptist Theological Seminary, 1982.

Borgen, P. "Catalogues of Vices, the Apostolic Decree, and the Jerusalem Meeting." In *The social World of Formative Christianity and Judaism*. Philadelphia: Fortress, 1988, 126–41. Edited by J. Neusner et al.

Boring, M. E. *The Continuing Voice of Jesus*. Louisville: Westminster/John Knox, 1991.

Boyle, M. O. "The Stoic Paradox of James 2:10," *NTS* 31 (1985): 611–17.

Brinktrin, J. "Zu Jak 2.1." *Bib* 35 (1954): 40–42.

Brown, S. K. *James: A Religio-Historical Study of the Relations between Jewish, Gnostic, and Catholic Christianity in the Early Period Through an Investigation of the Traditions about James the Lord's Brother*. Ann Arbor: University Microfilms, 1972.

Burchard, C. "Gemeinde in der strohernen Epistel: Mutmassungen über Jakobus." In *Kirche: Festschrift für Günther Bornkamm*. Edited by D. Lührmann and

G. Strecker. Tübingen: Mohr, 1980, 315–28.

———. "Zu Jak 2:14ff." *ZNW* 71 (1980): 27–45.

Burge, G. M. "'And Threw Them Thus on Paper': Recovering the Poetic Form of James 2:14–26." In *Studia Biblica et Theologica* 7 (1977): 31–45.

Burtchaell, F. W. *From Synagogue to Church: Public Services and Offices in the Earliest Christian Communities.* Cambridge: Cambridge University, 1992.

Bynum, C. W. *The Resurrection of the Body in Western Christianity, 200–1336.* New York: Columbia University, 1995.

Calvin, J. *Commentaries on the Catholic Epistles: James.* Translated and edited by J. Owen. Grand Rapids: Eerdmans, 1948.

Cambell, R. A. *The Elders: Seniority within Earliest Christianity.* Edinburgh: T & T Clark, 1994.

Carr, A. *The General Epistle of St. James.* CGT. Cambridge: University Press, 1930.

Cargal, T. B. *Restoring the Diaspora. Discursive Structure and Purpose in the Epistle of James.* Atlanta: Scholars Press, 1993.

Chadwick, H. "Justification by Faith and Hospitality." *TU* 79 (1961): 278–81.

Chester, A. "The Theology of James." In *The Theology of the Letters of James, Peter, and Jude.* Edited by A. Chester and R. P. Martin. Cambridge: University Press, 1994, 1–62.

Church, C. L. "A Forschungsgeschichte on the Literary Character of the Epistle of James." Ph.D. diss., Louisville, SBTS, 1990.

Condon, K. 'The Sacrament of Healing (Jas 5:14–15)." *SCR* 11 (1959): 33–42.

Cooper, R. "Prayer: A Study in Matthew and James." *Encounter* 29 (1968): 268–77.

Cranfield, C. E. B. "The Message of James." *SJT* 18 (1965): 182–93.

Cranford, L. L. "An Exposition of James 2." *SWJT* 29 (1986): 12–26.

Crotty, R. B. "The Literary Structure of the Letter of James." *ABR* 40 (1992): 45–57.

Davids, P. H. *The Epistle of James: A Commentary on the Greek Text.* NIGTC Grand Rapids: Eerdmans, 1982.

———. "The Epistle of James in Modern Discussion." *ANRW* II. 25.5 (1988): col. 3621–45.

———. "James and Jesus." In *Gospel Perspectives: The Jesus Tradition Outside the Gospels.* Edited by D. Wenham. Sheffield: JSOT, 1985, 63–84

———. "Tradition and Citation in the Epistle of James." In *Scripture, Tradition, and Interpretation: Essays Presented to Everett F. Harrison.* Edited by W. W. Gasque and W. S. LaSor. Grand Rapids: Eerdmans, 1978, 111–19.

Deppe, D. *The Sayings of Jesus in the Epistle of James.* Ph.D. diss., Free University of Amsterdam, 1989.

Dibelius, M. *James. Hermeneia.* Revised by H. Greeven. Translated by M. A. Williams. Philadelphia: Fortress, 1975.

Dillman, C. N. "A Study of Some Theological and Literary Comparisons of the Gospel of Matthew and the Epistle of James." Ph.D. diss., University of Edinburgh, 1978.

Donker, C. E. "Der Verfasser des Jak und sein Gegner: Zum Problem des Einwandes in Jak 2:18–19." *ZNW* 72 (1981): 227–40.

Dyrnes, W. "Mercy Triumphs over Justice: James 2:13 and the Theology of Faith and Works." *Themelios* 6/3 (1981): 11–16.

Easton, B. S. *The Epistle of James.* New York: Abingdon, 1957.

Eisenman, R. H. *James the Just in the Habakkuk Pesher. Studia Post-Biblica* 35. Leiden: Brill, 1986.

Elliott-Binns, L. E. "The Meaning of ΥΛΗ in Jas iii.5." *NTS* 2 (1956): 48–50.

Felder, C. H. "Partiality and God's Law: An Exegesis of James 2:1–13. *JRT* 39 (1982–83): 51–69.

———. "Wisdom, Law and Social Concern in the Epistle of James." Ph.D. diss., Columbia University, 1982.

Findlay, J. A. "James IV. 5,6." *ExpTim* (1926): 381–82.

Fine, H. "The Tradition of a Patient Job." *JBL* 74 (1955): 28–32.

Forbes, P. B. R. "The Structure of the Epistle of James." *EvQ* 47 (1975): 147–53.

Francis, F. "The Form and Function of the Opening and Closing Paragraphs of James and 1 John." *ZNW* 70 (1970): 110–26.

Frankemölle, H. "Das semantische Netz des Jakobusbriefes. Zur Einheit eines umstrittenen Briefes." *BZ* 34 (1990): 161–97.

———. "Zum Thema des Jakobusbriefes im Kontext der Rezeption von Sir 2,1–18 und 15,11–20." *BN* 48 (1989): 21–49.

Friesenhahn, H. "Zur Geschichte der Über lieferung und Exegese des Textes Bei Jak V,14f." *BZ* 24 (1938–39): 185–90.

Fry, E. "The Testing of Faith: A Study of the Structure of the Book of James." *BT* 29 (1978): 427–35.

Fung, R. Y. K. " 'Justification' in the Epistle of James." In *Right with God: Justification in the Bible and the World.* Edited by D. A. Carson. Grand Rapids: Baker, 1992, 146–62.

Gammie, J. G. "Paraenetic Literature: Toward the Morphology of a Secondary Genre." *Semeia* 50 (1990): 41–77.

Gard, D. H. "The Concept of Job's Character according to the Greek Translator of the Hebrew Text." *JBL* 72 (1953): 182–86.

Garrett, D. A. *Proverbs, Ecclesiastes, Song of Songs.* NAC. Nashville: Broadman & Holman, 1995.

George, T. " 'A Right Strawy Epistle:' Reformation Perspectives on James." *RevExp* 83 (1986): 369–82.

Gerhardson, B. *The Testing of God's Son.* ConBNT 2.1. Lunk: Gleerup, 1966.

Geyser, A. S. "The Letter of James and the Social Condition of His Addressees." *Neot* 9 (1975): 25–33.

Gordon, R. P. "KAI TO TELOS KYRIOU EIDETE (Jas. v. 11)." JTSNS 26 (1975): 91–95.

Gowan, D. E. "Wisdom and Endurance in James." *HBT* 15 (1993): 145–53.

Gushee, D. *The Righteous Gentiles.* Grand Rapids: Eerdmans, 1994.

Halson, B. R. "The Epistle of James: 'Christian Wisdom'?" *SE* 4 (1968): 308–14.

Hamerton-Kelly, R. G. *Sacred Violence: Paul's Hermeneutic of the Cross.* Minneapolis: Fortress, 1992.

Hanson, A. T. "Rahab the Harlot in Early Christian Tradition." *JSNT* 1 (1978): 53–60.

Hartin, P. J. "Exegesis and Proclamation. 'Come now, you rich, weep and wail . . .' (James 5:1–6)." *JTSA* 84 (1993): 57–63.

———. *James and the Sayings of Jesus. JSNT* 47. Sheffield: JSOT, 1991.

Haas, C. "Job's Perseverance in the Testament of Job." In *Studies on the Testament of Job.* Edited by M. A. Knibb and P. W. van der Horst. SNTSMS 66. Cambridge: University Press, 1989, 117–54.

Hadidian, D. Y. "Palestinian Pictures in the Epistle of James." *ET* 63 (1952): 228.

Hengel, M. "Der Jakobusbrief als antipaulinische Polemik." In *Tradition and Interpretation in the New Testament: Festschrift for E. E. Ellis.* Edited by G. F. Hawthorne with O. Betz. Grand Rapids: Eerdmans, 1987, 249–78.

———. *The "Hellenization" of Judaea in the First Century after Christ.* Translated by J. Bowden. London: SCM, 1989.

———. "Jesus as Messianic Teacher of Wisdom and the Beginnings of Christology." In *Studies in Early Christology.* Edinburgh: T & T Clark, 1995.

Hodges, Z. "'Dead Faith' What Is It? A Study on James 2:14–26." Dallas: Redencion Viva, 1987.

Hope, C. H. "Wisdom, Law and Social Concern in the Epistle of James." Ph.D. diss., Union Theological Seminary, 1982.

Hort, F. J. A. *The Epistle of St. James.* London: Macmillan, 1909.

Huther, J. E. *Critical and Exegetical Handbook to the General Epistles of James and John.* Edinburgh: T & T Clark, 1882.

Hymes, D. "The General Epistle of James." *IJSL* 62 (1986): 75–103.

Jacobs, I. "The Midrashic Background for James II.2103." *NTS* 22 (1975–76): 457–64.

Jeremias, J. "Jac 4:5: *epipothei.*" *ZNW* 50 (1959): 137–38.

———. "Paul and James." *ExpTim* 66 (1955): 368–71.

Johnson, D. K. "James's Use of the Old Testament." Th.D. diss., Dallas Theological Seminary, 1971.

Johnson, L. T. "Friendship with the World/Friendship with God: A Study of Discipleship in James." Edited by F. F. Sebovia. In *Discipleship in the New Testament.* Philadelphia: Fortress, 1985, 166–83.

———. "James 3:13–4:10 and the Topos PERI PHTHONOU." *NovT* 25 (1983): 327–47.

———. *The Letter of James.* Vol. 37A. AB. New York: Anchor, 1995.

———. "The Mirror of Remembrance (James 1:22–25)." *CBQ* 50 (1988): 632–45.

———. "The Social World of James: Literary Analysis and Historical Reconstruction." In *The Social World of the First Christians: Essays in Honor of Wayne A. Meeks.* Edited by L. M. White and O. L. Yarbrough. Minneapolis: Fortress, 1995, 180–97.

————. "Taciturnity and True Religion: James 1:26–27." In *Greeks, Romans, and Christians: Essays in Honor of Abraham J. Malherbe*. Edited by D. L. Balch, E. Ferguson, W. A. Meeks. Minneapolis: Fortress, 1990, 329–32.

————. "The Use of Leviticus 19 in the Letter of James." *JBL* 101 (1982): 391–401.

Kelly, F. X. *Poor and Rich in the Epistle of James*. Ph.D. diss., Temple University, 1973.

Kent, T. *Interpretation and Genre*. Lewisburg: Bucknell University, 1986.

Kilmartin, E. J. "The Interpretation of James 5:14–15 in the Armenian Catena on the Catholic Epistles: Scholium 82." *Orientalia Christiana Periodica* 53 (1987): 335–64.

Kirk, J. A. "The Meaning of Wisdom in James: Examination of a Hypothesis." *NTS* 16 (1969–70): 24–38.

Kittel, G. "Der geschichtliche Ort des jakobusbriefes." *ZNW* 41 (1942): 71–105.

Knowling, R. J. *The Epistle of James*. 2nd ed. London: Methuen, 1922.

Kugelman, R. *James and Jude*. NTM. Wilmington: Glazier, 1980.

Kutsch, E. "'Eure Rede aber sei ja, ja, nein, nein.'" *EvT* 20 (1960): 206–17.

Laws, Sophie. *A Commentary on the Epistle of James*. HNTC. San Francisco: Harper & Row, l980.

————. "Does Scripture Speak in Vain? A Reconsideration of James IV.5." *NTS* 20 (1973–74): 24–38.

Little, D. H. "The Death of James, the Brother of the Lord." Ph.D. diss., Rice University, 1971.

Lodge, J. C. "James and Paul at Cross-Purposes? James 2:22." *Bib* 62 (1981): 195–213.

Longenecker, R. "The 'Faith of Abraham' Theme in Paul, James, and Hebrews: A Study in the Circumstantial Nature of New Testament Teaching." *JETS* 20 (1977): 203–12.

Lorenzen, T. "'Faith without Works Does Not Count before God!' James 2:14–26." *ExpTim* 89 (1977–78): 231–35.

Luck, U. "Die Theologie des Jakobusbriefes." *ZTK* (1981): 1–30.

MacArthur, J. F., Jr. "Faith according to the Apostle James." *JETS* 29/1 (1986): 55–61.

Malherbe, A. J. "Ancient Epistolary Theorists." *Ohio Journal of Religious Studies* 5 (1977): 3–77.

————. "Hellenistic Moralists and the New Testament." *ANRW* II.II 26.1 (1992): 278–93.

Marcus, J. "The Evil Inclination in the Epistle of James." *CBQ* 44 (1982): 606–21.

Marshall, S. "*Dipsychos:* A Local Term?" *SE* 6 (1973): 348–51.

Martin, R. P. *James*. WBC. Waco: Word, 1988.

Maynard-Reid, P. U. *Poverty and Wealth in James*. Maryknoll: Orbis, 1987.

Mayordomo-Marin, M. "Jak 5,2.3a: Zukünftiges Gericht oder gegenwärtiger Zustand?" *ZNW* 83 (1992): 132–37.

Mayor, J. B. *The Epistle of St. James. The Greek Text with Introduction, Notes,*

Comments and Further Studies in the Epistle of St. James. 3rd. ed. London: Macmillan, 1913.

McKnight, S. "James 2:18a: The Unidentifiable Interlocutor." *WTJ* 52 (1990): 355–64.

Meinertz, M. "Die Krankensalbung Jak 5,14f." *BZ* 20 (1932): 23–36.

Milikowsky, C. "Which Gehenna? Retribution and Eschatology in the Synoptic Gospels and Early Jewish Texts." *NTS* 34 (1988): 238–49.

Milobenski, E. *Der Neid in der griechischen Philosophie.* Klassisch-Philologische Studien 29. Wiesbaden: Otto Harassowitz, 1964.

Minear, P. S. "Yes or No: The Demand for Honesty in the Early Church." *NovT* 13 (1971): 1–13.

Mitton, C. L. *The Epistle of James.* Grand Rapids: Eerdmans, 1966.

Moo, D. J. *James.* TNTC. Grand Rapids: Eerdmans, 1985.

Mussner, F. "'Direkte' und 'Indirekte' Christologie im Jakobusbrief." *Catholica* 24 (1970): 111–17.

———. Der Jakobusbrief. HTKNT 13. 5th ed. Freiburg: Herder, 1987.

Nicol, W. "Faith and Works in the Letter of James." *Noet* 9 (1975): 7–24.

Neitzel, H. "Eine alte crux interpretum im Jakobusbrief 2,18–19." *ZNW* 73 (1982): 286–93.

Noack, B. "Jakobus wider die Reichen." *ST* 18 (1964): 10–25.

Pearson, B. "James, 1–2 Peter, Jude." In *The New Testament and Its Modern Interpreters.* Edited by E. J. Epp and G. W. MacRae. Philadelphia: Fortress, 1989, 371–406.

Penner, T. C. *The Epistle of James and Eschatology: Re-reading an Ancient Christian Letter.* V. 121. JSNT. Sheffield: Academic Press, 1996.

Perdue, L. G. "Paraenesis and the Letter of James." *ZNW* 72 (1981): 241–56.

Plummer, A. *The General Epistles of St. James and St. Jude.* New York: Doran, 1920.

Polhill, J. B. "The Life-Situation of the Book of James." *RevExp* 66 (1969): 369–78.

———. "Prejudice, Partiality, and Faith: James 2." *RE* 83 (1986): 395–404.

Popkes, W. "New Testament Principles of Wholeness." *EvQ* 64 (1992): 319–32.

Porter, S. E. "Is *dipsychos* (James 1,8; 4,8) a 'Christian' Word?" *Bib* 71 (1990): 469–98.

———. "Jesus and the Use of Greek in Galilee." In *Studying the Historical Jesus: Evaluations of the State of Current Research.* Edited by B. Chilton and C. A. Evans. Leiden: Brill, 1994.

Pratscher, W. *Der Herrenbruder Jakobus und die Jakobustradition.* FRLANT 139. Göttingen: Vandenhoeck & Ruprecht, 1987.

von Rad, G. *Wisdom in Israel.* Nashville: Abingdon, 1972.

Rakestraw, R. V. "James 2:14–26: Does James Contradict Pauline Soteriology?" *CTR* 1 (1986): 31–50.

Reese, J. M. "The Exegete as Sage: Hearing the Message of James." *BTB* 12 (1982): 78–90.

Reicke, B. *The Epistles of James, Peter, and Jude.* AB 37. 1964.

———. "L'onction des malades d'après saint Jacques." *La Maison Dieu* 113 (1973): 50–56.

Robertson, A. T. *Studies in the Epistle of James.* Nashville: Broadman, n.d.

Ropes, J. H. *The Epistle of St. James.* ICC. Edinburgh: T & T Clark, 1916.

Sailer, J. "Jak 5,14 und die Krankensalbung." *TPQ* 113 (1965): 347–53.

Schille, G. "Wider dei Gespaltenheit des Glaubens—Beobachtungen am Jakobus-brief." *Theologische Versuche* 9 (1977): 71–89.

Schnabel, E. J. *Law and Wisdom from Ben Sira to Paul.* WUNT 2.16. Tübingen: Mohr, 1985.

Schmitt, J. J. "You Adulteresses! The Image in James 4:4." *NovT* 28 (1986): 327–37.

Schmidt-Clausing, F. "Die unterschiedliche Stellung Luthers und Zwinglis zum Ja-kobusbrief." *Reformatio* 18 (1969): 568–85.

Schökel, L. A. "James 5:2 [sic] and 4:6." *Bib* (1973): 73–76.

Seitz, O. J. F. "Afterthoughts on the Term 'Dipsychos.'" *NTS* 4 (1957–58): 327–34.

———. "Antecedents and Significance of the term *Dipsychos*." *JBL* 66 (1947): 211–19.

———. "James and the Law." *SE* 2 (1964): 472–86.

Sevenster, J. N. *Do You Know Greek? How Much Greek Could the First Jewish Christian Have Known?* NovTSup 19. Leiden: Brill, 1968.

Shepherd, M. H. "The Epistle of James and the Gospel of Matthew." *JBL* 75 (1976): 40–51.

Sidebottom, E. M. *James, Jude and 2 Peter.* NCB. London: Thomas Nelson, 1967.

Siker, J. S. *Disinheriting the Jews: Abraham in Early Christian Controversy.* Lou-isville: Westminster, 1991.

Sloyan, S. *The Letter of James.* PC. Philadelphia: Fortress, 1977.

Smit, D. J. "Show no partiality . . ." *JTSA* 71 (1990): 59–68.

Soard, M. L. "The Early Christian Interpretation of Abraham and the Place of James within That Context." *IBS* 9 (1987): 18–26.

Songer, H. "The Literary Character of the Book of James." *RevExp* 66 (1969): 379–89.

Soucek, J. B. "Zu den Problemen des Jakobusbriefes." *EvT* 18 (1958): 460–68.

Stagg, F. "An Analysis of the Book of James." *RE* 66 (1969): 365–68.

Stowers, S. K. *Letter Writing in Greco-Roman Antiquity.* Library of Early Chris-tianity. Philadelphia: Westminster, 1986.

Stulac, G. M. "Who Are 'The Rich' in James?" *Presbyterion* 16 (1990): 89–102.

Tamez, E. *The Scandalous Message of James: Faith without Works Is Dead.* New York: Crossroad, 1990.

Tasker, R. V. G. *The General Epistle of James.* TNTC 16. Grand Rapids: Eerd-mans, 1957.

Terry, R. B. "Some Aspects of the Discourse Structure of the Book of James." *JOTT* 5 (1992): 106–25.

Townsend, M. J. "Christ, Community, and Salvation in the Epistle of James." *EvQ* 53 (1981): 115–23.

Verseput, D. J. "Reworking the Puzzle of Faith and Deeds in James 2.14–26." *NTS* 43 (1997): 97–115.

Vokes, F. E. "The Ten Commandments in the New Testament and in First Century Judaism," *SE* 5 (1968): 145–54.

Vouga, F. *L'Epitre de Saint Jacques.* CNT. Vol. 13a. Geneva: Labor et Fides, 1984.

Wachob, W. H. "The Rich in Faith and the Poor in Spirit: The Socio-Rhetorical Function of a Saying of Jesus in the Epistle of James." Ph.D. diss., Emory University, 1993.

Wall, R. W. "James as Apocalyptic Paraenesis." *ResQ* 32 (1990): 11–22.

Ward, R. B. "The Communal Concern of the Epistle of James." Ph.D. diss., Harvard University, 1966.

———. "James of Jerusalem." *ANRW* II.26/1, 792–810.

———. "Partiality in the Assembly: James 2:2–4." *HTR* 62 (1969): 87–97.

———. "The Works of Abraham: James 2:14–26." *HTR* 61 (1968): 283–90.

Warrington, K. "Some Observations on James 5:13–18." *EPTA Bull* 8 (1989): 160–77.

———. "The Significance of Elijah in James 5:13–18." *EvQ* 66 (1994): 217–27.

Watson, D. F. "James 2 in Light of Greco-Roman Schemes of Argumentation." *NTS* 39 (1993): 94–121.

———. "The Rhetoric of James 3.1–12 and a Classical Pattern of Argumentation." *NovT* 35 (1993): 48–64.

Webber, M. I. 'IAKOBOS HO DIKAIOS: Origins, Literary Expression and Development of Traditions about the Brother of the Lord in Early Christianity." Ph.D. diss., Fuller Theological Seminary, School of Theology, 1985.

Wengst, K. *Humility: Solidarity of the Humiliated.* Translated by J. Bowden. Philadelphia: Fortress, 1988.

Westermann, C. *Prophetic Oracles of Salvation in the Old Testament.* Translated by K. Crim. Louisville: Westminster, 1991.

Williams, R. R. *The Letters of John and James.* Cambridge: University Press, 1965.

Wilkinson, J. "Healing in the Epistle of James." *SJT* 24 (1971): 326–45.

Witherington, B. *Jesus the Sage: The Pilgrimage of Wisdom.* Minneapolis: Fortress, 1994.

Wolmarans, J. L. P. "Making Sense out of Suffering: James 1:2–4." *Hervormde Teologiese Stud* 47 (1991): 1109–21.

Wolverton, W. I. "The Double-Minded Man in the Light of Essene Psychology." *ATR* 38 (1956): 166–75.

Wright, N. T. *The New Testament and the People of God.* Minneapolis: Fortress, 1992.

Wuellner, W. H. "Der Jakobusbrief im Licht der Rhetorik und Textpragmatik." *LB* 43 (1978): 5–66.

Young, F. W. "The Relation of I Clement to the Epistle of James." *JBL* 67 (1948): 339–45.

Selected Subject Index

Person Index

Selected Scripture Index